Impacts of Emerging Agricultural Trends on Fish and Wildlife Habitat

Committee on Impacts of Emerging Agricultural Trends on Fish and Wildlife Habitat

Board on Agriculture and Renewable Resources

Commission on Natural Resources

National Research Council

NATIONAL ACADEMY PRESS
Washington, D.C. 1982

NOTICE: The project that is the subject of this report was approved by the Governing Board of the National Research Council, whose members are drawn from the councils of the National Academy of Sciences, the National Academy of Engineering, and the Institute of Medicine. The members of the Committee responsible for the report were chosen for their special competences and with regard for appropriate balance.

This report has been reviewed by a group other than the authors according to procedures approved by a Report Review Committee consisting of members of the National Academy of Sciences, the National Academy of Engineering, and the Institute of Medicine.

The National Research Council was established by the National Academy of Sciences in 1916 to associate the broad community of science and technology with the Academy's purposes of furthering knowledge and of advising the federal government. The Council operates in accordance with general policies determined by the Academy under the authority of its congressional charter of 1863, which establishes the Academy as a private, nonprofit, self-governing membership corporation. The Council has become the principal operating agency of both the National Academy of Sciences and the National Academy of Engineering in the conduct of their services to the government, the public, and the scientific and engineering communities. It is administered jointly by both Academies and the Institute of Medicine. The National Academy of Engineering and the Institute of Medicine were established in 1964 and 1970, respectively, under the charter of the National Academy of Sciences.

This study was supported by the U.S. Department of Agriculture and the U.S. Department of the Interior.

Library of Congress Catalog Card Number 82-82033
International Standard Book Number 0-309-03283-0

Available from

NATIONAL ACADEMY PRESS
2101 Constitution Avenue, N.W.
Washington, D.C. 20418

Printed in the United States of America

COMMITTEE ON IMPACTS OF EMERGING AGRICULTURAL TRENDS ON FISH AND WILDLIFE HABITAT

Chester O. McCorkle, Jr. (Co-Chairman), University of California, Davis
John E. Halver (Co-Chairman), University of Washington
Malcolm W. Coulter, University of Maine
Jay D. Hair, National Wildlife Federation
Rolf Hartung, University of Michigan
Dean L. Haynes, Michigan State University
Niles R. Kevern, Michigan State University
R. Merton Love, University of California, Davis
Raymond J. Miller, University of Idaho
John Miranowski, Iowa State University
Carl L. Mosley, Ohio Department of Natural Resources
Carl H. Oppenheimer, University of Texas
Tony J. Peterle, Ohio State University
James G. Teer, Welder Wildlife Foundation
Robert Todd, University of Georgia
Milton W. Weller, University of Minnesota
Sylvan H. Wittwer, Michigan State University

Consultants

Sandra O. Archibald, University of California, Davis
Ronald W. Hardy, University of Washington
Frances P. Solomon, University of Washington

Staff

Philip Ross, Executive Secretary
Selma P. Baron, Staff Officer
Michael E. Berger, Senior Staff Officer
Mary L. Sutton, Administrative Assistant

Contents

Preface

At the request of the Fish and Wildlife Service (U.S. Department of the Interior) and the Soil Conservation Service (U.S. Department of Agriculture), the Board on Agriculture and Renewable Resources of the Commission on Natural Resources agreed to undertake a multidisciplinary study of the impact of emerging agricultural trends (including those in forestry and aquaculture) on fish and wildlife habitat. In addition to requesting assistance in developing policies and strategies that will minimize the negative impacts on fish and wildlife habitat and make the most of the positive ones, the sponsoring agencies also expressed concern about the environmental impacts of various agricultural practices. Hence the Environmental Studies Board of the Commission on Natural Resources participated in the early deliberations on this study.

The Committee on Impacts of Emerging Agricultural Trends on Fish and Wildlife Habitat was established by the Board on Agriculture and Renewable Resources. The Committee addressed the following tasks:

1. to review various existing projections of future agricultural trends over the next 10 to 50 years by land type (e.g., cropland, pastureland, rangeland, forests), practices (e.g., cultivation, irrigation, pest management), and geographic region;
2. to identify the types of impacts and habitat changes that are associated with the changing patterns of land and water use and changing agricultural practices, and to project the future impacts and changes that can be anticipated;
3. to define physical measures, policies, and strategies that might be used to offset or compensate for

these impacts, and wherever possible, to specify federal policies that could be adopted, particularly those that could be implemented within existing federal programs; and

4. to identify information and research needs.

To accomplish these objectives, the Committee divided into two teams and conducted the study in two phases. Phase I focused on identifying the agricultural trends likely to have significant impacts on fish and wildlife habitat. During Phase II of the study, the Committee analyzed the impacts, both positive and negative, on fish and wildlife habitat and identified research needs. These trends and impacts were examined in the broad sense for most species.

This report emphasizes game mammals, birds, and fish because of a need to focus and limit the scope of the study. The Committee recognizes, of course, that natural habitats contain many other types of mammals, birds, and fish, as well as insects, earthworms, fungi, and bacteria. Mammals, birds, and fish high in the trophic levels of natural ecosystems often feed on plants, insects, and microorganisms low in the system. These lower organisms are vital to the survival of the ecosystem, fulfilling such necessary functions as decomposing organic wastes and recycling the essential elements such as carbon, nitrogen, oxygen, phosphorus, and calcium. Loss of any of these vital groups of natural biota will damage habitat quality and may cause the loss of game mammals, birds, and fish that directly and indirectly depend upon these other biota.

Endangered species are not included in this analysis because the study of such species is a highly complex problem, often involving consideration of many regional and other limitations, and is thus outside the scope of this study.

This report is submitted in compliance with the terms of the agreement with the sponsoring agencies. It reflects the collective judgment of approximately 150 agricultural and wildlife scientists from many different disciplines and geographic locations throughout the United States. The Committee also reviewed an extensive literature during its investigation; but because many projections were required, the literature often served only as a base for informed conjecture.

The Committee appreciates the assistance of the BARR staff who contributed so generously to this effort. They include Selma P. Baron, Michael E. Berger, Sheridan E.

Caldwell, Philip Ross, Asha G. Rugimbana, Mary L. Sutton, Lawrence C. Wallace, and Michael D. Zagata. Consultants to the Chairmen were Sandra O. Archibald, Ronald W. Hardy, and Frances P. Solomon; they completed many details in the development of this study, and we appreciate their dedication and professional competence.

Chester O. McCorkle, Jr.
Co-chairman, Phase I
Agricultural Trends

John E. Halver
Co-chairman, Phase II
Impacts on Fish and
Wildlife Habitat

List of Contributors

The following contributors were helpful to the Committee in the preparation of this report, and the Committee is grateful for their assistance. The content of the report, however, and the views expressed in it remain the responsibility of the Committee.

Ernest D. Ables, University of Idaho
M. Wayne Adams, Michigan State University
Dennis Allen, Baruch Marine Laboratory
Eugene Allen, Montana Department of Fish, Wildlife and Parks
Chester Anderson, Wyoming Game and Fish Department
Fred Bakker-Arkema, Michigan State University
D. L. Bath, University of California-Davis
Bill Baxter, Nebraska Game and Parks Commission
Sidney Baynes, North Carolina Wildlife Resources Commission
Ruth Larsen Bender, Iowa State University
Eric Bolen, Texas Tech University
Gaylon Booker, National Cotton Council
G. E. Bradford, University of California-Davis
Galen Brown, Michigan State University
Robert H. Bruch, New Jersey Department of Agriculture
Jim Buckner, International Paper Company
F. E. Busby, University of Wyoming
Anthony Bywater, University of California-Davis
John N. Carr, Arizona Game and Fish Department
Suzanne Caturano, University of Maine-Orono
Marion Clawson, Resources for the Future, Inc.
Richard L. Cooper, Ohio Agricultural Research and Development Center
Ronald Cotterill, Michigan State University
Julian Crane, University of California-Davis

Hewlett S. Crawford, Jr., University of Maine
Pierre Crosson, Resources for the Future, Inc.
Michael J. Dellarco, U.S. Environmental Protection Agency
D. Decolesta, U.S. Fish and Wildlife Service
Joe Dell, New York Department of Environmental Conservation (retired)
John and Engelstad Douglas, Orvis National Fertilizer Development Center
Robert L. Downing, U.S. Fish and Wildlife Service
Harold Duebbert, U.S. Fish and Wildlife Service
Cathy Elliott, University of Maine-Orono
Eric L. Ellwood, University of California-Davis
Ralph A. Ernst, University of California-Davis
Ray Evans, Humboldt State University
Kenneth R. Farrell, U.S. Department of Agriculture
Richard Fisher, University of Florida
William P. Flatt, University of Georgia
Ron Fowler, South Dakota Game, Fish and Parks Department
K. D. Frederick, Washington State University
Leigh H. Frederickson, University of Missouri
Bruce L. Gardner, Texas A&M University
James G. Gosselink, Louisiana State University
William Graves, Kentucky Department of Wildlife Resources
Gordon Gunter, Gulf Coast Research Laboratory
Jim Hale, Wisconsin Department of Natural Resources
R. Hall, West Virginia Department of Natural Resources
Norman V. Hancock, Utah Division of Wildlife Resources
Clifford M. Hardin, Ralston-Purina
L. D. Harris, University of Florida
Stephen B. Harsh, Michigan State University
Richard B. Harwood, Organic Gardening Farming and Research Center
Virgil W. Hays, University of Kentucky
Joel W. Hedgpeth, Environmental and Editorial Analysis
Donald W. Hedrick, Humboldt State University
Harold Henneman, Michigan State University
Jimmye S. Hillman, University of Arizona
Howard W. Hjort, U.S. Department of Agriculture
Harold Hodgson, University of Wisconsin-Madison
B. F. Hoffman, Jr., University of Maine-Orono
George Hogabom, Michigan State University
Edward Horn, New York Department of Environmental Conservation
Eldridge Hunt, California Department of Fish and Game
Keith Huston, Ohio Agricultural Research and Development Center
Eugene Jakworski, Eastern Michigan University
James H. Jenkins, University of Georgia

Russell T. Johnson, Amstar Corporation
John A. Kadlec, Utah State University
James R. Karr, University of Illinois-Champaign
John Kelly, Michigan State University
William H. Kiel, King Ranch, Incorporated
Darrell L. King, Michigan State University
F. B. Knight, University of Maine-Orono
Lowell Kraft, Kraft, Incorporated
Ronald Labisky, University of Florida
Sylvia Lane, University of California-Davis
William H. Lawrence, Weyerhaeuser Company
Dale Lindsay, Tucson, Arizona
Jerry Longcore, U.S. Fish and Wildlife Service
R. M. Love, University of California-Davis
H. R. Lund, North Dakota State University
Robert C. Lund, New Jersey Department of Environmental Protection
Jack Lyon, U.S. Forest Service
J. P. Mahlstede, Iowa State University
Philip Martin, University of California-Davis
Alex A. McCalla, University of California-Davis
Chester McConnell, Wildlife Management Institute
D. L. McCune, International Fertilizer Development Center
John L. McHugh, State University of New York at Stony Brook
George E. Merva, Michigan State University
E. Charles Meslow, U.S. Fish and Wildlife Service
Fred Miller, Texas A&M University
Darrell Montei, Kansas Fish and Game Commission
Robert L. Morgan, North Dakota Game and Fish Department
Louis Nelson, Florence, Alabama
John D. Newsome, Louisiana State University
Louis G. Nickell, Velsicol Chemical Corporation
C. Niven, University of California-Davis
Richard Norrell, Idaho Fish and Game Department
Patrick O'Brien, U.S. Department of Agriculture
Joseph R. Orsenigo, Florida Sugar Cane League
Carlton M. Owen, Potlatch Corporation
Ray Owen, University of Maine-Orono
Don Paarlberg, University of Nebraska
Hugh Palmer, Pennsylvania Game Commission
Eugene Parks, New York Department of Environmental Conservation
C. L. Pelissier, University of California-Davis
Calvin Perkins, U.S. Soil Conservation Service
Patricia Perkins, California Department of Fish and Game
John C. Peters, U.S. Bureau of Reclamation
David Pimentel, Cornell University

Richard Poelker, Washington Department of Game
E. L. Proebsting, Washington State University
Alan R. Putman, Michigan State University
Lee Queal, Kansas Fish and Game Commission
D. W. Rains, University of California-Davis
Dennis Raveling, University of California
Harvey A. Roberts, Pennsylvania Game Commission
Lynn Robertson, Michigan State University
Elmer C. Rossman, Michigan State University
Dennis R. Rouse, Auburn University
Vernon Ruttan, St. Paul, Minnesota
Roy M. Sachs, University of California-Davis
Ernest D. Salo, University of Washington
Wayne W. Sandfort, Colorado Division of Wildlife
Sanford D. Schemnitz, New Mexico State University
Glenn O. Schwab, Ohio State University
Bernard S. Schweigert, University of California-Davis
William Seaman, Jr., University of Florida
George F. Seidel, Colorado State University
Douglas Sheppard, New York Department of Environmental Conservation
William Sims, University of California-Davis
Donald G. Smith, Colorado Division of Wildlife
Walter A. Snyder, New Mexico Game and Fish Department
Warren D. Snyder, Colorado Division of Wildlife
George R. Spangler, University of Minnesota
G. F. Sprague, University of Illinois-Urbana
J. W. Stansel, Texas A&M University
Ward Stone, New York Department of Environmental Conservation
Fred A. Stormer, Texas Tech University
Barbara Stowe, Michigan State University
Otto Suchsland, Michigan State University
Glen Suter, New York Department of Agriculture and Markets
James M. Sweeney, University of Arkansas-Monticello
Ross Talbot, Iowa State University
George Tanner, University of Florida
Mike Tesar, Michigan State University
Jack Ward Thomas, U.S. Forest Service
Edward Tolbert, Michigan State University
Larry W. Tombaugh, Michigan State University
Robert K. Towry, Jr., Colorado Division of Wildlife
George Tsukamoto, Nevada Department of Wildlife
Luther Tweeten, Oklahoma State University
Ray J. White, Montana State University
Kart T. Wright, Michigan State University
R. A. Young, Washington State University
Haig Zeronian, University of California-Davis

Summary, Conclusions, and Recommendations

The agricultural and forest industry is the largest modifier of the lands and waters that provide habitats for fish and wildlife. The size, scope, and nature of agricultural practices such as cultivating cropland, grazing rangeland, and harvesting forests have profoundly affected the quality of these habitats.

TRENDS IN AGRICULTURE

Agricultural land use and practices are changing. An increased demand for food and forest products is placing pressure on agricultural production and thus on our land and water. These pressures will remain high. The rising costs of production and declining net returns per unit of product place pressures on farmers to increase productivity further. In response, changes in farm size, production practices, and ownership patterns may occur that will affect wildlife habitats.

NEEDS FOR THE FUTURE

These changes will have both positive and negative impacts on fish and wildlife habitats. Agriculture and wildlife each have specific needs, and the direct relationship between agricultural practices and wildlife habitats must be more widely recognized. The value of fish and wildlife to society must be considered as well as the value of maintaining a productive agriculture. These values are not necessarily in conflict. They can be brought into better balance through careful planning, consistent policy, and appropriate incentives to landowners.

Political, social, economic, scientific, and technological trends greatly influence agricultural practices. Changes in some of these practices will increase habitat quality for fish and wildlife, whereas changes in others will decrease habitat quality. The trends and practices along with the impacts on habitats are summarized below.

CROPLAND AND PASTURE

Despite the diversity in types of crops and agricultural practices in the United States, several agricultural trends are apparent that could affect existing fish and wildlife habitats. The three major trends are as follows: (1) more intensive and efficient use of existing cropland, (2) conversion of lands currently in pasture, range, and forest into cropland, and (3) loss of prime farmland to other uses.

The use of agricultural chemicals, irrigation and drainage, double cropping, increased field size, and the improvement of plant species have led to more intensive and efficient use of cropland. These practices often have negative effects on habitats. Agricultural chemicals are toxic to many species and can disrupt ecosystems by eliminating certain plants or animals necessary to support wildlife. Replacement of wild pastures with tame pastures and widespread monoculture reduce the diversity of plant life and thus the diversity of wildlife. Double cropping and increased field size reduce habitats. More efficient use of pesticides, fertilizers, and water may reduce some of these effects. Integrated pest management and less tillage of land can improve fish and wildlife habitats.

FOREST LAND

Forest land is expected to be more intensively managed in the future as demands for timber products increase. The major forest land management practices that affect wildlife habitats are (1) those that alter the diversity of forest land, including conversion from one type of forest to another, (2) those that increase public or private access to remote forest land, and (3) those that create off-site impacts.

Forestry practices that often decrease plant species diversity include the conversion of hardwood forests to conifers, short rotations where trees are harvested at younger ages, and intensive use of new techniques for site preparation, planting, and culture of genetically superior planted stock. Increased grazing by livestock will accelerate degradation of forests for wildlife. In some regions there will be continued loss of forest land to agriculture or to reservoirs and other developments that reduce wildlife habitats.

Zoning that protects streams, steep slopes, and other sensitive areas and silvicultural treatments planned to retain a variety of vegetation zones will enhance habitats and result in a greater diversity of wildlife.

RANGELAND

Losses of habitats for fish and wildlife will occur through more intensive use of rangeland, conversion of rangeland to cropland and pasture, and fence-building in areas that are winter grazing lands for large mammals. Overuse of rangeland for recreation and intensive grazing of livestock in competition with wildlife will result in a degradation of habitats. Irrigation may result in lower water tables, and it reduces water in streams and further reduces the amount and quality of both riparian and upland habitats. The use of agricultural chemicals and certain mechanical practices to eliminate unwanted plants will alter the cover and food supply for wildlife. Rest-rotation grazing, where applicable, can improve wildlife habitats. Controlled burning to remove brushy species and encourage grass species will also affect wildlife habitats.

PONDS, LAKES, AND STREAMS

Agricultural practices that alter water flow or increase water runoff from agricultural land will affect the quantity and quality of pond, lake, and stream habitats for fish and wildlife. Channelization of streams to prevent flooding will change the diversity and abundance of fish and wildlife. Irrigation influences habitats by moving water from aquifers, ponds, lakes, and streams to agricultural lands. Agricultural practices that increase soil erosion greatly affect aquatic habitats by increasing the siltation and by carrying off nutrients that increase eutrophication. Chemical loading in ponds, lakes, and streams caused by runoff of agricultural chemicals can alter the ecological balance by killing certain plants or animals and thus changing the structure of the habitats. Grazing and cultivation may damage the riparian zones, reducing these unique wildlife habitats that are critical to the integrity of streams.

INTERIOR WETLANDS

Interior wetlands are affected by the same factors that influence ponds, lakes, and streams. In addition, the loss of wetland habitats through draining and conversion to agricultural uses continues, but its major remaining impact will be in southern fish and wildlife habitats, where the majority of new cropland will be developed.

COASTAL WETLANDS AND ESTUARIES

Coastal wetlands and estuaries are influenced by agricultural practices because they are downstream from farmland. Thus the quality of habitat in these areas is profoundly affected by runoff of agricultural chemicals and silt from agricultural lands. Coastal wetland habitats are indirectly affected by any change in the allocation of acreage to cropland or pasture. Estuarine areas are the nurseries for most of the coastal and Gulf fish stocks. Increased agricultural use of the estuarine habitats may affect bay, river mouth, and shallow coastal areas. At the present time, the water quality of estuaries is subject to regulation by the government. The estuaries are fertilized by land runoff, but, at the same time, harmful chemicals are being transported and deposited. A proper balance of nutrients and chemicals is critical for the biomass and the fish and wildlife habitats of the estuary.

THE FUTURE IN PERSPECTIVE

The future for wildlife and their habitats is not encouraging in those areas where intensive practices are employed to produce larger amounts of food and fiber. There is urgent need to balance the value of using the most efficient and economical agricultural practices--beneficial to our national welfare--and the value of maintaining or improving wherever possible the quality and quantity of fish and wildlife habitats--one critical index of quality of human life in our country. These are not mutually exclusive values, and much can be done with deliberate, intelligent planning plus effective stewardship and management of our natural resources.

The development of the United States occurred under the general assumption that land and water resources were nearly unlimited. Our production systems under this assumption attempted to maximize the agricultural output per unit of area. Agriculture, like other sectors of the economy, now is faced with the need to protect and enhance resources, not only for agricultural use but for other uses and values as well.

As a nation we are learning that we must optimize, or make the best possible use of, all our resources instead of maximizing the output of agriculture alone. Optimization requires consideration not only of a longer time period, but also of a broader array of both positive and negative outcomes of production systems, including impacts on habitats for fish and wildlife.

The Committee's recommendations center on three requirements for optimization: (1) changes in attitudes and values, (2) additional critical research, and (3) public policies that are consistent and that make use of incentives.

With respect to the requirement for changes in attitudes and values toward the use of our resources to achieve multiple objectives including agricultural production and wildlife habitats, the following recommendations are offered:

1. Promote, through all types of education, public understanding of the multiple values and benefits, including economic, recreational, aesthetic, and ecological, of improved stewardship of fish and wildlife resources.

2. Increase public understanding and awareness, through research and extension, of how present agricultural and forestry practices affect wildlife habitats.

3. Through public policy and education, encourage the adoption of management practices and systems such as soil and water conservation that can both sustain high levels

of agricultural and forestry output and increase fish and wildlife populations.

4. Educate policymakers, producers, and the public as to the critical importance of timing in dealing with the dynamics of biological populations, in changing production practices, and in developing and implementing public policies designed to bring into better balance the national objectives of enhancing agricultural and forestry productivity and improving habitats for fish and wildlife.

5. Encourage habitat development plans for specific wildlife in local areas. Local fish and wildlife conservation groups should be encouraged to develop plans for habitat enhancement with the assistance and expertise of federal, state, regional, county, and local agencies and universities.

The major critical research needs fall in four broad categories with specific needs under each. Specific research needs for cropland and pasture habitats, forest habitats, western rangeland habitats, lake and stream habitats, interior wetland habitats, and coastal wetland and estuary habitats are given at the ends of Chapters 6 through 11. The major categories of research needs are as follows:

1. Assess the effects of present agricultural and forestry practices and systems on productivity and on fish and wildlife habitats.

(a) resolve definitional and measurement questions related to classification and inventory techniques for wildlife habitats.

(b) identify the shared critical parameters in agricultural and forestry production on the one hand and fish and wildlife habitats on the other.

(c) develop more comprehensive concepts to use in the measurement of agricultural productivity that account for outcomes beyond the physical production of agricultural and forestry products, such as the cost to the environment, the cost of energy used, and the impact on rural development.

2. The social, political, and economic aspects of land management should be considered in efforts to develop agricultural and forestry practices that operate efficiently to reduce erosion, reduce water and energy

requirements, reduce the use of toxic substances, and maintain long-term quality of the resource base.

3. Develop new strains of plants and animals with greater stress tolerance (to pests and diseases, weather, and adverse soil and water conditions) and increased yields (improved photosynthetic efficiency, nitrogen fixatives, and so on), ensuring conservation of resources and improving the quantity and quality of fish and wildlife habitats.

4. Study how to use incentives as well as regulations to bring about optimal resource use to meet multiple purposes. Such incentives include (a) taxation, (b) subsidization, and (c) the creation of markets to value previously nonpriced outputs from land and water resources.

It is not within the Committee's charge to propose specific and detailed policies for enhancing fish and wildlife habitats. In general, however, policies, to be effective, must be internally consistent and mutually supportive of other related policies. This is not currently true. For example, the federal government guarantees that producers receive certain minimum prices for some commodities. This encourages production of these commodities even when supplies exceed demand, which leads to continued production on marginal agricultural lands and the conversion of other lands to agricultural production. Also, the federal government often provides technical and/or financial assistance for draining wetlands even as other agencies are purchasing wetlands or wetland easements. Such inconsistent and conflicting programs not only waste scarce funds but also are detrimental to wildlife values. Many conflicting policies were developed independently in response to specific problems, but they now must be reexamined to ensure that they are in the overall public interest.

Any policies developed must recognize the interdependencies of agriculture, forestry, fish and wildlife, and other sectors of the national economy. None is of such overriding importance that it can be considered independently of the others.

Public policies must recognize that agricultural land use and practices and their impacts on fish and wildlife habitats vary from region to region. Guiding principles are best set by national policy, but the diversity of needs and opportunities mandates that specific programs implementing these principles be developed at community and regional levels.

The most important component of successful existing agricultural policies is incentive. In most cases, producers are rewarded for taking specific actions. Too often, wildlife and habitat conservation programs lack financial incentives and instead rely on penalties. Such approaches have not worked well. New wildlife and habitat conservation programs must be developed, funded by fees from users or beneficiaries, which will allow wildlife to be considered on an equal basis along with other products of the land, and which will, in turn, motivate individuals and communities to move toward optimal use of national resources given the multiple objectives of society.

1 Introduction

Habitat is the environmental setting in which an animal or plant normally lives, grows, and reproduces. Agricultural land use, including grazing, crop production, and forestry, affects the quality and quantity of the water and land available for food, cover, space, and living and reproducing sites for fish and wildlife. This report examines agricultural trends and their likely impacts on fish and wildlife habitats.

HABITAT FEATURES OF IMPORTANCE TO WILDLIFE

To understand how agricultural and forestry activities affect habitat, it is necessary first to understand how wildlife are attracted to and use various natural habitats. The complexity and infinite diversity of wildlife habitats make the categorization of the habitat characteristics of numerous species an imposing and impractical task. Patterns of use in this study will be illustrated by examples, instead of by attempting to address the multiplicity of types observable in various species or groups of animals.

Some comprehensive, broad habitat characteristics have been identified by scientists. Key habitat characteristics were presented as early as 1938 (King 1974). These include the availability and adequate interspersion of cover, food, and water. The special requirements associated with reproduction include special foods (often protein rich), den or nest sites, and the territorial spacing often associated with breeding. Such spacing depends on the social system of the animal; some colonial species like herons cluster in limited habitat during breeding periods and disperse at other times, whereas other birds flock during the winter and become highly territorial during breeding.

The habitat needs of resident species may differ from those of migratory ones. Where changes from season to season due to climate or rainfall are severe, mobile species find the resources they need by moving to different habitats. Muskrats may do this locally, but birds annually migrate long distances to exploit resources. Anadromous fish swim from the ocean or a lake to streams to breed.

Recent studies of animal communities have identified certain patterns of vegetation important to wildlife (Thomas 1979). It long has been known that borders, or edges, between two vegetative types are rich in number of species (diversity) and sometimes in numbers of individuals of a species (abundance). Many contiguous different types of vegetation and the edges between them form a horizontal pattern, which is attractive to wildlife. Vertical layering, such as in forests, is another habitat pattern that induces use by a variety of species, and this is regarded as beneficial to wildlife.

The habitat diversity of an area may be a result of natural, local, climatically controlled vegetation, but it also is influenced by time. Natural or man-made disturbances of vegetation induce a succession, which begins with pioneering plants that are subsequently replaced with change in microclimate and soil conditions, including nutrient level and nutrient exchange. Different wildlife communities have adapted to these various vegetative stages because of the different food and cover available in each. Thus wildlife communities are dynamic. In streams and lakes, similar processes occur that are influenced by physical conditions, age, and nutrient level.

There are other general patterns in fish and wildlife communities. In communities with few species, the species occupy broad niches. In more complex communities with many species, the niches are narrow (MacArthur and Wilson 1967). Essentially, competition for resources induces specialization and reduces niche breadth. A more complex vegetative structure then produces more potential sites for animals with different requirements while it reduces competition. Hence habitat diversity generally produces a greater diversity of fish and wildlife.

Natural processes such as fire, flood, and grazing cause a continuing plant succession, and hence wildlife diversity, in natural systems. However, severe natural effects such as fire can decrease wildlife diversity. The management practice of temporarily lowering the water level in a marsh, known as drawdown, produces this effect also. Management goals often include setting back succession to stimulate and hold a particular plant community, such as quail habitat management by fire or management of an endangered species habitat in which a reduced habitat would be further endangered by natural succession toward local mature communities.

EFFECTS OF AGRICULTURAL ACTIVITIES ON WILDLIFE HABITAT

Agricultural activities on cropland, rangeland, pasture, and forest land have been altering wildlife habitat, in both positive and negative ways, throughout America's history. Agricultural and forestry production has increased to meet the growing demands of an expanding and more affluent population for food, fiber, and forest products. During the early periods, the clearing of forests for small, scattered farms created habitat diversity that provided a fertile environment for species like robins, woodchucks, and bobwhite quail. But, at the same time, it decreased favorable habitat for other native populations, such as wild turkeys, black bears, and moose. The migration westward brought a drastic modification of prairie habitat to the detriment of some wildlife (bison, elk, and pronghorn) and to the benefit of others (rodents and lagomorphs). These early changes were gradual in relation to the rate of transformation brought on by the advent of mechanized agriculture. In the early periods, wildlife had time to adapt to "changing conditions . . . [or] . . . to retreat to nearby undisturbed areas. But [modern] agriculture in America rapidly affected vast areas . . . giving most wildlife species no time to adapt and no place to retreat" (Brokaw 1978).

Modern agricultural technology, together with economic forces, has favored large contiguous fields devoted to single crops. The increasingly efficient drainage of lowlands, improved varieties of crops capable of growing on marginal soils, increased and more efficient use of fertilizer and pesticides, and development of irrigation have expanded cropland at the expense of natural ecosystems. The variety of habitat essential to wildlife is now often lacking. Species that responded positively to earlier patterns of agriculture have now declined. The ring-necked pheasant is an excellent example: the large pheasant populations typical in the Midwest and Northern Plains 30 years ago have dwindled rapidly with the intensification of agricultural operations.

Many specific agricultural and forestry land use practices affect the potential of an area to support wildlife. A unit of land planted to row crops or grain and plowed immediately after harvest results in poor habitat for most wildlife. If the same unit is cropped using conservation tillage practices or is used for pasture, it becomes more attractive to several species. Crop and forest diversity, plant spacing, presence of weeds, spillage of harvested crops, crop and forest residues, timing of farming and silvicultural operations, field size, and distribution of fields in relation to one another and to uncultivated bottomlands, woodlots, and similar areas that are relatively undisturbed all determine the attractiveness of an area to wildlife. Often, small changes in land use practices can result in major differences in the amount of habitat available to wildlife.

Other practices result in changes in the quality of aquatic habitats. Silt from erosion and runoff from organic wastes, fertilizers, and chemicals, as well as such techniques as irrigation, channelization, ponding, and cutting on steep slopes, affect aquatic systems and hence the species diversity of fish and wildlife dependent on these habitats.

Some practices that increase agricultural production enhance fish and wildlife habitats; others are detrimental. For example, diversifying crop and tree species may increase yields and build soil texture and fertility and at the same time create wildlife habitats far superior to those of similar areas that support single-species crops. Erosion control often directly and indirectly improves terrestrial habitats and protects water quality while benefiting agricultural production. Fall plowing, double cropping, extensive clearcutting, and increased use of herbicides aid production, but usually at the expense of wildlife habitat.

Whenever a change in agricultural or forestry practices provides food or cover for wildlife, a variety of species are usually quick to adjust to the new resources. Canada geese winter by the thousands in areas where there is little water or natural food but where corn has been spilled during the harvest in extensive fields. Similar responses to new sources of food or shelter can be observed in songbirds and other nongame species. In contrast, species can be eliminated by agricultural practices that fragment their habitats. Some insect-eating songbirds need large forested areas during the breeding season, and practices that break up forests are likely to be detrimental to them.

THE STRUCTURE OF THIS REPORT

This report falls roughly into two parts. The first part, Chapters 2 through 5, identifies the major agricultural trends in the United States. Chapter 2 focuses on the incorporation of wildlife values in land and water use decisions and the measurement and valuation issues associated with the private and public policy decisions that will affect the nature of the impacts of agricultural trends. Chapter 3 discusses the major forces that shape agricultural trends particularly important to wildlife habitat. Chapter 4 provides information about land and water resources and discusses trends for future land and water use as well as the quality and availability of these resources. Chapter 5 examines agricultural and forestry management practices that affect fish and wildlife habitats and the likelihood of their continued use. The second part, Chapters 6 through 11, examines the impacts of the identified trends on each of the major habitat types.

LITERATURE CITED

Brokaw, H.P., ed. 1978. Wildlife and America. Council on Environmental Quality, Washington, D.C.

King, R.T. 1974. The essential of a wildlife range. Pages 335-341 in J.A. Bailey et al., eds., Readings in wildlife conservation. The Wildlife Society, Washington, D.C.

MacArthur, R.H., and E.O. Wilson. 1967. The theory of island biogeography. Princeton University Press, Princeton, N.J.

Thomas, J.W., ed. 1979. Wildlife habitats in managed forests--the Blue Mountains of Oregon and Washington. U.S. For. Serv. Agric. Handbk. No. 553. 512 pp.

2

Measuring and Incorporating Wildlife and Habitat Values in Land and Water Use Decisions

RELATIONSHIPS BETWEEN AGRICULTURAL TRENDS AND WILDLIFE HABITAT

Farming, be it for fish or corn, is an activity in which natural environments are modified to enhance production of harvestable goods. In addition to the benefits of farming, there may also be adverse consequences. For instance, environmental modifications undertaken to increase crop flows may result in disturbances that reduce the availability of wildlife habitat. The habitat may be destroyed as a direct result of tillage and harvesting activities, or it may be reduced in quality as a result of residual flows into water bodies resulting in sedimentation and chemical loads. Some changes in farming practices may have a positive effect on fish and wildlife habitats, enhancing the flow of fish and wildlife goods.

The relationships between agricultural trends and wildlife habitats fall into three categories:

1. One value is substituted for another. Increasing the agricultural output reduces habitat availability or quality (e.g., the draining of marginal wetlands for crop production).
2. The two values are complementary. Changing certain agricultural practices increases habitat availability or quality (e.g., shifting to reduced tillage practices increases wildlife food, cover, and water quality).
3. The two values are independent of each other. Changing certain agricultural practices has no impact on habitat availability or quality (e.g., changing row crop rotation has no effect on general habitat characteristics).

NATIONAL VERSUS REGIONAL IMPACTS

The trends in U.S. agriculture being assessed in this report may not be unidirectional for all regions of the country. For example, if rising energy prices provide incentives for food production closer to major population centers, then food and livestock production may become more diverse around cities and less intensive in other areas. Likewise, increased irrigation east of the Mississippi River is anticipated, whereas reduced irrigation is expected in the West. These changes will likely benefit wildlife in the West and be to the detriment of wildlife in some areas in the East.

One factor associated with or responsible for the regional differences is the shifting comparative advantages of the agricultural locations. Changing economic conditions, such as rising energy prices, influence transportation and irrigation costs and, in turn, the types of crops most profitably grown in a given region. There are regional differences in the intensity and nature of production as well.

Ecosystems in some regions are more fragile and sensitive to changing trends than are those in other regions. Supplemental irrigation may have a smaller impact on water quality and quantity in the eastern states than in the western states.

It is important to consider regional trends in production as well as national changes. Once the regional trends are identified, their potential impacts can be assessed in terms of the particular regional habitat characteristics and situation. In assessing the habitat impacts it is important to remember that the whole is the sum of its parts and that some of the parts may be quite different.

INCORPORATING VALUES IN DECISIONS

The major impediment to the inclusion of wildlife and habitat values in land use decisions is that these values are difficult to measure. Without an accepted unit of value, wildlife and habitat values cannot be expressed in dollars for comparison with other land use values. At present, it is possible to measure, or measure by proxy, some wildlife habitat values such as recreation, but the more intangible aesthetic and philosophical benefits may be impossible to measure.

Although Congress has declared that "Fish and wildlife are of ecological, educational, aesthetic, cultural, recreational, economic, and scientific value to the Nation" (Fish and Wildlife Conservation Act of 1980), other decisionmakers have often failed to share this recognition. Inclusion of wildlife values in decisionmaking is further complicated by the fact that they are often external to private interests and included only in social or public interests.

This "public good" nature of wildlife is related to the doctrine of public ownership that governs wildlife in the United States. The difficult question of who owns wildlife presents a major obstacle to valuation. In this country, wildlife is determined to be owned by all Americans. The ownership right is limited, however, by the power of both state governments and the federal government to protect and control wildlife in the interests of the public and future generations. One answer to the ownership question was put succinctly but paradoxically by Russell Train when he said, "Wildlife is owned by everybody and by nobody . . . " (Brokaw 1978). Thus attempts at valuation founder on the fact that one person's use of wildlife resources affects another's, sometimes positively, often negatively. Yet these elusive external costs and benefits (i.e., those not taken into account by individuals) must somehow be included in estimates of wildlife resource values.

In economic terms, the desired level of investment in wildlife habitat improvements is determined by pushing such investments to the level where the added benefits of improvement are equal to the added costs of improvement. These costs of improvement include the outlays for habitat improvement as well as the foregone net returns from agricultural output or other competing uses. In the past there have been at best only partial assessments of benefits and costs of wildlife resource decisions, and the assessments can only be improved with a more acceptable measure than we have at present.

VALUE OF WILDLIFE AND HABITATS

Consumptive values of wildlife are those associated with the harvesting of wildlife resources. Consumptive values can be divided into commercial and recreational values.

Commercial value is the direct income from the sale of wildlife or wildlife products or from a business directly related to a wildlife resource (for example, the fur trade and commercial fisheries). These are explicit values that can be measured in dollars.

Recreational value refers to the enjoyment derived from recreational activities such as sport hunting and sport fishing in which wildlife resources are harvested. It should be noted that, while the hunter or fisherman gains consumptive value from "harvesting" a deer or fish, he or she also benefits from the nonconsumptive values associated with the total recreational experience. It should also be noted that whereas a few individual creatures are removed from the population, strict regulations ensure that adequate numbers remain to produce offspring. Thus, even though harvested, the wildlife resource replenishes itself for the enjoyment and use of future beneficiaries.

Nonconsumptive values are those associated with activities that do not preclude later use of the same resource. Nonconsumptive values include recreational value, biological value, environmental quality value, educational and philosophical values, and aesthetic value.

Recreational value is associated with the enjoyment gained from many recreational activities involving wildlife and wildlife habitats, such as birdwatching, hiking, camping, photography, and the nonconsumptive benefits enjoyed by hunters and sport fishermen. It relates to the "pleasure, adventure, and enhanced physical and mental health from outdoor activities . . . (that people gain from) . . . the pursuit or sometimes accidental enjoyment of wildlife and its habitat" (Bailey 1981).

The biological value of wildlife and its habitats is derived from their contribution to genetic research, their potential for providing now unknown benefits in the future, and their crucial role within their delicately balanced ecosystem.

The environmental quality value is the contribution made by wildlife and wildlife habitats to the overall environmental quality or health of the ecosystem. To the environmentalist, the presence of wildlife and its habitats is a valuable indicator of the overall environmental quality. Wildlife resources are of educational value because they can be used for research into areas such as genetics, provide answers to many questions confronting humans, and "enhance people's understanding of their environment" (Bailey 1981). The study of wildlife and its habitats is also valuable "to philosophy because wildlife ecology is the study of life and serves as one basis for speculation on human purposes, values, ethics, and destinies" (Bailey 1981).

Aesthetic value refers to aspects of the wildlife resource that provide visual, intellectual, spiritual, and artistic satisfaction and inspiration.

Three other types of values are also recognized: option, existence, and negative values. Option value is that associated with the knowledge that a resource is available for use sometime in the future. An option value holder is one who is willing to pay a premium for the assurance of future use of a resource. Existence value is gained by someone who benefits from the knowledge that a wildlife resource is available in an area, whether or not he or she ever uses it. Negative values of wildlife refer to damage done to property by wildlife, such as livestock lost to predators, or damage to crops from foraging animals and birds, or threats to human and animal health through the transmission of disease. Campaigns against bald eagles and coyotes by certain property owners are an expression of negative value as are the costs of controlling damages involved in fencing, trapping, and patroling.

There are two stumbling blocks in the way of more explicit quantification of wildlife habitat benefits for purposes of analyzing their worth to society. First, explicit values for wildlife resources are scarce because the markets that would define them seldom exist. Second, impacts on wildlife habitat are often not a factor in many decisionmaking processes. For example, farmers are often unable to quantify benefits to themselves from improved habitat and for this reason ignore wildlife when making production decisions.

The first stumbling block does not rule out decisions on the basis of imperfect information; the result is less than desirable levels of wildlife habitat. The second argues for public intervention to point up public benefits of wildlife when they are more important than the private benefits to the farmer. Only limited public intervention has occurred where private lands were involved.

MEASURING WILDLIFE AND HABITAT VALUES

Losses of wildlife habitat because of agricultural and other activities should be evaluated both biologically and economically to assess the seriousness of loss, to determine ways to minimize impacts, and to decide upon the best alternative use of the land. Methods for making such evaluations have developed slowly because of the complexity and expense of readily assessing the density, richness, and dynamics of natural communities, and the difficulty of making economic comparisons of aesthetic and non-product losses with other kinds of loss. Recently, however, environmental protection laws coupled with the development of special agency groups to enforce them have spurred evaluation efforts, while, at the same time, techniques have been evolving for assessing other nonmarket goods and services that can be applied to wildlife habitat values.

There are a variety of measurement techniques that can be used to quantify wildlife numbers and habitat quality. These techniques encompass fish and wildlife population surveys, wildlife community enumerations, and habitat assessments.

A diversity of techniques has been devised to estimate fish and wildlife density (i.e., the number of individuals of one species per unit area or volume). Some are indexes that allow only year-to-year or area-to-area comparisons; others are total censuses that purport to count an entire population. These techniques are best summarized for wildlife by Schemnitz (1980) and for fish by Bagenal (1978). Traditionally, these estimates have been time-consuming, covering several seasons or years, a span rarely allowed for in current impact assessment work. Even methods like the Peterson-Lincoln index require the marking of a significant number of animals and a high rate of recapture. Newer indexes that also convert to density estimates are being developed and tested, so that ultimately such population assessment may demand less time and money and fewer people (Burnham et al. 1980).

To assess the density of the numerous wildlife species coexisting in an area is an enormous task. Nevertheless, some effort must be made to determine the numbers of different species that occur (species richness) and their relative abundance. Whereas line or spot censuses may provide information on species richness, data necessary for total censuses (for calculating species density indexes) are difficult to obtain. With small birds, mist netting has been used regularly, and fisheries scientists have used nets and traps of various sizes. Mammalogists have combined live and dead traps to assure representation of all species for an index to relative abundance. All these techniques have problems of inaccuracy and are time-consuming, but they are being improved.

Standard vegetation assessment techniques have been used to sample the habitats of terrestrial wildlife. These include cover maps, quadrats, transects, and bisects. Aquatic habitats are most difficult to appraise and involve physical parameters such as depth, size of substrate, chemistry, and vegetation. All are difficult to relate to how fish and wildlife use the habitat, and many assessments of habitat use fish or wildlife density as a measure of carrying capacity and, thereby, quality of the habitat. Again, these measurements are time-consuming and often require several seasons of study because they involve observational rather than experimental approaches.

New qualitative approaches to habitat assessment have been developed by several federal agencies, which are often pressured to make judgments or plan for future resource management needs with little scientific justification. The U.S. Fish and Wildlife Service is now testing a system called the Habitat Evaluation Procedure (HEP) (Schamberger and Farmer 1978). This is a community-oriented approach to habitat evaluation involving qualitative assessments of the suitability of a habitat for each relevant species. The process involves mapping, use of selected species as indicators, trial runs in sample areas, and, ultimately, the calculation of a suitability index from 0 to 1.0 for each characteristic of the habitat. Considerable qualitative judgment is involved based on the experience and knowledge of the evaluator.

The Lower Mississippi River Division of the U.S. Army Corps of Engineers is developing another system called the Habitat Evaluation System (HES). While it is not yet in operation, it will be ecosystem-oriented and perhaps more comprehensive in the way it appraises such natural processes as succession. Whitaker and McCuen (1976), Thomas et al. (1976), and Lines and Perry (1978) have developed other systems tailored to special local or regional tasks.

These systems, when perfected, will be useable by different researchers and agencies. The methods will be comparable, and it will be possible to compare the data they generate on habitat evaluation, impact assessment, and long-range planning for wildlife resources. Still further agreement on methodology needs to emerge from these experimental approaches, however, so that quantification and modeling feasibility can be improved.

ECONOMIC VALUATION METHODS

A number of valuation methods designed to measure recreational values are applicable to values of wildlife resources even though some of them have serious shortcomings. Such methods of evaluation include the direct expenditures method, market value of harvested game, cost approach, unit day value method, and the willingness-to-pay techniques.

The direct expenditures method seeks to value wildlife activities on the basis of the total amount spent by participants in wildlife-related activities. Usually a questionnaire is mailed to a randomly selected population to elicit information on dollars spent on wildlife resource activities, such as food, lodging, travel, equipment, and license fees. The method is based on the assumption that the value of wildlife-related activity is equal to or greater than the amount spent in the enjoyment of the activity. Nobe and Gilbert (1970) used this approach to estimate the economic value of hunting and fishing in Colorado, which they concluded had amounted to $250 million in 1968.

A major criticism of this approach is that it measures gross value instead of a net increase in value added by increases in the opportunity to enjoy wildlife resources, or conversely, the added costs of declining opportunities (Davis 1963).

Another technique estimates the value of activities related to the wildlife resource by using the market value of the harvested game. For example, it is argued that the measure of the value of fishing is the market value of the fish caught. The method fails to assess the wide range of benefits associated with activities related to wildlife and assumes that the sole benefit of the activity is derived from harvesting the wildlife (Davis 1963). Also, for many species harvested for sport a commercial market may not exist.

The cost approach proposes that the value of a wildlife resource is equal to the cost of developing and maintaining it. The technique does not enable us to identify added gains or losses from wildlife resource development or destruction, and it can be a good example of circular reasoning (Brown et al. 1973).

One of the three methods approved by the Water Resources Council for valuing wildlife use, the unit day approach, uses expert or informed opinion and judgment to estimate the value of a unit day of activity. These values are typically based on the commercial value associated with different activities related to wildlife resources. The chief problems of this approach are (1) uniform values are not appropriate for both commercial and public wildlife resource use; (2) the values assigned are arbitrarily chosen; and (3) even though subject to adjustment, the values frequently do not adequately reflect variations in quality in the recreation experience.

The previous methods all fail to arrive at an estimate of wildlife resource value that satisfactorily covers most, if not all, of the appropriate values and offers an assessment of the added costs and benefits of different wildlife resource decisions. Some measure is needed of the maximum amount consumers would be willing to pay to continue an activity or to create a new one. The goal is to measure the total willingness to pay of consumers for a given level and quality of wildlife resources (or, in economic terms, the area under the demand curve). Two techniques are available to provide this estimate--the travel cost method and the interview or contingent valuation method.

The objective of the travel-cost method is to estimate a demand curve for wildlife resources by analyzing variations in the number of visits to a wildlife area and by measuring the associated variation in travel costs. This method proposes that the cost of travel to a wildlife resource area for a visitor from a distance is equal to the value that the local user receives but does not need to pay for in travel expenses. A basic problem with this method is its assumption that the sole cost of traveling is in money when, in fact, other costs such as time and the inconvenience are also relevant (Davis 1963).

The interview or survey method estimates the value of wildlife resource use with the aid of interviews or questionnaires that ask how much a person would be willing to pay to use a certain wildlife resource. A model is then developed to predict willingness to pay for a given wildlife resource. The quality of the wildlife-related experience in an area is positively related to the willingness to pay for the opportunity to visit that area. The major problem with this technique is that the individual's responses to the interview or survey questions may reflect significant biases (Schulze et al. 1981).

Several studies have laid the foundation for wildlife resource valuation by willingness-to-pay techniques.

Hammack and Brown (1974) looked at the value of waterfowl hunting as a function of the number of waterfowl shot and bagged during the season, along with other causal variables. Cocheba and Langford (1978) related the willingness to pay for waterfowl hunting to the number of waterfowl shot and bagged, and the number of shots missed. Capel and Pandey (1973) expressed willingness to pay for deer hunting in terms of total number of days spent hunting in a season, expenditures for hunting in a season, and hunter's residence. Their results showed that the more often a hunter uses a site, the less he or she is willing to pay per day, and that hunters who spend more during the season to hunt at a specific site are more willing to pay more per day.

Comparisons in both the Capel and Pandey (1973) study and the Davis (1963) study of travel cost and interview methods reveal similar results for the two valuation techniques. In any event, we need further research in the application of these techniques, in the refinement of variables measuring the quality of experiences related to wildlife resources, and in ways of incorporating more wildlife resource values, such as option and existence values.

ALTERNATIVES FOR MAINTAINING HABITAT

Although the discussion of the optimal mix of agriculture and wildlife was based on the assumption that the most efficient or cost-effective means of attaining improvements would be used, there are a number of alternative approaches to providing wildlife habitat when government intervention is deemed necessary. It is not the purpose of this section, however, to provide a comprehensive accounting of these alternatives or even to suggest the most appropriate ones.

There are two general categories of policy approaches: direct public intervention and incentive schemes for private action. One form of direct intervention involves restrictions on hectares of cropland, on land that could be used for cropland, or on agricultural exports. These restrictions would leave more land available for varied wildlife habitat and could change the nature of cultural practices. Another form of direct intervention would restrict cropping and livestock practices. Reduced tillage and grazing intensity would improve habitat but likely at the expense of agricultural output. Finally, the public sector could intensify wildlife management on public lands and acquire more public lands to compensate for deterioration in quantity or quality of habitat on private lands.

The incentive approach for improved habitat on private lands could be used for wildlife farming per se or for joint production of agricultural products and wildlife through modified management of existing agricultural land. Recent research lends support to the incentive approach (Burger and Teer 1981).

Finally, more research is needed on the trade-offs between intensively managed habitat on a limited land base and limited management on a vast land base. It is conceivable that a larger supply of wildlife habitat may result from management at the intensive rather than the extensive margin. These factors require careful scrutiny as impacts on habitat are considered.

LITERATURE CITED

Bagenal, T.B., ed. 1978. Methods for assessment of fish production in fresh waters. IBP Handbk. No. 3. 3rd ed. Blackwell Scientific Publications, London. 365 pp.

Bailey, J.A. 1981. Principles of wildlife. Unpublished textbook manuscript. Department of Wildlife Biology, Colorado State University.

Brokaw, H.P., ed. 1978. Wildlife and America. Council on Environmental Quality, Washington, D.C.

Brown, W.G., A. Singh, and N. Castle. 1973. An economic evaluation of the Oregon salmon and steelhead sport fishing. Oreg. Agric. Exp. Stn. Tech. Bull. No. 74, pp. 2-41.

Burger, G.V., and J.G. Teer. 1981. Economic and socioeconomic issues influencing wildlife management on private lands. Proceedings of symposium, Wildlife Management on Private Lands. Wisconsin Chapter, The Wildlife Society. (In press.)

Burnham, K.P., D.R. Anderson, and J.L. Laake. 1980. Estimation of density from line transect sampling of biological populations. Wildl. Monogr. Vol. 72. 202 pp.

Capel, R.E., and R.K. Pandey. 1973. Evaluating demand for deer hunting: a comparison of methods. Can. J. Agric. Econ. 21:6-14.

Cocheba, D.J., and W.A. Langford. 1978. Wildlife valuation: the collective good aspect of hunting. Land Econ. 54:490-504.

Davis, R.K. 1963. Value of outdoor recreation: an economic study of the Maine woods. Ph.D. thesis, Department of Economics, Harvard University.

Hammack, J., and G.M. Brown, Jr. 1974. Waterfowl and wetlands: toward BW economic analysis. Johns Hopkins University Press for Resources for the Future, Baltimore, Md.

Lines, I.L., and C.J. Perry. 1978. A numerical wildlife habitat evaluation procedure. Trans. North Am. Wildl. Nat. Resour. Conf. 43:284-301.

Nobe, K.C., and A.H. Gilbert. 1970. A survey of sportsmen expenditures for hunting and fishing in Colorado, 1968. GFP-R-T-24. Colorado Division of Game, Fish, and Parks, Denver.

Schamberger, M., and A. Farmer. 1978. The habitat evaluation procedures: their application in project planning and impact evaluation. Trans. North Am. Wildl. Nat. Resour. Conf. 43:274-283.

Schemnitz, S.D., ed. 1980. Wildlife management techniques manual. 4th ed. The Wildlife Society, Washington, D.C.

Schulze, W.D., R.C. d'Arge, and D.S. Brookshire. 1981. Valuing environmental commodities: some recent experiments. Land Econ. 57(2):151-172.

Thomas, J.W., R.J. Miller, H. Black, J.E. Rodiek, and C. Maser. 1976. Guidelines for maintaining and enhancing wildlife habitat in forest management in the Blue Mountains of Oregon and Washington. Trans. North Am. Wildl. Nat. Resour. Conf. 41:452-475.

Whitaker, G.A., and R.H. McCuen. 1976. A proposed methodology for assessing the quality of wildlife habitat. Ecol. Model. 2:251-272.

3
Forces Shaping Agricultural Trends in Land and Water Use and Management Practices

American agriculture is influenced by many factors, the most important of which are the economic forces. How will the demand for agricultural products be affected by continued population growth, both domestic and foreign? Will relative income grow along with population, thereby sustaining or increasing the demand for agricultural products? Will consumption preferences for agricultural products remain stable, or will there be major shifts in per capita consumption of various products or marked changes in the way some commodities are consumed? For example, will more or less grain be produced and how much will be used for direct human consumption, for animal consumption, or for alcohol production? Will farm size continue to increase? What effect will farm size have on ownership patterns, profitability, and the way land is used? Will the changing geographical distribution of the U.S. population continue to cause the conversion of agricultural lands to urban purposes? Will prices of land, labor, energy, chemicals, and other production inputs continue to escalate? What effect will foreign exchange rates have on the relative value and desirability of U.S. agricultural goods?

Social and political forces are becoming more important in shaping American agriculture. Will "tight money" be a continuing economic policy? Will present price policies for agriculture continue? Will restrictions on the uses of pesticides and herbicides and other environmental safeguards be strengthened or relaxed? Will agricultural products be a greater or lesser lever in U.S. foreign policy?

The future role of science and technology in shaping agriculture is unknown. Can new plant varieties with greater yields, shorter maturity, or greater disease resistance be counted on to alter agricultural output and production practices? Will fertilizer and pesticides be looked to as the major sources of expanded productivity? Will new production practices be found, or known ones extended, to reduce soil loss and arrest degradation and depletion of water resources?

These major social, economic, political, and technological questions are addressed in this chapter as a basis for projecting agricultural trends in land and water use and management practices.

TRENDS IN POPULATION AND INCOME AND THEIR IMPLICATIONS FOR U.S. AGRICULTURE

World Population

World population is a significant force affecting the demand for U.S. agricultural products. There is disagreement about the present trend of world population, and the disagreement increases as projections are made farther into the future. Projections for the year 2000 can differ by more than three quarters of a billion people, depending on whether a 2.5 percent or a 1.7 percent growth rate per year is applied (Table 3-1). Most of the discrepancy is in the projections for the less developed countries. In the more developed countries, present population levels are better known, and growth rates can be more accurately predicted.

The major importers of U.S. agricultural products are Western Europe, Asia (including the People's Republic of China), Africa, Latin America, Japan, and the Soviet Union. Estimates of increases in population from 1975 to 2000 range from a low of 10 percent in Western Europe to a high of 104 percent in Africa (Council on Environmental Quality and U.S. Department of State 1980). If the assumptions used to support the high projection in Table 3-1 materialize, world population will increase by 50 percent by the year 2000. If the low-level assumptions hold true, world population will increase by 35 percent. For the purposes of this report, the Committee arbitrarily accepts the medium-level projection of 42 percent. If this projection is used, the population of the major importers of U.S. agricultural commodities will increase by nearly 60 percent between 1975 and 2000; that is, the population of these areas will increase by about 2.2 billion people by the year 2000.

TABLE 3-1 World Population Projections (billions of people)

	1980			1990			2000		
	High	Medium	Low	High	Medium	Low	High	Medium	Low
World	4.549	4.471	4.384	5.545	5.340	5.140	6.797	6.351	5.922
More developed countries	1.174	1.170	1.166	1.276	1.252	1.231	1.377	1.323	1.274
Less developed countries	3.375	3.301	3.218	4.269	4.088	3.909	5.420	5.028	4.648

SOURCE: Council on Environmental Quality and U.S. Department of State 1980.

Irrespective of the accuracy of the estimates, the fact remains that world population is increasing, and given the current agricultural production and potential capacity in these areas the demand for U.S. agricultural products will also increase. In 1980, the production from one of every three hectares in the United States was exported. Therefore competition for land for agricultural uses arises not only from the domestic demand for food but also from the growing foreign demand.

In addition to the increased demand for food grains as a result of population growth in importing countries, there are also rising demands for feed grains as rising affluence stimulates meat consumption. This demand will be influenced not only by population levels, but also by changes in per capita gross national product (GNP), oil prices, levels of agricultural production, and public policies toward development. For example, estimates that per capita GNP in importing developing countries will increase over the next decade depend upon the successful transition to a world of high and increasing oil prices. If a GNP growth rate of 3.2 percent is realized, an increase over the 2.6 percent rate of increase of the 1970s (Schnittker Associates 1979), the demand by importing developing countries for feed grains to produce meat will increase. If, on the other hand, per capita GNP grows at a lesser rate than 3.2 percent or declines, the demand for grain for human consumption could increase. Care must be exercised in using any GNP growth rates for planning purposes.

Changes in patterns of international trade will also affect future demand for agricultural products. For example, between 1975 and 1979 there were marked shifts in the destinations of U.S. agricultural exports (Table 3-2). While the percentages of total exports to developed, developing, and centrally planned nations remained basically unchanged, agricultural exports showed a shift from developed nations to centrally planned economies. There was also an important and marked reduction in the percentage of grains and soybeans that went to developed countries and a substantial increase in the percentage purchased by centrally planned nations.

Shifting relative levels of per capita income among countries will change the pattern of exports of U.S. agricultural commodities. Exports to OPEC nations have increased dramatically from 1972 to 1978 (USDA, Economics, Statistics, and Cooperatives Service 1979a). During those years, exports of wheat to OPEC countries nearly

TABLE 3-2 Destination of U.S. Agricultural Exports, 1975-1979 (percentage)

	Total Exports	Agricultural Exports	Grain Exports				Soybean Exports
			Total	Wheat and Products	Rice	Feed Grains	
Developed countries							
1975	61	57	46	26	17	62	90
1976	62	60	48	25	29	65	86
1977	62	62	50	25	26	70	84
1978	61	56	39	25	22	53	81
1979	61	52	37	24	24	48	74
Developing countries							
1975	36	35	42	60	81	14	9
1976	35	30	35	64	68	10	9
1977	36	31	37	58	71	18	10
1978	36	33	41	60	77	20	12
1979	34	31	36	52	74	20	12
Centrally planned							
1975	3	8	12	14	2	24	1
1976	3	10	17	11	3	25	5
1977	2	7	13	17	3	12	5
1978	3	11	20	15	1	27	7
1979	5	17	27	24	2	32	14

SOURCE: USDA, Economics, Statistics, and Cooperatives Service 1979a.

doubled, and exports of corn, a primary feed grain, increased by more than 10 times as per capita income in these countries has increased.

U.S. Population

The U.S. population is projected to increase by about 24 percent between 1975 and 2000 (U.S. Water Resources Council 1978). More significant than the increase will be the geographic redistribution of the population. During the past decade when the U.S. population (exclusive of Alaska and Hawaii) grew by 11 percent, there were major population shifts among regions (Table 3-3). Several Northeast states actually lost population, and others gained only marginally. The Northern Plains, Corn Belt, and Lake States grew at rates well below the national average. Mountain, Pacific, and Southeast states sustained large population increases, with California, Texas, and Florida accounting for 40 percent of the net population growth between 1970 and 1980.

Since 1970, nonmetropolitan areas have grown more rapidly than metropolitan areas, reversing one of the nation's long-established population trends. The population of the standard metropolitan statistical areas (SMSAs) increased by 0.8 percent annually between 1970 and 1978, whereas the nonmetropolitan population increased by 1.3 percent annually (U.S. Department of Commerce, Bureau of the Census 1980). The nonmetropolitan counties closest to cities grew more rapidly in both the 1960s and the 1970s, whereas the more remote counties, with longer commuting distances, grew more slowly. Such trends indicate that part of the nonmetropolitan population growth is due to metropolitan development beyond the official SMSA boundaries. However, since 1970 the gap in growth rates between the different nonmetropolitan categories has narrowed. Even those counties far removed from cities are now growing more rapidly than metropolitan areas or the nation as a whole.

The continuation of such a trend is likely to cause the conversion of significant amounts of prime agricultural land to nonagricultural uses and result in the conversion of rangeland, pasture, and forest land to cropland or the increased use of marginal land for producing agricultural products. Such conversions, in turn, drive up the cost of agricultural land and stimulate more intensive use of existing farmland, including greater use of chemicals and water to sustain production.

TABLE 3-3 U.S. Population by Region in 1970 and 1980

	1980	1970	Percent Change
Pacific			
Washington	4,130,163	3,413,244	21.0
Oregon	2,632,663	2,091,533	25.9
California	23,668,562	19,971,069	18.5
Total (average)	30,431,388	25,475,846	(19.5)
Mountain			
Idaho	943,935	713,015	32.4
Montana	786,690	694,409	13.3
Wyoming	470,816	332,416	41.6
Utah	1,461,037	1,059,273	37.9
Colorado	2,888,834	2,209,596	30.7
Nevada	799,184	488,738	63.5
Arizona	2,717,866	1,775,399	53.1
New Mexico	1,299,968	1,017,055	27.8
Total (average)	11,368,330	8,289,901	(37.1)
Northern Plains			
North Dakota	652,695	617,792	5.6
South Dakota	690,178	666,257	3.6
Nebraska	1,570,006	1,485,333	5.7
Kansas	2,363,208	2,249,071	5.1
Total (average)	5,276,087	5,018,453	(5.1)
Southern Plains			
Oklahoma	3,025,266	2,559,463	18.2
Texas	14,228,383	11,198,655	27.1
Total (average)	17,253,649	13,758,118	(25.4)
Lake States			
Minnesota	4,077,148	3,806,103	5.1
Wisconsin	4,705,335	4,417,821	6.5
Michigan	9,258,344	8,881,826	4.2
Total (average)	18,040,827	17,105,750	(5.5)
Corn Belt			
Iowa	2,913,387	2,825,368	3.1
Illinois	11,418,461	11,110,285	2.8
Indiana	5,490,179	5,195,392	5.7
Ohio	10,797,419	10,657,423	1.3
Missouri	4,917,444	4,677,623	5.1
Total (average)	35,536,890	34,466,091	(3.1)
Delta States			
Louisiana	4,203,972	3,644,637	15.3
Mississippi	2,520,638	2,216,994	13.7
Arkansas	2,258,513	1,913,322	18.8
Total (average)	8,983,123	7,774,953	(15.5)

TABLE 3-3 (continued)

	1980	1970	Percent Change
Northeast			
Maine	1,124,660	993,722	13.2
Vermont	511,456	444,732	15.0
New Hampshire	920,610	737,681	24.8
Connecticut	3,107,576	3,032,217	2.5
Massachusetts	5,737,037	5,689,170	0.8
Rhode Island	947,154	949,723	-0.3
New York	17,557,288	18,241,391	-3.8
New Jersey	7,364,158	7,171,112	2.7
Pennsylvania	11,866,728	11,800,766	0.6
Delaware	595,225	548,104	8.6
Maryland	4,216,446	3,923,897	7.5
West Virginia	1,949,644	1,744,237	11.8
District of Columbia	637,651	756,668	-15.7
Total (average)	56,535,633	56,033,420	(0.89)
Appalachian			
Kentucky	3,661,433	3,220,711	13.7
Tennessee	4,590,750	3,926,018	16.9
Virginia	5,346,279	4,651,448	14.9
North Carolina	5,874,429	5,084,411	15.5
Total (average)	19,472,891	16,882,588	(15.3)
Southeast			
South Carolina	3,119,208	2,590,713	20.4
Alabama	3,890,061	3,444,354	12.9
Georgia	5,464,265	4,587,930	19.1
Florida	9,739,992	6,791,418	43.4
Total (average)	22,213,526	17,414,415	(27.6)

SOURCE: U.S. Department of Commerce, Bureau of the Census 1981.

ECONOMIC TRENDS AND THEIR IMPLICATIONS FOR DEMAND AND SUPPLY OF U.S. AGRICULTURAL PRODUCTS

The primary economic trends in agricultural production are related to the large increase in capital required to engage in modern technologically based agriculture. These increased requirements reflect (1) greater reliance on purchased inputs such as chemicals and machinery, (2) rising land values, and (3) relative changes in energy prices.

During the past 30 years, the importance of capital to farm production has increased significantly (Figure 3-1). Agricultural producers have increased their expenditures for machinery and chemicals to maximize returns and to reduce uncertainty. In doing so, they have become vulnerable to fluctuations in the prices of these increasingly important capital expenses. Today, farmers must borrow heavily to meet the large annual requirements for cash. When the prices of the items needed for production that are purchased off the farm rise more rapidly than the prices received for the products--as has been the case during the recent period of high inflation--more and more farmers become financially stressed. If inflation continues, the financial viability of many farmers will become precarious. The availability and cost of capital are now, and will continue to be, an important factor in determining the level of supply of U.S. agricultural products.

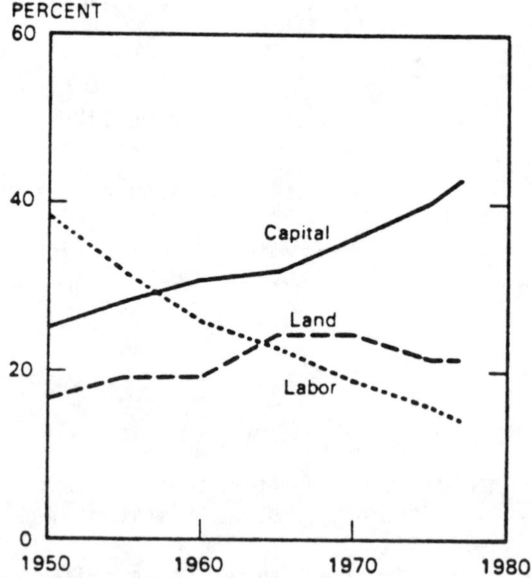

FIGURE 3-1 Resources used in farming, 1950-1980. SOURCE: USDA, Economics, Statistics, and Cooperatives Service 1979c.

The per hectare value of farmland remained reasonably stable until the mid-1960s, but it has increased dramatically since the early 1970s (Figure 3-2). Some of this increase is due to inflation, including speculation by developers paying high prices for residential or industrial sites. It also reflects the drive by farmers to expand their operations to maintain present incomes. High land prices are preventing many would-be farmers from purchasing land since they cannot pay for an entire farm from the agricultural operation. Entry into American agriculture is not guaranteed, if it ever was, and the traditional passing of a farm from generation to generation within a family is becoming increasingly difficult because of inheritance taxes. The present trend of leasing farmland is likely to continue, and this may influence land use patterns, production decisions, and output levels, which, in turn, can affect the quality of land and water resources.

Two of the most important economic factors shaping the future of American agriculture are the supply and the price of energy. Rising energy prices boost production costs and narrow profit margins; they influence what crops are grown, as well as how, where, and when they are produced.

Since the mid-1970s, fuel cost per hectare has doubled for nearly all commodities. The cost of fuel has increased by nearly 50 percent as a share of farmer's variable costs. Some experts foresee a decline in the

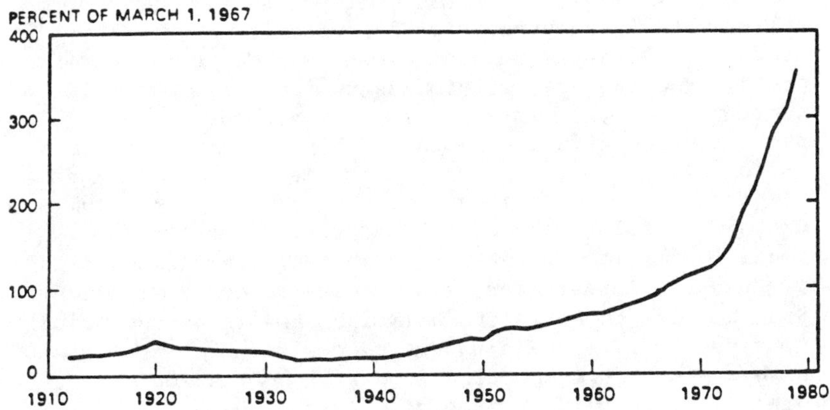

FIGURE 3-2 Index of U.S. farm real estate value.
SOURCE: USDA, Economics, Statistics, and Cooperatives Service 1979c.

use of fossil fuels. There is evidence that land preparation practices (plowing and cultivating) are being modified to reduce fuel consumption. New production practices will likely require energy, though less per hectare than present practices. The total energy consumption for agriculture, however, may rise as total output rises to meet new demands. High energy prices have already affected the economics of irrigation throughout the United States. Unless commodity prices increase to compensate for higher energy costs, groundwater use may be limited in certain regions, depending on how much water must be lifted. It is projected that deep-well pumping and supplemental irrigation will become restricted to high-value crops; supplemental irrigation in regions such as the Corn Belt will continue to be profitable. Higher energy costs are also stimulating changes in irrigation practices. More energy- and water-conserving systems, such as drip irrigation and low-pressure mobile systems, are being used.

A future trend, the direction and impact of which are still in dispute, is the degree to which substitutes for fossil fuels will come from agricultural products. Current federal policy subsidizes the production of ethanol, and this could lead to a competition for grain between exporters and buyers for domestic use. This competition increases the demand for land to grow corn. If deregulation of domestic oil and natural gas increases supplies and stabilizes prices, it seems unlikely that ethanol production will increase. Even with continued moderate increases in fossil fuel prices, it seems unlikely that the production of fuels from agricultural products will increase significantly. Conversion of some grain, crop residue, or biomass to fuel will probably continue to supplement on-farm energy needs and may partially substitute for other fuels on a regional basis.

The rising cost of transportion may lead to changes in the location of production for some commodities. Bulky crops with tolerance for a broad range of natural conditions (e.g., potatoes and apples) are already being produced in larger quantities closer to consumer markets. Some believe those shifts will increase if energy prices continue to rise. Rising energy costs and the resulting high costs of transporting food will be a stimulus for greater regional independence. At the same time, if greater reliance on integrated farming systems emerges, such as intercropping with legumes to restore soil nitrogen, feeding crop residues to livestock, and employing less chemically intensive pest management strategies, could also lead to greater diversification of agricultural operations. If diversification regionally and on individual farms evolves, greater diversity for fish and wildlife habitats would result.

STRUCTURAL ISSUES IN U.S. AGRICULTURE AFFECTING LAND USE AND MANAGEMENT PRACTICES

The most important structural changes taking place in U.S. agriculture include a continued reduction in the total number of farms, an increase in average farm size, and changes in the pattern of farm ownership.

Since 1935 the absolute number of farms has declined by about one third. In 1935, 86 percent of all farms had fewer than 89 ha (220 acres); by 1974 this figure had decreased to 70 percent. Likewise, in 1935 only 1.3 percent of all farms were larger than 405 ha (1000 acres); by 1974 5.4 percent of all farms exceeded 405 ha (USDA, Economics, Statistics, and Cooperatives Service 1980).

Projections indicate that the total number of farms will decline by nearly 40 percent between 1974 and 2000 (Table 3-4). This decline would be even greater if the

TABLE 3-4 Most Likely Projection of the Number of Farms by Size of Farm (thousands of farms)

Size of Farm	Actual 1974	1985	1990	1995	2000
Fewer than 40 ha (less than 100 acres)	1357	1096	990	895	827
40-88 ha (100-219 acres)	650	476	404	346	302
89-202 ha (220-499 acres)	502	387	339	296	264
203-404 ha (500-999 acres)	211	202	193	187	183
405-809 ha (1000-1999 acres)	93	97	98	100	102
810 ha and over (2000 acres and over)	62	65	66	67	71
All farms	2875	2323	2090	1891	1749

SOURCE: Adapted from USDA, Economics, Statistics, and Cooperatives Service 1980.

definition of a farm as a unit having sales of more than $1000 is employed. By the year 2000, small farms, defined as those having fewer than 89 ha (220 acres), will decline slightly to make up 65 percent of all farms, and large farms, having more than 405 ha (1000 acres), will increase to make up almost 10 percent of all farms.

If these projections are realized, small farms and large agricultural enterprises will dominate in the future. By 2000, it is estimated that the 50,000 largest farms, approximately 3 percent of the 1.75 million farms, will produce about two thirds of the agricultural products and the largest 1 million farms, approximately 57 percent of all farms in that year, will produce almost all the agricultural products (USDA, Economics, Statistics, and Cooperatives Service 1980).

The declining numbers but relatively stable percentage of farms of less than 40 ha (100 acres) projected indicates that a number of people will choose to live in rural agricultural settings and farm part-time to supplement other income. Although these farm units are projected to continue to make up about 47 percent of all farms, they will not produce a significant proportion of the total output and will not produce the types of commodities that will enter the export trade.

By the year 2000, most commercial farms will still be owned by families, although the present trend toward incorporation of the family farm for tax advantages and ease of bequeathment is likely to continue. However, the trends and projections indicate that increasing farm size tends to result in more part-ownership (Table 3-5). Whereas over 50 percent of farms with sales of $100,000 and more were part-owned in 1974, projections are that more than 70 percent of such farms will be part-owned in the year 2000. On the other hand, the trend for farms with sales of less than $100,000 is increasing toward full-ownership by the year 2000. Expansion of existing larger agricultural units is likely to involve the leasing, rather than the purchase, of additional land.

The asset balance of farmers will be affected by the continued increase in land values. Farm real estate now accounts for nearly 75 percent of all farm assets, and the value of real estate per farm has increased by a factor of more than 40 in the past 35 years, reflecting both increasing farm size and rising land values. This shift in the asset balance has provided a base for additional borrowing for both short- and long-term purposes. High-technology agriculture relying on

TABLE 3-5 Tenure Structure by Sales Class (percentage)

	Less than $20,000	$20,000 to $99,999	$100,000 and Over	All Farms
Full owners				
1964	61.8	31.5	34.2	57.9
1969	69.4	35.1	35.3	62.5
1974	74.3	39.3	29.3	61.5
2000	93.0	59.0	16.0	63.0
Part owners				
1964	21.7	50.3	51.6	24.9
1969	26.9	47.8	51.4	24.6
1974	16.6	44.8	57.2	27.2
2000	4.0	28.0	72.0	30.0
Tenants				
1964	16.5	18.1	14.1	17.2
1969	17.1	17.1	13.3	12.9
1974	9.1	15.9	13.5	11.3
2000	3.0	12.0	12.0	7.0

SOURCE: USDA, Economics, Statistics, and Cooperatives Service 1979c.

purchased inputs can continue, and further investments in land improvement and capital equipment can be made only if capital is available. With capital, more land can be drained, supplemental irrigation developed, and new and more efficient machinery employed. On the other hand, high interest rates could serve as a deterrent to borrowing, shorten the acceptable payback period for any capital expenditure, and slow the adoption of new technology.

Continuing increases in the average level of education of agricultural producers should speed acceptance and application of new scientific and technological information, including practices that may help to conserve resources as well as be economically efficient. Such ownership forms as incorporation to facilitate the transfer of a farm between generations could encourage a more farsighted perspective in the stewardship of land and water resources.

U.S. PUBLIC POLICY ISSUES AFFECTING LAND USE AND MANAGEMENT PRACTICES

Agriculture in the future will be affected by a broader array of public policies than in the past. As exports increase, the influence on agriculture of both U.S. and foreign policies affecting international trade will increase. The greater amounts of capital necessary to finance agricultural production will make monetary and fiscal policy more important to agriculture. Farmers' decisions will be influenced by other nonagricultural domestic policies in such areas as environmental protection and occupational safety and health. Domestic policies directly benefiting agriculture have been, and will remain, important, though their future will be influenced by relative political strength, changing values, and the relative importance of agriculture in the national economy.

Current cultural practices will continue to prevail until available technology (e.g., no-till agriculture and drip irrigation) becomes economically profitable to adopt or until new, economically viable technology is developed (e.g., new seed varieties, greater photosynthetic efficiency in plants, nitrogen-fixing capability in nonleguminous plants, growth regulators, and pest and disease control systems). The major short-term change most likely to occur will be a change in individual farm and regional cropping patterns, primarily in response to fluctuations in product and factor prices and secondarily in response to concerns about soil use, water use, and income stability. Governmental policy, including the availability of credit and levels of research expenditure, can affect the rates at which innovative practices are adopted and new technologies are developed.

Agricultural production in the United States will continue to be influenced by the rising importance of export markets and hence the domestic policies of foreign countries. Most projections of international trends suggest an increased international demand for U.S. agricultural exports. The government's use of exports to help meet balance of payments deficits resulting from dependence on foreign energy sources continues to encourage increased agricultural output. As more products enter international markets, the instability of those markets, tied as they are to the domestic policies of foreign nations, will be felt in U.S. markets. This may foster greater price variability for agricultural products, particularly those important in the export trade.

Since 1940, agricultural imports, measured in dollars, have increased nearly twelvefold and the agricultural portion of total U.S. imports has declined steadily. During the same period, agricultural exports increased by eightyfold (USDA 1980). Thus, today, U.S. agriculture not only supplies a much larger portion of domestic needs, but it also makes a large contribution to U.S. export trade. Because of its increasing contribution to the economy, pressures for the maintenance or expansion of agriculture production for export markets will continue.

Governmental policies on agricultural exports will affect how much is sold abroad in the future. A policy that emphasizes feeding a growing world population will encourage more and more crop production. On the other hand, a policy that uses food and fiber as tools in the conduct of foreign policy (e.g., grain embargoes, trade agreements, and import restrictions) may lead to a decline in exports in the future because of uncertainty on the part of the buyer about the United States as a supplier. Although food can be a powerful tool in conducting international relations, it has not heretofore been employed extensively as such. Two recent exceptions were the grain embargo against the U.S.S.R. and the withholding of food aid to Poland. The United States views the Agricultural Trade Development and Assistance Act of 1954, as amended (PL 480), as a surplus disposal program, not as a food aid program. This view could change, however, if there were to be a massive world crop failure resulting in starvation.

Governmental policies on interest rates and capital availability will affect the number of hectares farmed, cropping patterns, production practices, adoption of new technology, replacement of equipment and structures, farm size, and even the rate at which industry develops new technology and materials needed by agriculture to meet growing demands efficiently and effectively.

Environmental policies, too, will affect agricultural output and land use. At present, some agricultural chemicals are banned or restricted. Although there are a large number of chemicals available, the need for new and different chemicals to control pests and weeds, stimulate growth, and aid in harvesting is growing, but regulatory constraints and costs have impeded their development. Without efficacious chemicals to control specific insect pests and unwanted plant species, more land would be needed to maintain present levels of output. Concerns for the quality of land and water resources can be expected over time to lead to new public policies designed to reduce soil losses and the runoff of fertilizer and pesticide residues that can have both harmful and beneficial effects on nonagricultural activities.

A variety of public subsidies or expenditures, such as price supports, technical assistance for drainage or construction of small impoundments, loan guarantees, and construction of irrigation projects, currently assist the agricultural sector. In coming years, agriculture is expected to fare reasonably well under American domestic policies. Although there are likely to be fewer farmers in the years ahead, the political strength of the farm sector is not expected to diminish. Its strength will be maintained because the demand for farm products will remain strong, the need for domestic price stability will continue, and many powerful business interests will continue to share objectives with the farm sector. It is expected that farmers and their political allies will press for policies that will maintain adequate farm income in the face of rising production costs and uncertain prices. For example, price protection for major export commodities will be sought, since fluctuations in export demands subject domestic prices to greater potential variation. Lack of price stability could result in larger fluctuations in amount of land cropped from year to year, particularly the more marginal lands. Lack of price support programs could also encourage greater diversification as farmers attempt to protect their incomes from excessive fluctuations and risk.

Large expenditures of public funds for water developments with subsidies for irrigation characteristic of the past may be less popular in the future. Yet, as population density continues to shift westward and southwestward, competition for water between those needing it for nonagricultural uses and those needing it for agricultural uses will increase. Public policy will emphasize water development and conservation, but agriculture will be increasingly pressed in the long run to pay a larger proportion of the bill for the water it draws from public projects.

In the future, policies on technical and financial assistance to operators may be more closely tied to resource-conserving practices. Areas of particular concern are soil erosion and the runoff of fertilizers and other chemicals into waterways, the off-farm disposal of wastes, and the burning of crop residues. Farmers will have to remain sensitive to the impacts of their activities on others.

Domestic policies also will affect the future of publicly held noncrop agricultural land. For example, the levels of future production from public rangeland and forests will be directly affected by the amounts of money appropriated under the terms of the Resources Planning Act of 1974 (PL 93-378), which provides for improving the productivity of these resources.

There are several viewpoints as to how development and production objectives and environmental protection can be accommodated. Some believe that the differences will become more severe and will be resolved by single-interest political or legal decisions more often than by reliance on economic or biological analyses and negotiation. Others believe that conflicts will become less intense and that resolutions will be reached more easily. A third view is also emerging: that increased production and environmental enhancement are not mutually exclusive and that both can be achieved with the proper set of coordinated public policies.

Future agricultural policies will be influenced by public recognition of opportunities for multiple use of natural resources, concern about the stewardship of public and private resources, and changing values toward the family farm. Americans have become aware that efficiencies from new agricultural technologies resulting in increased size and increases in productivity per farm employee coming from large capital investments have permanently changed the structure of American agriculture.

As the public becomes more concerned about the allocation of land and the enhancement and protection of the natural resource base, land use planning will gain momentum. These new issues will result in new policy directions.

TRENDS IN SCIENCE AND TECHNOLOGY AND THEIR IMPLICATIONS FOR U.S. AGRICULTURE

Developments in science and technology have always been an important force in increasing productivity. Improvements in agricultural technology over the last 50 years have resulted in impressive gains in food and fiber yields, dramatic increases in the deployment of capital equipment, and a sharp decline in direct labor requirements. Most experts, while continuing to be optimistic about the possibilities for continued improvements in the efficiency and productivity of American agriculture, share the view that "satisfactory" future growth of productivity in agriculture cannot be taken for granted. The NRC's Board on Agriculture and Renewable Resources has held this position for some time. Despite continued debate over questions of productivity measurement, evidence from a variety of sources indicates that the rate of productivity growth has slowed, with the average rate per year for this past decade being approximately 1.2 percent (Farrell 1981) contrasted to an average of 1.85 percent over the previous two decades. Without continued increases in productivity, increasing amounts of land will be required to meet increased demand.

Agricultural research and extension expenditures are crucial to continued productivity growth. The real growth rate of research and extension dollars from 1939 to 1972 was 3 percent per year, but since 1972 the real growth rate has been either zero or negative. With a zero growth rate for research expenditures, the growth rate in agricultural productivity between 1980 and 2000 would be approximately 1 percent per year (USDA, Economics, Statistics and Cooperatives Service 1979b). If real research and extension expenditures grew at a real rate of 7 percent per year, an annual growth rate of 1.2 percent could be maintained.

There are promising prospects. Genetic engineering to achieve greater plant efficiency and to breed plants with increased resistance to environmental stresses, diseases, pests, and toxic chemicals can greatly enhance productivity. Current research is also focusing on improving productivity by increasing the photosynthetic efficiency of plants, but major breakthroughs are not yet on the horizon. Research on the enhancement of soil fertility through the development of nitrogen-fixing plants continues to show great promise. Increasing the number of multiple births in livestock will enhance the efficiency of meat and milk production. It is hoped that economical ways will be developed to help continue to close the gaps between experimental and average yields.

Often overlooked is the fact that many past scientific achievements have depended directly on the uninterrupted availability and low cost of fossil fuels, especially natural gas and oil. The technology that evolved during an era of declining real energy prices is now being reevaluated in a new context. The real cost of energy resources must be taken into account in planning for the future.

Energy costs are stimulating science and technology to look for ways in which energy input can be reduced and greater efficiency of the resources employed can be achieved. For example, use of equipment that improves the speed and precision with which farming operations can be accomplished (laser-leveling equipment) is becoming more widespread, as are practices to obtain precise applications of chemicals. Equipment that incorporates several operations to reduce tillage and the number of cultivation passes is in use. These trends are expected to continue. Furthermore, technology that emphasizes concepts of "organic farming"--such as the use of weed residues and conservation tillage systems to reduce inputs and enhance total crop productivity--is likely to result from higher energy prices and a continued commitment to protection of the environment.

"Integrated farming systems" are becoming more widespread and profitable as concerns for the environment spread and energy costs rise. The use of legumes for nitrogen replacement is likely to increase, either through intercropping or as winter covers. Also, crop residues are being used by livestock for feed, and "nutrient" cycling is being reintroduced on individual farms.

If farms increase in size, tractors may, too. Efficiency per unit of output and per hectare will be sought, and "appropriate technology" to meet this goal is likely to result in the use of a greater diversity of equipment as well as new types of mechanized harvest equipment, the greatest expansion coming in the harvesting of perishable commodities.

Electronics will play a greater role in farming in helping to increase the precision, and thus the efficiency, of operations. Remote sensing devices, on-farm computer-controlled feed operations, and microprocessors to monitor and regulate energy and water use are possible applications.

Scientific research and technological development can improve crop and livestock productivity, particularly by increasing the efficiency with which resources are converted into food, fiber, wood products, and industrial commodities. Substantial gains in productivity could lead to a decreased need for agricultural lands, but this will depend heavily on research funding, international

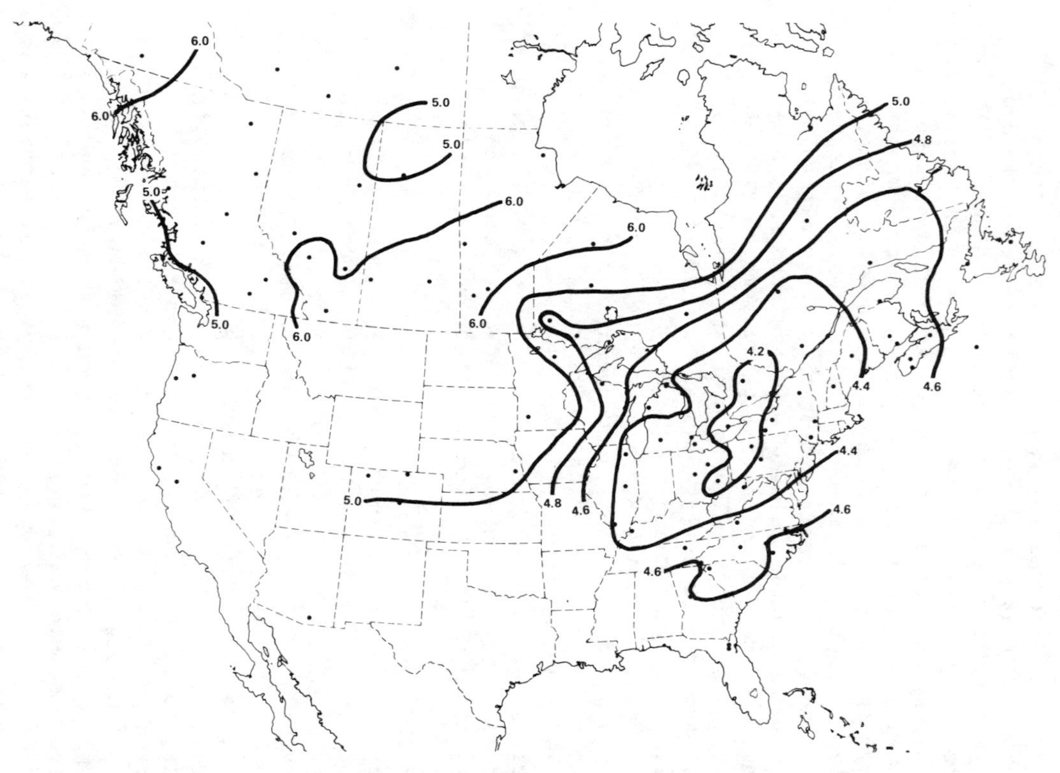

FIGURE 3-3 Acidity of precipitation in the United States (pH).
SOURCE: National Research Council 1981.

production and trade conditions, domestic energy prices relative to commodity prices, and other policies related to use of natural resources. Without such gains, it is probable that more land will have to be cultivated to maintain current levels of output. The political, social, and economic aspects should be considered in order to provide the incentives for the management of soil and water on a sustained basis for meeting domestic food needs and export demand.

REGIONAL DIFFERENCES AND CONSTRAINTS

Climatic factors, water availability, soil type, water use, and land use shape agricultural trends on a regional level.

No clearly defined trends in climatic variability have been identified yet within major agricultural areas. The amount of atmospheric carbon dioxide is increasing, and although its future impact on climate is still uncertain, its potential impacts are tremendous. A rise in world temperature of only a few degrees Celsius could reduce polar ice, raising sea levels and inundating coastal regions, increasing evaporation, creating or expanding deserts, and reducing river flows. Rainfall patterns will also be affected. On the other hand, a world warming would lengthen growing seasons and enable agriculture to expand into areas now locked in permafrost. Acid rain currently is a problem in certain areas (Figure 3-3), and the increasing use of coal will add more oxidized nitrogen and sulfur to the atmosphere, causing more acid rain in the Northwest, Northeast, and East, and in isolated areas elsewhere. The adverse effects of acid rain on lakes and wetlands are discussed in Chapters 9 and 10.

Attempts to alter the effects of climate on agriculture will certainly continue. For example, plastic mulches and controlled environments will be used to modify temperature. Cloud seeding may be effective regionally, but it is difficult to control precisely where the water will fall, and the concomitant rain shadows are detrimental to agriculture downwind.

In general, precipitation is a greater constraint in the West than in the East and Southeast. (A map showing average annual precipitation can be found in U.S. Water Resources Council (1978).) Temperature is a greater constraint in the North, where it limits the length of the growing season, than in the South. Soil differences among regions are also important. The deep, fertile soils of the Midwest and Plains are more productive for major commodities than are shallow, sandy alkaline, acid, or saline soils elsewhere, which may require large inputs of fertilizers or other chemicals.

Water use and water availability constrain agricultural production in several regions. Crops grown in areas that are marginally productive are more vulnerable to adverse climatic effects, especially drought. The importance of supplemental irrigation in such areas may encourage further multipurpose development of water resources.

Land use decisions can also act as regional constraints upon agriculture. Urbanization and suburbanization will continue to break up agricultural areas and remove land from production. Given the different migration rates in the United States, different regional constraints on the availability of land for further agricultural development are likely. Recreational uses would also reduce the availability of some lands for agriculture.

Agricultural practices currently in use regionally and by individual crop and livestock enterprises set the pattern for future changes. Existing capital equipment--machinery, irrigation systems, and other equipment--is a substantial deterrent to change, particularly when the salvage or current value declines as new technology becomes available. Farmers will keep existing equipment and irrigated systems until it pays to change and until more efficient new machinery and systems become available.

Constraints will be imposed on future food and fiber production by resources other than energy. Time is one such resource. If adequate time is not available for solving problems or for developing new technology, production capacity may decrease. For example, it takes an average of 10 years to develop a new crop variety. An adequate lead time must be allowed for in a rapidly changing and highly uncertain economic environment if the premature obsolescence of capital stock and other unacceptable social and economic costs are to be avoided.

THE NATURE OF CHANGE

Future changes in agricultural practices, as well as in the level and the location of agricultural activity, are likely to proceed in divergent directions. For example, increases in specialized agriculture may occur at the same time that agriculture is becoming more diversified on a regional basis. Agricultural production near large metropolitan areas could become more diversified, especially if energy prices stimulate some production of seasonal commodities close to the consuming areas. Some animals could be raised near consumption centers if changing cropping patterns increase feed supplies locally. This development could reduce the need to ship certain types of livestock to given regions--for example, pork to the Northwest. Renewed interest in crop rotation, intercropping, and double cropping will lead to greater diversification but more intensive land use as well. Other forces will promote monoculture in some regions. An example of the potential increases in specialization is the trend toward fewer and larger high-technology dairy farms. In this case, as in others, the high cost of control measures for environmental protection favors large farms.

The prediction of future changes in agriculture is difficult under any circumstances, but uncertainty over future energy prices adds to the complexity. Two perspectives have evolved regarding trends in farm size and input in response to higher energy prices. Proponents of one argue that farm size and mechanization will continue to increase and that capital will continue to be substituted for labor. Supporters of the other maintain that agriculture will become more labor intensive and diversified, with little or no increase in size of farms and machinery. More research is needed if these perspectives are to be reconciled.

DISCONTINUITY IN TRENDS

Trends in land use and production practices likely to result from these economic, political, and social forces can be identified. But the assumptions underlying these trends may be invalidated. Major economic or political changes could have serious effects on the future of agriculture. For example, serious interruptions in fossil fuel supplies at any time could sharply alter the levels of input of petroleum-based chemicals and output of food and fiber. Should food become a strategic tool in international policy on the part of the United States or any other major producing or consuming region, the impacts on trends in animal agriculture could be great and unpredictable. Finally, world conflict would so totally alter the domestic demand for agricultural products and the structure of world trade that any attempt to identify trends would be fruitless.

AGRICULTURAL TRENDS INFORMATION DATA

In the Committee's view, the National Agricultural Lands Study (Council on Environmental Quality 1981) is the best source of information on agricultural trends to date. Other related references that deal with trends include Resources and Environmental Impacts of Agriculture in the United States (Crosson and Brubaker 1982), The Nation's Water Resources: 1975-2000 (U.S. Water Resources Council 1978), Soil and Water Resources Conservation Act (U.S. Department of Agriculture 1981), An Assessment of the Forest and Range Land Situation in the United States (USDA, Forest Service 1980), Wildlife and America (Brokaw 1978), and Farmland or Wasteland (Sampson 1981).

LITERATURE CITED

Brokaw, H.P., ed. 1978. Wildlife and America. Council on Environmental Quality, Washington, D.C. 532 pp.

Council on Environmental Quality. 1981. National agricultural lands study: final report. Government Printing Office, Washington, D.C. 108 pp.

Council on Environmental Quality, and U.S. Department of State. 1980. The global 2000 report to the President. Vol. I, Entering the twenty-first century. 47 pp. Vol. II, The technical report. 766 pp. Washington, D.C.

Crosson, P.R., and S. Brubaker. 1982. Resources and environmental impacts of agriculture in the United States. Resources for the Future, Washington, D.C. (In press.)

Farrell, K.R. 1981. Productivity in U.S. agriculture. Economics and Statistics Service Staff Report AGE 55810422. U.S. Department of Agriculture, Washington, D.C.

National Research Council. 1981. Atmosphere-biosphere interactions: toward a better understanding of the ecological consequences of fossil fuel combustion. National Academy Press, Washington, D.C.

Sampson, R.N. 1981. Farmland or wasteland: a time to choose. Rodale Press, Pa.

Schnittker Associates. 1979. Trade issues relative to world hunger. A report prepared for the Presidential Commission on World Hunger. Washington, D.C.

U.S. Department of Agriculture. 1980. U.S. foreign agricultural trade statistical report, calendar year 1980. Washington, D.C.

U.S. Department of Agriculture. 1981. Soil and Water Resources Conservation Act, 1980 Appraisal, pts. I and II. Government Printing Office, Washington, D.C.

U.S. Department of Agriculture, Economics, Statistics, and Cooperatives Service. 1979a. FATUS: foreign agricultural trade of the United States. Washington, D.C.

U.S. Department of Agriculture, Economics, Statistics, and Cooperatives Service. 1979b. Prospects for productivity growth in U.S. agriculture. Ag. Econ. Rep. 435. Washington, D.C.

U.S. Department of Agriculture, Economics, Statistics, and Cooperatives Service. 1979c. Structural issues of American agriculture. Rep. 438. Washington, D.C.

U.S. Department of Agriculture, Economics, Statistics, and Cooperatives Service. 1980. U.S. farm numbers, sizes, and related structural dimensions: projections to year 2000. Tech. Bull. 1625. Washington, D.C.

U.S. Department of Agriculture, Forest Service. 1980. An assessment of the forest and range land situation in the United States. FS 345. Government Printing Office, Washington, D.C. 631 pp.

U.S. Department of Commerce, Bureau of the Census. 1980. Current population reports. Population estimates and projections: estimates of the population of counties and metropolitan areas, July 1, 1977 and 1978. Ser. P-25, No. 873. Government Printing Office, Washington, D.C.

U.S. Department of Commerce, Bureau of the Census. 1981. 1980 census of population and housing. Government Printing Office, Washington, D.C.

U.S. Water Resources Council. 1978. The nation's water resources, 1975-2000: second national water assessment. Washington, D.C.

4
Trends in the Use of Land and Water

How land is used and the availability and quality of water have direct impacts on fish and wildlife habitats. Current land and water management practices have both positive and negative impacts on fish and wildlife habitats. The interrelationships of agricultural practices with water quality and quantity are discussed in various chapters of this report. It is important to note that food production does not require the sacrifice of other resource values such as fish and wildlife habitats. Agriculture continues to have a responsibility to maintain the quality of fish and wildlife habitats. This chapter examines the trends in land and water use that are the most likely to affect fish and wildlife habitats. Appendix A summarizes by geographic regions the major trends in agricultural land use identified by the Committee.

THE LAND, SOIL, AND WATER BASE

The extent and use of America's land base are portrayed in Figure 4-1. Over two thirds of the total land in the United States is in nonfederal ownership. Of this, over 90 percent is used for agricultural purposes. Of the federal land, about two thirds is used for agriculture and is almost exclusively rangeland and forest land. There is more nonfederal than federal rangeland and forest land in spite of the extensive federal holdings in the West (see Figure 4-2 for a definition of geographic regions). Nonfederal lands are divided into three major use categories--cropland, rangeland, and forest land--each of which offers potential wildlife habitat. Over one half of the cropland is located in the North Central region,

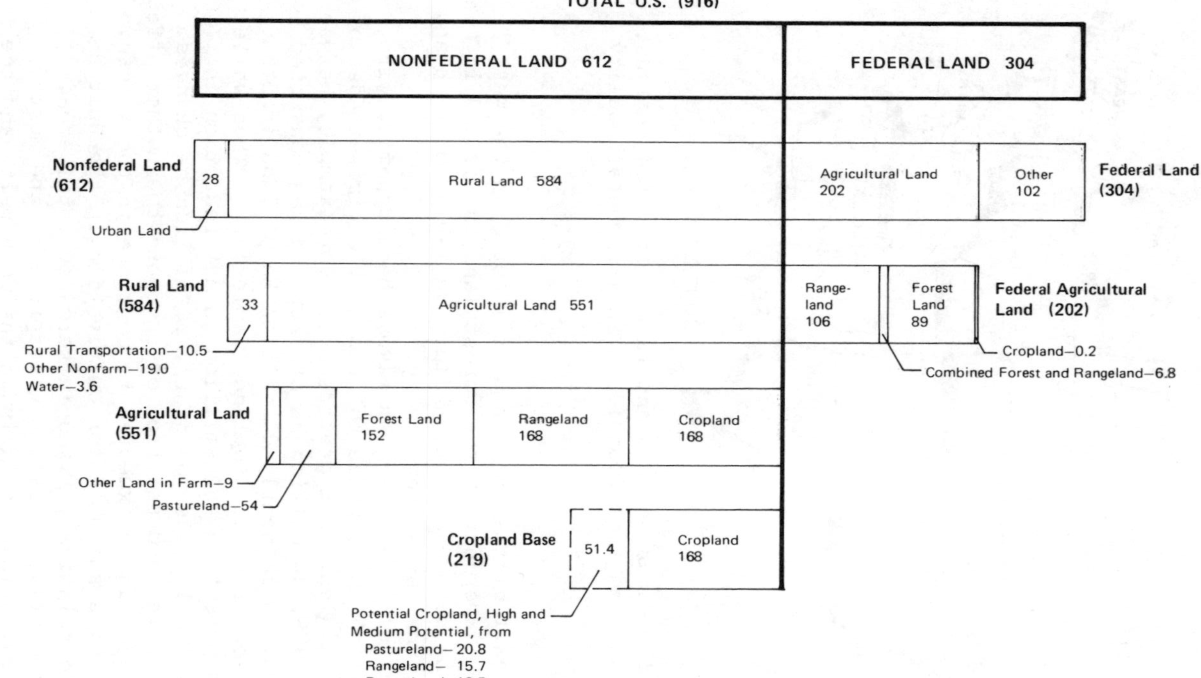

FIGURE 4-1 America's land base in 1977 (million hectares). Figures do not sum correctly because of conversion to metric units. SOURCE: Adapted from Council on Environmental Quality 1981.

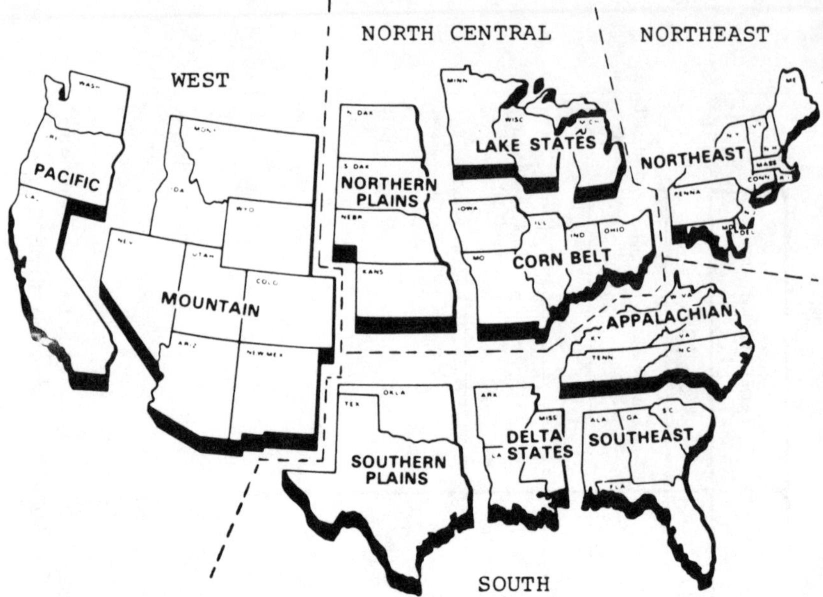

FIGURE 4-2 Census regions and farm production regions. SOURCE: Adapted from Council on Environmental Quality 1981.

over one half of the rangeland is located in the West, and about 40 percent of the forest land is located in the South. The nature of the habitat available for fish and wildlife thus varies regionally.

Agricultural land use has always been dynamic, with uses changing in response to prices, the vicissitudes of climate, and landowner preferences. For example, between 1967 and 1975, 30 million ha of cropland was converted to other uses, while nearly 20 million ha of land in other uses was converted to cropland (Table 4-1). Thus while there was more than a 10-million-ha net reduction in cropland, the land use on nearly 50 million ha changed. Such shifts in land use from one purpose to another affect wildlife and can be expected to continue in the future.

Those soils suitable for cultivation in the United States are relatively fixed in terms of total area. Highly productive soils are widespread in the North Central region (particularly in the Corn Belt) and the South, though there are highly productive soils in all parts of the United States (Figure 4-3). Soils of

TABLE 4-1 Agricultural Land Shifted Into and Out of Cropland, by Selected Census Regions, 1967-1975 (million hectares)

Shift	West	North Central	South	Northeast	Total
Out of cropland	4.6	11.5	11.2	2.8	30.0
Into cropland	3.3	7.6	7.3	1.5	19.7
Total hectares shifted	7.9	19.1	18.5	4.3	49.7
Net shift out of cropland	1.3	3.9	3.9	1.3	10.3

NOTE: Figures do not sum correctly because of conversion to metric units. SOURCE: Adapted from Council on Environmental Quality 1981.

marginal suitability for cropland are distributed fairly equally across the nation (10 to 13 percent of the total area in each region) with the exception of the Southeast and Lake States (23 percent in each). Soils unsuitable for cultivation occur nationwide, but most frequently in the East and West. Soils unsuitable for cultivation are of marginal suitability at best for wildlife. Similarly, the most productive lands--those in demand as cropland--hold the greatest potential for development as wildlife habitats.

As Table 4-2 indicates, there are regional differences in both quantity and type of surface water available in the United States. Although surface waters are more scarce in the West and Southwest than in the South and East and small water areas are less abundant than large water areas nationwide, each region has potentially adequate surface water to provide habitats for a variety of fish and aquatic wildlife. Their usefulness as habitats cannot be finally determined, however, until other factors such as temperature, salinity, pH, turbidity, flow rate, depth, bottom composition, and associated vegetation are considered.

TRENDS IN LAND AND WATER USE

Trends in land and water use are categorized by major land use type: cropland, forage land, and pastureland; rangeland; forest land; and wetlands and aquatic areas.

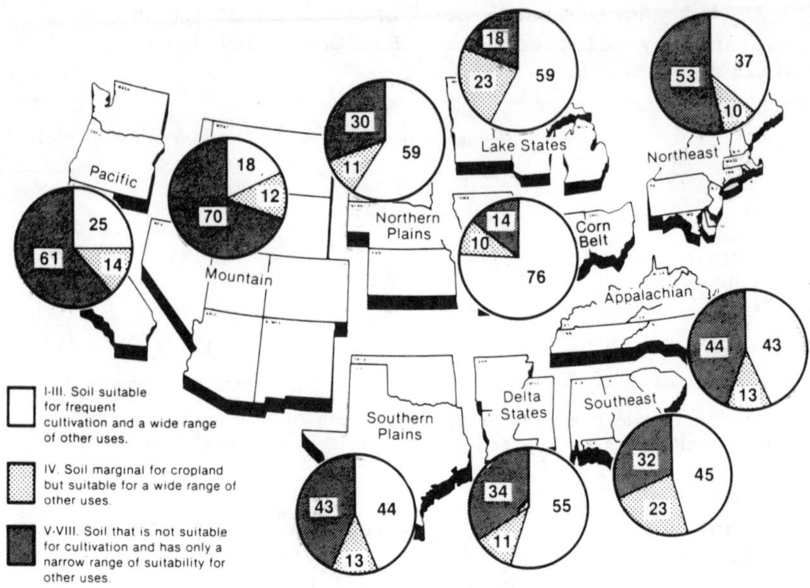

FIGURE 4-3 Percentages of soil in soil capability classes I-VIII, by farm production region. SOURCE: USDA 1981a.

Cropland, Forage Land, and Pastureland

The total land area cultivated for crops in the United States declined between the end of the 1930s and the mid-1970s, but total farm productivity over this period increased by nearly 100 percent. These gains have been attributed to new technology, which substituted other inputs such as fertilizers, new plant breeds, and water for land. A sharply expanding grain and soybean export market in the 1970s reversed this nearly 40-year trend of declining cropland use (Table 4-3).

Regardless of whether or not the total amount of cropland continues to increase, changes in land use will continue to occur. New land will be brought into agricultural production to replace cropland lost to urbanization, and regional shifts in land use will take place in response to economic forces. The _National Agricultural Lands Study_ (Council on Environmental Quality 1981) estimates that over 1 million ha of prime agricultural farmland is taken out of agricultural production each year. However, much more than this is

TABLE 4-2 Water Areas of the United States by Type, Region, and Subregion (thousand hectares)

	Inland Waters				Great Lakes,
Estuaries	Total Water Area	Total Inland Water	Large Areas[a]	Small Areas[b]	Coastal Waters, Bays, and
Northeast	4,715	2,068	1,765	302	2,647
North Central					
Northern Plains	1,350	1,350	976	374	0
Lake States	15,558	2,387	2,062	325	13,171
Corn Belt	2,321	971	572	399	1,350
Total	19,228	4,708	3,610	1,098	14,520
South					
Appalachian	2,412	2,021	1,726	295	391
Southeast	3,030	2,388	1,899	489	642
Delta States	2,111	1,704	1,339	365	407
Southern Plains	1,978	1,957	1,677	280	21
Total	9,532	8,070	6,640	1,429	1,462
West					
Mountain	2,397	2,397	2,150	247	0
Pacific	2,114	1,463	1,268	195	651
Total	4,511	3,860	3,419	442	651
TOTAL					
United States	37,986	18,705	15,434	3,271	19,281

[a]River 1/5 km wide and water over 16 ha.
[b]Streams less than 1/5 km and water less than 16 ha.

NOTE: Figures do not sum correctly because of conversion to metric units. SOURCE: Adapted from USDA, Forest Service 1980, pages 26-27.

required each year to offset the loss since the land being substituted generally is of lesser quality. The amount of available land of sufficient quality to support economical production is, however, limited. About 50 million ha can be identified as having high or medium potential for conversion to cropland (Table 4-4). Of this, 41 million ha, or 82 percent, is in the North Central region and the South: 18 million is currently in pasture, 11 million is in forests, and 10 million is in rangeland. The other 9 million ha is mostly in rangeland and pasture in the West. If these lands are converted to cropland, there will be substantial changes in the amounts and character of wildlife habitats. From 1967 to 1975, 23 million acres of agricultural land was converted to

TABLE 4-3 Trends in U.S. Cropland Area (millions of hectares)

Year	Cropland
1910	134
1920	149
1930	155
1940	149
1950	153
1959	145
1969	135
1974	146
1977	152[a]

[a]Reported in Council on Environmental Quality 1981, p. 6.

SOURCE: USDA 1981b, Table 602 (excludes idle cropland and cropland in forage and pasture).

nonagricultural uses. About 70 percent of this land was converted to urban and transportation uses, and 30 percent to man-made reservoirs, lakes, and other water-impounding facilities. Of the average annual conversion of 3 million acres, 675,000 acres was from cropland; 537,000 acres was from range and pastures; 825,000 acres was from forest land, and 875,000 acres was from other land uses (Council on Environmental Quality 1981).

The uncertainties likely to influence the amount of cropland needed in the future are numerous and make prediction difficult. For example, if the price of energy continues to increase, irrigation water could become prohibitively expensive, particularly in the West, necessitating increases in cropland area to maintain output levels. If population continues its westward and southwestward shift, competing demands for the limited water available could make water for agricultural uses more expensive or unavailable and again result in increases in cropland in other areas. If the demand for wood and wood products increases, prices will rise and current trends to convert forests to cropland could diminish. Whether or not the demands for export of agricultural products remains strong is a function not only of population and economic growth but also of attitudes and politics of the governments in the importing regions toward self-sufficiency. Export levels are heavily influenced by domestic farm policy as well as by

TABLE 4-4 Use of Agricultural Lands in 1977 and Potential Conversion to Cropland by Source and Region, Excluding Hawaii and Alaska (millions of hectares)

	Pasture	Rangeland	Forest	Other	Total Regional Potential Conversion	Current Cropland	Total Potential Cropland
West							
Current	5.1	92.8	25.6	0.6		26.6	
Potential	1.6	5.7	0.4	0.1	7.9		34.6
North Central							
Current	16.8	28.8	28.0	2.9		92.5	
Potential	7.6	5.1	2.8	0.8	16.3		108.8
South							
Current	29.4	46.0	73.5	0.8		41.1	
Potential	10.8	4.9	8.3	0.3	24.3		65.4
Northeast							
Current	2.3		25.2	0.6		6.8	
Potential	0.8		0.9	0.2	1.9		8.7
TOTAL							
United States							
Current	53.7	167.5	152.3	4.9		167.1	
Potential	20.8	15.7	12.5	1.4	50.4		217.5

NOTE: Figures may not sum correctly because of conversion to metric units. SOURCE: Council on Environmental Quality 1981, and USDA 1980.

foreign policy. The level of agricultural research directly affects productivity and the amount of cropland needed. The level of domestic demand is influenced by the state of the economy, which is influenced in part by monetary and spending policies.

After considering these uncertainties as well as other projections and research, the Committee concluded that if export demand continues at the high levels of the past decade, if current patterns of exports, commodities, and importing countries prevail, and if the growth rate of agricultural productivity remains at present levels, an increase in total cropland of between 10 and 15 percent (16 to 24 million ha) can be expected by 2010. The Committee considers this to be an upper bound, given the nature of the assumptions on which it is based. It represents a conversion of about two thirds of the land currently classified as having high or medium potential for conversion to cropland.

An increase in cropland area is likely to occur in all regions of the United States with the exception of the Northeast. Almost 50 percent of the land with medium and high potential for conversion is in the South. Conversion of that land could as much as double the area now in crops in the South, given the potential for conversion in that region. Expansion of cropland in this area would mean that a substantial amount of forest and pastureland would be lost, and in the Delta States it would probably mean the draining of more wetlands.

In some areas, land currently in pasture could be converted to cropland. Conversion from forest to pasture may also be expected if high feed grain prices make it more profitable to produce livestock from pasture than from grain feed. Of course, the net return per hectare from livestock grazed would have to be greater than that from forest products.

The amount of pastureland is expected to increase nationally to feed additional numbers of dairy and beef cattle and sheep. Permanent pasture in the Southeast, Delta States, and the seaboard states of the Appalachian region has not been fully exploited for beef production. To achieve the full potential would require more fertilizer, use of improved forage cultivars, and improved management. In general, conversion to pastureland from other uses will be economically feasible in regions with more rainfall and longer grazing seasons since these are areas that can sustain heavier use by livestock.

The amount of land in forage is not expected to decline since forage crops are an important part of the rotation scheme on many farms. Forage lands could increase to meet demands for livestock feedstuffs or as part of more intensive efforts to control erosion. Economic forces alone, however, are not likely to cause the expansion of lands devoted to forage.

Rangeland

From 1967 to 1977, nearly 14 million ha of rangeland, or 7 percent of all lands classified as nonfederal rangeland, was lost to water improvements and to urban expansion--an irreversible loss of almost 1.4 million ha per year (USDA 1980). Grassland and shrub land are the basic vegetative types of rangeland, together composing about 90 percent of all rangeland. Chaparral and pinyon-juniper ecotypes constitute the other 10 percent (Table 4-5). These two major ecotypes, grassland and shrub land, do not occur evenly throughout the United States. Grassland tends to dominate the range in the more mesic East and Northern Plains, while shrub land is more frequent in the more xeric West and Southwest. The Mountain region of the West is the most important rangeland area of the country, containing nearly half of all grassland and about 60 percent of all rangeland.

The potential for conversion of rangeland to cropland is influenced by, among other factors, the ownership of the rangeland. Over half the rangeland in the Mountain region and nearly 70 percent of the rangeland in the Pacific region are federally owned; thus these lands are unlikely candidates for large-scale conversion to cropland. In the Northern Plains, 95 percent of rangeland is privately owned, and this, coupled with more favorable climatic conditions, increases the possibility of conversion of rangelands to other uses in the future.

Both rangeland to cropland and cropland to rangeland conversion will occur. Where underground water becomes too expensive to pump for irrigation, land will probably revert to rangeland. However, where precipitation is sufficient or water can be obtained from surface or underground sources at reasonable cost, conversion to cropland will occur. The Northern Plains is the most likely area to experience conversion from rangeland to cropland, but conversions of lesser magnitude also could occur in the South and North Central regions.

TABLE 4-5 Rangeland in the Contiguous States by Ecosystem and Region, 1976 (1000 hectares)

	Total Range-land	Grass-land	Percent of Total	Shrub Land[a]	Percent of Total	Other Forest Land	Percent of Total
Northeast	59	59	100	--	--	--	--
North Central	31,527	31,524	100	-- 1	--	2	--
Northern Plains	39,859	30,856	100	-- 1	--	2	--
South	42,140	22,774	54	19,366	46	--	--
Southern Plains	40,834	21,468	53	19,366	47	--	--
West	189,467	64,083	34	99,979	53	25,406	13
Mountain	154,668	54,067	35	80,347	52	20,254	13
Pacific	34,800	10,016	29	19,631	56	5,152	15
TOTAL of all contiguous states	263,195	118,441	45	119,346	45	25,408	10

[a]Chaparral mountain shrub and pinyon-juniper.

SOURCE: Adapted from USDA, Forest Service 1980, Table 2.8.

Given the increasing population and its resultant increasing demand for meat and the increased export demand for feed grains, the demand for rangeland for livestock grazing will probably increase sharply. Demand for grazing land in the contiguous 48 states has been estimated to increase by about 30 percent above the 1976 level by 1990 and by over 50 percent by 2030 (USDA, Forest Service 1980). These projections assume traditional patterns of grazing and constant levels of productivity. However, this anticipated demand for grazing land far exceeds the capability of current rangeland. This will lead to more intensive use of rangeland. Since conversions of rangeland to cropland must come from the privately owned 60 percent, the pressure will be on public rangeland to increase livestock production.

Projections indicate that about 24 million ha of rangeland will be lost to other uses such as crop and pastureland by 2030. Of this, only about 16 million ha of nonfederal rangeland has high to medium potential for conversion to cropland, and of that only about 600,000 ha appears to be in the highly productive land classes.

Economic pressures will continue to lead to the consolidation of rangeland holdings into larger and larger units, particularly in areas of low precipitation. This process is complicated by the fact that the land resources used in livestock ranching in the West are composed of both publicly and privately owned lands, and therefore consolidations are usually subject to public policies regarding terms of transfer and intensity of use.

Exploration for and mining of mineral and energy resources on rangeland may locally reduce land available for grazing livestock, placing greater demands on the remaining land. Rangeland is also used for recreational activities (e.g., hiking, trail riding, hunting, and off-road vehicle use). The demand for these uses is increasing, further restricting the opportunities for ranchers to intensify the use of federal rangeland for livestock and providing incentives for using private rangeland less intensively for livestock grazing in favor of other uses.

Forest Land

Nonfederal forest land has been decreasing since 1952 as forests are converted to cropland, pastureland, and urban uses. Between 1967 and 1975, 14 percent of forest land was converted to pastureland and rangeland, 2 percent to cropland, 2 percent to water and urban use, and 3 percent to other uses, for a total loss of about 20 percent. Some conversions to forest land occurred during this period, so that the result was a net loss in forest land of about 15 percent. Future projections call for a continuation of past declines in forests at least through the 1980s, with total forest area stabilizing thereafter.

A variety of factors will influence whether forests will be retained in the future. Forests are likely to decline in areas where grazing and cropping are more profitable, where forests are in predominately private ownership, and where opportunities are limited for increasing income through improved forest management. In other words, the net return per acre will largely determine whether forests are maintained or converted to other uses. The greatest potential for conversion of forest to cropland and other uses is in the South, which contains about 35 percent of all the forests in the lower contiguous United States; over 90 percent of southern forests are in private ownership (Table 4-6).

Natural forest types vary by region (Table 4-7), with hardwood species dominating in the Northeast, North Central, and South regions and softwood and other species (chaparral and pinyon-juniper) dominating in the West. It is primarily in regions other than the West that 15 million ha of high and medium potential agricultural soils is currently occupied by forests. Nearly half of

TABLE 4-6 Total Federal and Nonfederal Forest Land in the Contiguous 48 States by Region and Ownership (1000 hectares)

	Total Forest Land	Federal	Percent of Total	Nonfederal	Percent of Total
Northeast	28,927	922	3	28,005	97
North Central	33,882	4,703	14	29,180	86
South	93,366	7,455	8	85,911	92
West	92,888	57,042	61	35,846	39
TOTAL	249,064	70,122	28	178,942	72

SOURCE: Adapted from USDA, Forest Service 1980, Table 2.3.

TABLE 4-7 Forest Land Area in the United States by Region and Major Type (1000 hectares)

	Total	Softwoods	Hardwoods	Other
Northeast	33,649.6	8,665.2[a]	24,175.8[b]	808.3
North Central	32,062.2	5,732.1[a]	25,383.5[b]	946.6
South	88,643.9	26,434.2[a]	54,932.9[b]	7,276.8
Rocky Mountain	55,192.8	30,524.9[c]	3,096.7[d]	21,578.5[e]
Great Plains	1,820.1	608.7[c]	34.4[d]	233.6[e]
Pacific Coast	37,695.0	25,074.8[c]	3,605.1[d]	9,015.1[e]

[a]Includes white, red, and jack pines, fir-spruce, longleaf slash, loblolly shortleaf.
[b]Includes oak-pine, oak-hickory, oak-gum cypress, elm-ash-cottonwood, maple-beech-birch, aspen-birch.
[c]Includes Douglas fir, Ponderosa pine, western white pine, fir-spruce, hemlock-sitka spruce, larch, lodgepole pine, redwood, other softwoods.
[d]Western hardwoods.
[e]Includes nonstocked, chaparral, pinyon-juniper, other.

SOURCE: Adapted from USDA, Forest Service 1980, Tables 2.7 and 2.9.

this is prime agricultural land (USDA 1980). Therefore any conversion of forest land to other uses would be largely at the expense of hardwood in the South and North Central regions.

Analysis of demand and supply indicates that increased demand will result in higher prices for both softwoods and hardwoods (USDA, Forest Service 1980). However, the price of softwoods will rise more rapidly than that of hardwoods. These price rises will probably encourage more intensive management of commerical forests.

Approximately 11 million ha of prime agricultural land in the South is occupied by forests (USDA 1980). This represents about 65 percent of the pastureland, forage land, and rangeland in the South that has the potential for conversion to cropland (Crosson and Brubaker 1982). The land with the greatest potential for conversion to cropland is also the most productive land for forests. Considering that the total national demand for additional cropland could be as much as 24 million ha, it is possible that one third or more could come from the forests of the South.

Wetlands and Aquatic Areas

A number of attempts have been made to classify wetlands and aquatic areas (e.g., Shaw and Fredine 1956, Cowardin et al. 1979), and unfortunately all have limitations. In a most general sense, wetlands are basins that hold water (temporarily or permanently) and that have plant communities tolerant or in need of wet soils. Wetlands range in size from very small, temporarily flooded depressions to extensive wooded swamps and are found in all regions of the United States.

Because of the difficulties in identifying and defining wetlands, estimates of their extent are not precise. In 1956 Shaw and Fredine (1956) estimated that the lower 48 states contained about 33 million ha of wetlands. In 1977 the Soil Conservation Service (USDA 1980) estimated there was about 28 million ha of wetlands. By using these estimates, the annual average loss over the 20-year period is calculated to be about 200,000 ha.

In definitions of land that is used for agricultural purposes, wetlands are often included in pastureland, forest land, or rangeland (see Chapters 6, 7, and 8). One classification scheme for agricultural soils has wet soils as a category, of which wetlands is a subcategory. Wet soils constitute 109 million ha, of which 42 million is cropland, 23 million is pastureland and rangeland, and 45 million is forest and other. Since only the portion in cropland is likely to be drained at present, the undrained wet soils constitute about 60 percent of the total.

Since many of the wetlands of the Corn Belt were long ago drained and converted to cropland, estimates are that almost 95 percent of Iowa's wetlands have been destroyed (Bishop 1981). It is unlikely that additional losses will occur in Iowa. The most extensive conversions of wetlands are likely to occur in the bottomland hardwood swamps and overflow wetlands of the South. Nearly 80 percent of such areas have been lost in the Lower Mississippi Valley (MacDonald et al. 1979), and as the South becomes more important in the production of agricultural commodities, 25 percent of the remaining area likely could be drained by 1995.

WATER QUANTITY AND QUALITY

Quantity

Agriculture is the largest single user of water in the United States. In 1975, agriculture accounted for nearly half of withdrawals of freshwater for offstream use (Table 4-8). This compares with 26 percent of withdrawals for steam electricity generation, 17 percent for manufacturing and minerals, and 9 percent for domestic and commercial uses. In terms of consumption (allowing for evapotranspiration and incorporation into products), agriculture and livestock accounted for 83 percent of the functional use of water in 1975, whereas steam generation consumed less than 1 percent, manufacturing and minerals about 8 percent, and domestic and commercial uses 7 percent. By 2030, total freshwater withdrawals are expected to decline slightly (7 percent) and consumption is projected to increase by about 60 percent. This reflects an increase in the ratio of consumption to withdrawal from about 30 percent to over 50 percent.

The greatest water withdrawals in 1975 for irrigation were in California with over 34 billion gallons per day, the Pacific Northwest water resource region with 33 billion, the Missouri region with 32 billion, and the Texas Gulf region with almost 12 billion (Table 4-9). Consumption as a percent of withdrawals for irrigation purposes was approximately 55 percent in 1975.

Almost 17 million ha--approximately 10 percent of U.S cropland--was irrigated in 1974, almost twice as much as was irrigated 30 years earlier (Table 4-10). Twenty states account for over 95 percent of all irrigated hectares. Western and Plains states alone account for almost 90 percent of all irrigated hectares. The trend of increasing irrigation is not an entirely western phenomenon; irrigated land in the East increased by nearly 75 percent from 1967 to 1977 (Table 4-11).

The types of land being irrigated, the sources of the water (surface or ground water), and the irrigation methods differ from area to area in the West (Table 4-12). Given that water conservation is critical to the future of agriculture in these regions, the efficiencies of on-farm and off-farm conveyance are particularly important. These efficiencies indicate where changes can be made, and what the magnitude of the changes should be, to conserve water. Rising costs of pumping water, concern over depletion of reserves, and growing competition from

TABLE 4-8 Freshwater Withdrawals and Consumption in the United States in 1975 and Projected Demand (Alaska, Hawaii, the Caribbean included) in 2030 by Major Use (million gallons a day)

	Withdrawals				Consumption			
	1975		2030		1975		2030	
	Million gal/day	Percent of Total	Million gal/day	Percent of Total	Million gal/day	Percent of Total	Million gal/day	Percent of Total
Irrigation	158,743	47	148,518	47	86,391	81	99,972	59
Steam electric	88,916	26	70,472	23	1,419	1	21,373	13
Manufacturing	51,222	15	26,392	8	6,059	6	25,117	15
Domestic and commercial	28,786	9	47,081	15	7,377	7	11,875	7
Minerals	7,055	2	16,465	5	2,196	2	5,203	3
Livestock	1,912	.5	3,211	1	1,912	2	3,316	2
Public lands and other	1,866	.5	3,200	1	1,236	1	2,326	1
TOTAL	338,500	100.0	315,339	100.0	106,182	100.0	169,182	100.0

SOURCE: Adapted from U.S. Water Resources Council 1978, as extended in USDA, Forest Service 1980.

TABLE 4-9 Freshwater Withdrawals and Consumption for Irrigation in the Contiguous 48 States in 1975, by Water Resource Region, with Projections of Demand in 2030 (million gallons a day)

TABLE 4-9a Withdrawals

Water Resource Region	1975	1985	1990	2000	2010	2020	2030
New England	35	41	39	46	46	45	37
Middle Atlantic	265	366	350	481	481	473	466
South Atlantic Gulf	3,464	4,008	3,829	4,509	4,509	4,436	4,363
Great Lakes	145	211	202	282	282	277	273
Ohio	47	68	65	91	91	89	88
Tennessee	14	18	17	21	21	21	20
Upper Mississippi	192	283	270	387	386	381	374
Lower Mississippi	4,580	4,559	4,355	4,444	4,444	4,372	4,300
Souris-Red Rainy	46	144	138	434	434	427	420
Missouri	31,636	39,376	37,613	36,236	36,736	36,142	35,550
Arkansas-White-Red	9,980	10,483	10,014	9,776	9,776	9,618	9,460
Texas Gulf	11,538	9,333	8,915	7,427	7,427	7,307	7,187
Rio Grande	5,684	5,498	5,252	4,873	4,873	4,794	4,716
Upper Colorado	6,400	7,223	6,900	6,672	6,672	6,564	6,457
Lower Colorado	7,989	7,299	6,872	6,343	6,343	6,240	6,138
Great Basin	6,969	6,120	5,846	5,825	5,825	5,731	5,637
Pacific Northwest	33,181	34,639	34,088	29,961	29,961	29,477	28,994
California	34,539	34,863	34,302	34,764	34,764	34,356	33,281
TOTAL	156,776	164,532	159,067	152,572	153,847	150,261	147,285

TABLE 4-9b Consumption

Water Resource Region	1975	1985	1990	2000	2010	2020	2030
New England	25	29	29	33	34	35	36
Middle Atlantic	196	269	265	354	367	375	384
South Atlantic Gulf	2,752	3,184	3,132	3,597	3,724	3,812	3,899
Great Lakes	114	169	166	232	240	246	251
Ohio	37	53	51	74	77	78	80
Tennessee	11	14	14	17	18	18	18
Upper Mississippi	153	230	226	323	334	342	350
Lower Mississippi	3,065	3,204	3,152	3,272	3,388	3,467	3,546
Souris-Red Rainy	37	116	114	350	373	371	390
Missouri	14,214	17,597	17,312	17,607	18,232	18,922	19,083
Arkansas-White-Red	7,048	7,468	7,347	7,125	7,378	7,550	7,722
Texas Gulf	9,347	7,597	7,474	6,100	6,317	6,464	6,611
Rio Grande	3,886	3,920	3,717	3,570	3,696	3,783	3,869
Upper Colorado	2,194	2,657	2,614	2,741	2,838	2,905	2,971
Lower Colorado	4,026	3,962	3,898	3,720	3,852	3,942	4,032
Great Basin	3,225	3,082	3,032	3,196	3,309	3,387	3,464
Pacific Northwest	11,026	13,363	12,981	13,213	13,279	15,001	14,321
California	24,282	25,134	24,727	26,311	27,245	28,881	28,218
TOTAL	85,638	92,047	90,251	91,835	94,701	99,579	99,245

SOURCE: Adapted from USDA, Forest Service 1980.

TABLE 4-10 Top 20 States in the Number of Hectares Irrigated

	1974 Rank	Irrigated Hectares (thousands) 1944	1954	1964	1974
California	1	2,004	2,852	3,075	3,136
Texas	2	534	1,905	2,584	2,669
Nebraska	3	256	474	878	1,605
Colorado	4	1,092	916	1,089	1,163
Idaho	5	820	941	1,134	1,157
Kansas	6	39	134	406	813
Montana	7	629	765	766	712
Oregon	8	457	603	651	632
Florida	9	90	173	493	631
Wyoming	10	548	511	636	591
Washington	11	210	315	465	530
Arizona	12	294	476	455	467
Utah	13	455	434	442	393
Arkansas	14	117	347	394	384
New Mexico	15	217	263	329	351
Nevada	16	273	229	334	315
Louisiana	17	217	287	235	284
Oklahoma	18	[a]	44	122	208
Mississippi	19	[a]	53	50	66
South Dakota	20	21	36	53	62
All other states		34	200	406	524
TOTAL for 50 states		8,312	11,960	14,997	16,691

[a]Fewer than 202 ha.

SOURCE: Adapted from USDA 1980, Table 3C-1.

nonagricultural users are forces encouraging greater efficiencies. It is the increase in efficiency that leads to the downward projections in withdrawal for irrigation in the future. Projections to 2030 indicate that irrigation will continue to account for about half of all withdrawals (Table 4-8). The greatest absolute decreases in withdrawal for irrigation are projected to be in the Texas Gulf, Lower Colorado, Great Basin, Pacific Northwest, and Rio Grande water resource regions (Table 4-9). It is likely that in these regions greater efficiencies in the use of water will be realized, so that the area of irrigated land will not be reduced. The possible exception is the Texas Gulf, where water consumption for irrigation is expected to decline by nearly 30 percent. The appropriate implementation of

TABLE 4-11 Irrigated Land in the Eastern United States, 1967 and 1977 (1000 hectares)

	1967	1977
Northeast	178	150
Appalachia	--	168
Corn Belt	84	450
Missouri	48	314
Other Corn Belt	36	136
Lake States	52	391
Southeast	686	1386
Delta	1425	1624
TOTAL	2425	4169

SOURCE: Hanson and Pagano 1980.

political, social, and economic incentives may help to achieve a balance between recharge and withdrawal.

Electrical energy is used for on-farm pumping of water on over 44 percent of all hectares irrigated with on-farm pumped water; 30 percent rely on natural gas, 11 percent on diesel fuel, and 14 percent on liquefied petroleum gas and gasoline (Sloggett 1977). The costs of these inputs are rising rapidly and will force adjustments in practices and quantities used. In nearly all areas where stream water is used, there are seasonal inadequacies resulting from depleted stream flows. Stream flows of 40 percent of mean annual minimum flow seriously affect fish and wildlife (Bayha 1976).

Quality

Hydrologic basins are affected primarily by agricultural and urban runoff as nonpoint sources of pollution (Table 4-13). Sixty-eight percent of the basins in the United States report water pollution caused by agricultural activities, with basins in the North Central, South Central, and Southwest water resource regions most seriously affected. The primary agricultural pollutants in water are salt, pesticides and herbicides (and other materials including animal wastes), nutrients (e.g., nitrogen and phosphorous), and sediments.

Salinity results from the leaching of saline soils and evaporation and transpiration from irrigation. These

TABLE 4-12 Irrigation Characteristics in the 17 Western States

	Irrigation Situation	Water Source	Irrigation Methods	Present Average Irrigation Efficiencies (percent) On-farm	Off-farm Conveyance	Instream Flow	Water Quality
Northwest Oregon Washington Idaho	Intermediate Valley	70% surface 30% ground water	About equally divided between sprinkler surface (border, furrow, basin, corrugations), some trickle	25-70	60-95	Seasonal inadequacies in streams and estuaries	Seasonal temperature fluctuations dissolved gases and sediment
	Mountain Meadow	100% surface	Wild flood	25-40	55-70	Inadequate streamflows in dry years	Excellent
Southwest California Arizona Southern New Mexico	Lower Valley	80% surface 20% ground water	Surface (border, basin, corrugations, furrow), sprinkler and some trickle	50-70	70-95	Severely depleted streams and estuary inflows	Salinity increases downstream
Southwest Texas	Intermediate Valley	90% surface 10% ground water	Surface (border, contour ditch, furrow and corrugations)	45-65	70-80	Seasonal inadequacies	Good
	Plains (with on-farm water supply)	100% ground water	Surface (border, basin, corrugations, furrow) some sprinkler and trickle	60-70	none	Inadequacies	Ground water good to poor
Intermountain Nevada Utah Northwest New Mexico	Intermediate Valley	80% surface 20% ground water	Surface (border, contour ditch, furrow corregations), some sprinkler	35-50	70-95	Seasonal inadequacies	Salinity increases downstream
	Mountain Meadow	100% surface	Wild flood	25-50	50-80	Localized areas with inadequate flows in dry years	Excellent

TABLE 4-12 (continued)

	Irrigation Situation	Water Source	Irrigation Methods	Present Average Irrigation Efficiencies (percent) On-farm	Off-farm Conveyance	Instream Flow	Water Quality
Rocky Mountain Portions of Colorado Wyoming Montana Idaho Northern New Mexico	Mountain Meadow	100% surface	Wild flood	25-50	50-80	Localized areas with inadequate flows in dry years	Excellent
	Intermediate Valley	95% surface 5% ground water	Surface (border, contour ditch, corrugations and furrow), some sprinkler	40-55	50-95	Seasonal inadequacies	Salinity increases downstream
Northern Great Plains Montana North Dakota South Dakota Nebraska Eastern Wyoming Eastern Colorado	Plains (with on-farm water supply	90% ground water 10% surface (overdraft)	About equally divided between sprinkler and surface (furrow)	40-65	none	Seasonal inadequacies	Ground water good
	Intermediate Valley	90% surface 10% ground water	Surface (border, contour ditch, corrugations and furrow), some sprinkler	40-55	40-95	Seasonal inadequacies	Water summer temperatures and sediment problems
Southern Great Plains Southern Kansas Oklahoma Texas Eastern New Mexico	Plains (with on-farm water supply	95% ground water (severe overdraft)	About equally divided between sprinkler and furrow and basin	50-70	none	Seasonal inadequacies	Ground water good to poor
	Lower Valley	50% surface 50% ground water	Surface (furrow, border and basin), some sprinkler	65-75	40-95	Severely depleted streams and estuary inflows	Low to high salinity

SOURCE: Adapted from USDA 1980, Table 3C-7.

TABLE 4-13 Percentage of Hydrologic Basins Affected By Nonpoint Sources of Pollution in the United States, by Region, Source, and Type of Pollution

	Number of Hydrologic Basins	Source of Pollution									
		Urban Runoff	Construction	Hydrologic Modification	Silviculture	Mining	Agriculture	Solid Waste Disposal	Individual Disposal	Bacteria	Oxygen Depletion
Northeast	40	70	15	20	10	20	55	35	63	70	53
Southeast	47	57	2	21	30	15	62	9	40	66	74
Great Lakes	41	54	7	2	15	41	59	15	39	51	54
North Central	35	54	6	3	6	40	89	9	29	69	66
South Central	30	50	0	23	13	53	87	13	40	53	43
Southwest	22	23	0	18	5	36	79	0	35	36	14
Northwest	22	23	23	23	27	23	55	9	32	64	18
Islands	9	67	67	22	0	0	78	22	89	89	44
TOTAL	246	62	9	15	15	30	68	14	43	61	51

TABLE 4-13 (continued)

	Number of Hydro-logic Basins	Type of Pollution						
		Nutri-ents	Sus-pended Solids	Dis-solved Solids	pH	Oil and Grease	Toxics	Pesti-cides
Northeast	40	63	65	10	18	15	33	18
Southeast	47	57	34	4	9	4	11	21
Great Lakes	41	44	56	27	37	20	34	15
North Central	35	63	80	51	20	0	51	37
South Central	30	63	37	70	23	3	47	40
Southwest	22	45	32	68	14	14	27	0
Northwest	22	55	64	14	9	5	32	0
Islands	9	44	100	0	0	0	22	44
TOTAL	246	56	54	30	18	9	32	22

NOTES: Percentage is based on the number of basins affected, either wholly or in part. As little as 3 percent or as much as 100 percent of an individual basin could be affected and the basin would be included.

processes can raise the salt concentration in the soil to levels intolerable to agricultural crops. Erosion of soils with a high salt content contributes 82 to 91 million metric tons (90 to 100 million tons) of salt to the water supplies of the eleven western states annually. Also, overdraft of ground water in coastal areas invites the intrusion of saltwater into underground aquifers as the hydrostatic pressure changes.

Of the approximately 680,000 metric tons (750,000 tons) of biocides produced in 1977, farmers used 60 percent (USDA 1980). Farmers are expected to increase their use of biocides in the future. The concentrations of insecticides and herbicides applied are usually low and relatively small quantities either drift or run off into fish and wildlife habitats, but even very small amounts can be toxic to aquatic life. If these materials do not readily or rapidly degrade or if they degrade into other toxic and persistent forms, their threat to wildlife can be long-lived. Another severe, albeit localized, pollution source is animal wastes from feedlots.

In 1976, farmers applied approximately 44.5 million metric tons (49 million tons) of fertilizer (USDA, Forest Service 1980). Estimates of how much of the nitrogen, phosphorous, and potassium in these fertilizers reached the water vary widely. Estimates of nitrogen in surface water range from 15 to 54 percent of the amount applied (USDA, Forest Service 1980). Land use and nutrient concentrations in streams are directly related (Figure 4-4). Land devoted almost exclusively to crops contributes significantly more nitrogen to streams. A shift from monoculture to integrated agriculture could improve stream quality.

Cropland is also the greatest single contributor to stream sediment (about 40 percent), the exact amount depending on rates of soil erosion. Therefore as forests and rangeland are more intensively managed or as they are converted to cropland, more runoff of pesticides, more nutrient loading of streams, and possibly more sedimentation can be expected.

SOIL QUANTITY AND QUALITY

Quantity

In the United States, lands suitable for continuous cultivation of crops as well as for pasture, forage, or

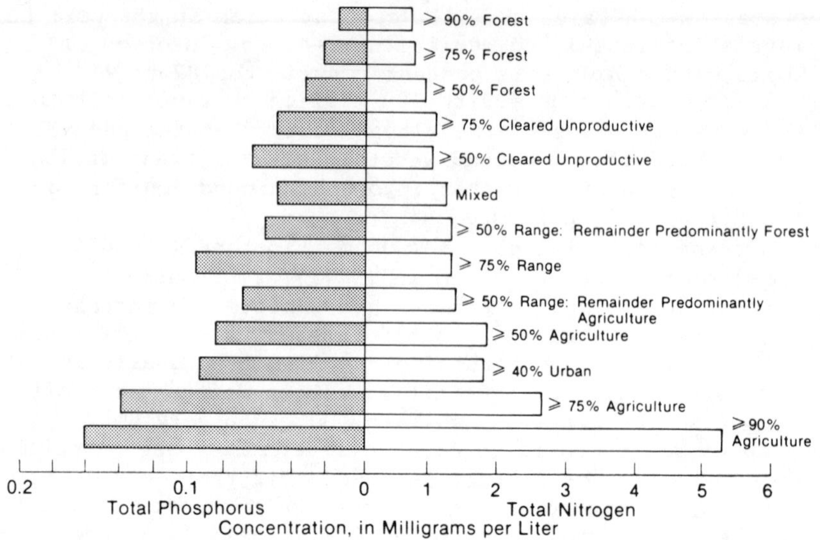

FIGURE 4-4 Relationships between land use and nutrient concentrations in streams. SOURCE: USDA, Forest Service 1980.

forests make up over 40 percent of all nonfederal land, or about 250 million ha. Lands of marginal capacity for cultivation, but with acceptable properties for other uses constitute about 13 percent of nonfederal land, or over 75 million ha. Other lands, generally unsuitable for cultivation, make up over 40 percent of nonfederal lands, or about 250 million ha (USDA 1980).

Only a portion of all soil is useable for agricultural production (Figure 4-3). The proportion of high-quality agricultural soils to total land area is highest in the Corn Belt, Northern Plains, Lake States, and Delta States, where roughly 50 to 75 percent of the soils are considered Class I to Class III soils. In the South, where cropland increases are expected to be greatest, the proportion of soils in Classes I to III is approximately 50 percent.

Quality

Soil formation is a relatively slow process depending on vegetation, climate, use, parent material, living organisms, and topography. Forest soils develop at a rate of 1 inch in 1000-plus years; agricultural soils at a rate of 1 inch in 100 years. The quality of U.S. soils generally is being reduced by a number of factors, including erosion from water and wind, compaction and deterioration of the soil structure, loss of nutrients and minerals, and soil-water interaction, as well as air pollution and its impact on soil pH.

Erosion is a serious problem on more than half of the nation's cropland, although geographic variations make generalizations regarding its extent difficult. The seriousness of the problem at any particular site is a function of soil depth and the rate of soil regeneration. Thus erosion rates that are alarming in one area may be only slightly worrisome in another location (National Research Council 1980). With this qualification in mind, it is noted that in 1977 erosion exceeded 22 metric tons per hectare (10 tons per acre) on about 30 percent of row cropland in the Southeast, 10 percent in the Northeast, and 20 percent in the Corn Belt. If present erosion rates continue or increase, corn, soybean, and cotton yields in several important areas could be reduced substantially, other factors being equal, over the next 50 years. And because erosion is the main source of sediment in streams, it is also responsible for the transfer of agricultural chemicals to waterways.

The increased size and weight of farm equipment have resulted in soil compaction, impeded water penetration, and promoted increased runoff and sedimentation. Although fall plowing is an important means of remedying compaction, it leaves the land vulnerable to wind and water erosion during the nongrowing season. While increasing energy costs will probably encourage less tillage of all types, thus reducing erosion and the pollution of surface waters, they also will necessitate the use of greater quantities of herbicides and perhaps insecticides. This, coupled with the possibility of greater infiltration and leaching, may lead to more pollution of surface and ground water or runoff water in the future.

As long as we are farming the extensive land area and using current production practices, including large-scale machinery, there is no reason to believe that the high rate of erosion is going to diminish. If appropriate social, political, and economic incentives are implemented, soil erosion may be significantly reduced.

LITERATURE CITED

Bayha, K. 1976. Instream flow--the big picture. Pages 95-131 in The symposium and specialty conference on instream flow needs, Vol. 1. American Fisheries Society and the American Society of Civil Engineers.

Bishop, R.A. 1981. Iowa's wetlands. Proc. Ia. Acad. Sci. 88:11-16.

Council on Environmental Quality. 1981. National agricultural lands study: final report. Government Printing Office, Washington, D.C. 108 pp.

Cowardin, L.M., V. Carter, F.C. Golet, and E.T. LaRoe. 1979. Classification of wetland and deepwater habitats of the United States. U.S. Fish and Wildlife Service, Office of Biological Services, Washington, D.C. 103 pp.

Crosson, P.R., and S. Brubaker. 1982. Resource and environmental impacts of agriculture in the United States. Resources for the Future, Washington, D.C. (In press.)

Hanson, J., and J. Pagano. 1980. Growth and prospects for irrigation in the eastern United States. Unpublished paper. Resources for the Future, Washington, D.C.

MacDonald, P.O., W.E. Frayer, and J.R. Clauser. 1979. Documentation, chronology, and future projections of bottomland hardwood habitat loss in the lower Mississippi alluvial plain. Vol. I, Basic report. HRB Singer, Inc., State College, Pa. 133 pp.

National Research Council. 1980. Report of the soil transformation and productivity workshop. Photocopy. National Academy of Sciences, Commission on Natural Resources, Washington, D.C. 15 pp.

Shaw, S.P., and C.G. Fredine. 1956. Wetlands of the United States. U.S. Fish Wildl. Ser. Cir. 39. 67 pp.

Sloggett, G. 1977. Energy in U.S. agriculture: irrigation pumping. Ag. Econ. Rep. 376. U.S. Department of Agriculture, Washington, D.C.

U.S. Department of Agriculture. 1980. Soil and Water Resources Conservation Act, 1980 appraisal, review draft, pt. II. Government Printing Office, Washington, D.C.

U.S. Department of Agriculture. 1981a. Soil and Water Resources Conservation Act, 1980 appraisal. Pt. I, Soil, water, and related resources in the United States: status, condition, and trends. Government Printing Office, Washington, D.C.

U.S. Department of Agriculture. 1981b. Agricultural statistics 1980.

U.S. Department of Agriculture, Forest Service. 1980. An assessment of the forest and range land situation in the United States. FS 345. Government Printing Office, Washington, D.C. 631 pp.

U.S. Water Resources Council. 1978. The nation's water resources, 1975-2000: second national water assessment. Washington, D.C.

5
Trends in Cropland, Range, and Forest Cultural and Management Practices

CROPLAND PRACTICES

Conservation Tillage (Cultivation)

The term conservation tillage covers a broad range of tillage methods that generally require less soil disturbance during seedbed preparation, planting, and crop growth than the conventional soil inversion systems associated with moldboard plows and offset discs. Some conservation tillage practices actually require no tillage and others involve very little.

With no tillage, seeding is accomplished without preparation of the seedbed, and the crop is not cultivated during the production period. In 1976 there was about 3 million ha (7.5 million acres) being farmed with no-till techniques in the United States, more than double the area (3.3 million acres) in 1972. Estimates are that 10 to 20 percent of all cropland (13 to 26 million ha) will be farmed by no-till methods by 2010 (Development Planning and Research Associates 1978). In conjunction with this trend, total fertilizer and herbicide usage is estimated to increase by 15 percent and insecticide usage by 10 percent over the same period. Such increases in no-till farming should substantially reduce soil losses (50 to 95 percent) and thus reduce turbidity of streams. However, pesticide runoff is likely to increase because of the greater quantities applied and because the materials will remain longer on the soil surface.

With reduced tillage there is limited preparation of the seedbed for planting combined with use of chemicals for weed control. No moldboard plowing is done, and crop residues are normally left on the soil surface or mixed into the topsoil or both. In 1977, almost 24 million ha

(58.8 million acres) was farmed by reduced tillage, and another 16 million ha (40 million acres) was farmed with less than conventional tillage techniques (Development Planning and Research Associates 1978). Estimates are that reduced or conservation tillage is currently employed on 22 to 32 million ha (55 to 79 million acres) (Table 5-1), and projections indicate that these practices will be implemented on 50 to 60 percent of U.S. cropland by 2010, primarily for corn, soybean, and wheat crops (Crosson and Brubaker 1982). Most researchers conclude that conservation tillage will reduce erosion but not necessarily nutrient runoff or waterway nutrient flow, because there will be greater concentrations of fertilizers in the uppermost layers of soil most subject to erosion. Multiple cropping of land will increase with the growth of reduced tillage, and thus output will increase on a yearly per hectare basis. Use of fertilizers will increase, but not by as much per hectare

TABLE 5-1 Alternate Estimates of Land in Conservation Tillage in the United States (million hectares)

	USDA Estimates	Percent of Harvested Cropland	"No-Till Farmer" Estimates No-Till[a]	Minimum Till	Total	Percent of Harvested Cropland
1965	2.7	2.3	NA	NA	NA	NA
1973	11.9	9.3	2.0	15.8	17.8	13.9
1975	14.5	10.8	2.6	20.1	22.7	17.0
1976	15.9	11.8	3.0	21.1	24.1	18.0
1977	19.2	14.1	3.0	25.4	28.3	20.7
1978	20.9	15.6	2.9	27.4	30.3	22.6
1979[b]	22.3	16.1	3.1	29.0	32.1	23.2

[a]Defined as "where only the intermediate seed zone is prepared. Up to 24 percent of surface area could be worked. Could be no-till, till-plant, chisel plant rotary strip tillage, etc. Includes many forms of conservation tillage and mulch tillage."
[b]Preliminary.

NA = not available.

SOURCES: USDA estimates are from Gerald Darby, conservation agronomist, Soil Conservation Service, personal communication (based on reports from SCS county field offices). "No-Till Farmer" estimates are from Anonymous 1979. Harvested cropland data for 1965-1976 are from USDA, January 1980, informal communication; and for 1977-1979 from Tom Frey, USDA, personal communication.

as on lands not tilled. In the same way, the use of herbicides and pesticides will have to increase. Implementation of reduced tillage practices will cause less soil loss through erosion than is caused by conventional tillage, but the loss will still be greater than the loss that occurs under no tillage.

Conservation tillage will be favored particularly in areas with well-drained soils, where weeds are easily controlled with herbicides, and where growing seasons are long enough to sustain double cropping. The percentage of tillable land with drainage characteristics favorable for conservation tillage increases as we move from east to west in the Corn Belt (Table 5-2), and sufficient land remains for significant expansion of this practice.

If projected increases in the extent of conservation tillage materialize, the losses of nitrogen fertilizer from land planted to corn, wheat, and soybeans will increase; but they will be significantly less than the projected gross increases in the amounts applied (Crosson and Brubaker 1982). It is likely that phosphorous runoff will increase, but again it will be by an amount less than the projected gross increases in amounts applied. The effect of phosphorous on water resources as a result of conservation tillage is not clear, but, whatever the effect, the additional phosphorous from fertilizer should not make a significant contribution to the total. Fertilizer runoff as a result of reduced tillage will increase in regions where nitrogen application increases,

TABLE 5-2 Percentages of Land Amenable to Conservation Tillage and in Conservation Tillage in Ohio, Indiana, Illinois, and Iowa

	(1) Percent Amenable to Conservation Tillage	(2) Percent in Conservation Tillage, 1979
Ohio	47.5	8.0
Indiana	53.4	22.8
Illinois	65.9	28.0
Iowa	76.4	38.9

SOURCES: Column (1): Cosper 1979. Land is "tillable acres," and for each state is almost exactly the same as the sum of cropland and pasture as reported in USDA, Soil Conservation Service 1977. Column (2): Anonymous 1979.

i.e., the South, Southeast, Southwest, and Mountain areas. Since much of the expansion of cropland and crop production, and thus fertilization, will occur in the Southeast, this area may feel the strongest impact.

The trend toward conservation tillage will be driven by the cost of energy and the necessity to conserve soil resources. As a result, tractor fuel and labor needs for agriculture may be reduced, and new equipment may evolve designed to replace tractors now in use. More herbicides will be required, but emphasis on preemergent materials will decline as more selective postemergent treatments are developed. Increasing use of surface mulches--including plastics--in irrigated areas should help conserve water as well as reduce the need for tillage for crops of high value, particularly in the West. Discovery of allelopathic attributes in several mulches of cereal grains may provide an additional dimension to no-till systems. Properly dessicated, the mulches of these crops can greatly reduce weed populations through release of phytotoxic compounds. Good management of cover crops in conjunction with no-till culture may become an important and practical means of controlling weeds as well as conserving water, soil, and energy. Thus there are emerging production practices that could reduce the need for herbicides currently projected to accompany the trend toward conservation tillage.

Control of Erosion

The use of contour farming had been increasing as an erosion control practice, but between 1964 and 1969 it declined by about 25 percent (Development Planning and Research Associates 1978). Since 1969 it has declined even further. Yet in addition to reducing soil losses, contour farming can reduce runoff of nitrates and phosphorous, as well as pesticide residues, into surface waters. It is likely that the need to control nonpoint sources of water pollution will stimulate increased return to contour farming.

Use of terraces or soil embankments to control erosion and divert or store surface runoff will increase slightly, particularly on moderate to steep slopes. Grassing of waterways that carry surface water from croplands would promote water infiltration, reduce erosion, and help reduce sediment loads in streams.

Spring plowing is a practice that should become more prevalent and replace fall plowing to some extent. Plowing croplands in spring rather than fall can reduce soil loss in most areas by 10 to 20 percent by allowing crop residues to remain on the land through the winter.

Reducing the distance between rows of seeded crops can reduce erosion by increasing the area of soil stabilized by plant root systems and reducing the area of bare ground between rows. Currently, the use of narrow rows, which increases yields per hectare, is more prevalent in corn (25 percent) than in other crops, but adoption of the practice is expected to increase.

Planting winter cover crops could reduce soil erosion, particularly in areas where fall plowing is prevalent. It would also enable farmers to take a second crop from the land for little additional cost.

Irrigation and Drainage Practices

Factors that can influence decisions regarding the type of irrigation practice adopted include the source and quality of water, and the cost of delivering and distributing it, crop requirements, topography, and drainage conditions. The overriding trend in irrigation is toward greater efficiency in the application and use of water through improved practices and conservation. Falling water tables, increasing energy costs, and competition from nonagricultural users are forcing these changes. The trend appears to be away from furrow, basin, and corrugation irrigation and toward more sprinkler and drip irrigation, although some increased efficiencies in use of water through furrow irrigation seem possible with new land-leveling techniques and other practices.

In 1969 about half the cropland irrigated was irrigated by furrow methods. Average water use with furrow irrigation was slightly more than 0.61 ha-m per hectare (2 acre-ft per acre). The efficiency of this method was 35 percent (Development Planning and Research Associates 1978). Improved land grading, better timing of application, and other practices can reduce water use by 40 percent, thus reducing sediment and runoff pollutants as well. The salinity is greater with furrow irrigation, and improved grading may increase nitrate penetration into ground water. Any form of irrigation tends to increase nitrate concentrations in water. Careful timing of application and control of amount applied can reduce nitrate penetration.

Again in 1969, nearly 20 percent of hectares irrigated were sprinkled; the average water application was about 0.4 ha-m per hectare (1.39 acre-ft per acre), and the efficiency of water use was 50 to 60 percent. Sprinkling results in less loss of soil, reduced runoff of pesticides and nutrients, less ground-water pollution, and less soil salinity. However, if highly saline water is used, sprinkling can leave toxic and often lethal deposits on plant surfaces.

Drip irrigation is a system particularly well adapted to certain perennial crops. Drip irrigation operates with less energy if water is pumped from a significant depth, and, in addition, it almost eliminates soil runoff and excessively deep percolation. The method may, however, concentrate salts if the water source contains dissolved salts.

It is estimated that professional soil-plant-water managers or consultants can reduce water application by 10 percent through more careful scheduling and application. But only 1 percent of the farmers who irrigate employ professional help. If use of professional assistance increases, as it is likely to as costs rise, runoff and salinity buildup in surface and ground water should fall. Lining of surface ditches can reduce water losses by an estimated 20 percent, since much is lost in conveying the water to and from the fields.

Drainage of wet soils has long been practiced in both irrigated and nonirrigated areas. Subsurface drainage of wet areas increased markedly during the 1970s for a number of reasons, including the needs to crop wetlands and certain other wet soils for increased production, to assist in flushing salts to attain a balance tolerable by plants, to mitigate flooding if or when rain followed irrigation, and to facilitate earlier initiation of cultivation and later harvest. Such draining was made more feasible by the development of new materials, particularly corrugated perforated plastic tubing, which has largely replaced clay and concrete tiles. Laser beam installation of tubing is being used to establish the grade for drainage systems so that flows are more even and certain.

Agricultural Chemicals

Fertilizers and pesticides are the most common of the materials usually referred to as agricultural chemicals. Pesticides can be subdivided into such categories as herbicides, insecticides, fungicides, or miticides; other chemicals include fumigants, defoliants, dessicants, and plant growth regulators.

For more than two decades now, fertilizer has been one of the most important inputs used by farmers to increase food and fiber production. Without increasing amounts of nitrogen, phosphate, and potash there is no way that, given the current state of management practices, genetic understanding, and other technology, U.S. farmers could have produced as they have. Total fertilizer use in the United States in the past 20 years has tripled, growing from less than 7 million metric tons of plant nutrients to about 20.3 million metric tons (Table 5-3). The largest increase has been in nitrogen, up from 2.5 million metric tons to nearly 10 million metric tons--an increase of approximately 300 percent. Use of phosphate increased over 100 percent, from 2.33 million metric tons to 5.03 million metric tons. Use of potash increased nearly 200 percent, from 1.95 million metric tons to about 6 million metric tons. Most of these increases occurred during the 1960s, when total use of plant

TABLE 5-3 Total Consumption of Fertilizer Plant Nutrients, United States, 1960-1979 (million metric tons plant nutrients)

	N	P_2O_5	K_2O	Total
1960	2.4	2.3	2.0	6.8
1970	6.8	4.2	3.7	14.6
1971	7.4	4.4	3.8	15.6
1972	7.3	4.4	3.9	15.6
1973	7.5	4.6	4.2	16.4
1974	8.3	4.6	4.6	17.6
1975	7.8	4.1	4.0	15.9
1976	9.4	4.7	4.7	18.9
1977	9.7	5.1	5.3	20.1
1978	9.0	4.6	5.0	18.7
1979	9.7	5.0	5.6	20.3

SOURCE: Adapted from Bridges 1979.

nutrients increased by more than 100 percent or 8 million metric tons. Thus the annual rate of increase on a compounded annual basis was about 8 percent. During this period, use of nitrogen increased on an annual compounded rate of about 10 percent, while increases of phosphate and potash amounted to about 6.0 and 6.5 percent, respectively.

Use of fertilizer continued to increase in the 1970s, but at a slower rate. Total use increased by about 6 million metric tons from 1970 to 1979, less than 4 percent on a compounded annual basis. About half this increase was in nitrogen, with another third of the increase in potash, and a gain of less than 1 million metric tons in phosphate. These lower rates of increase suggest that use of fertilizer has reached a more mature stage in some areas and for some principal crops.

Use of fertilizer has increased in almost all geographic areas during the past two decades, but much more in some areas than in others (Table 5-4). Generally, in geographic areas where fertilizer use has long been a common practice, increases were smaller. As a result, although total fertilizer use has increased, these areas now consume a smaller share of the total market than they did in 1960. For example, the Atlantic Coast states, an area of comparatively long-standing use, decreased its share of the market by almost 14 percent, while the North Central states, an area of comparatively recent use, increased its share by almost 20 percent. The trend toward increased fertilizer use may well be approaching maturity, and, although increases in absolute amounts used in the future are expected, the rate of increase is certainly lower than that of the past. There is still potential for substantial increase in fertilizer applications on at least two major U.S. field crops. Only two thirds of the wheat acreage and less than half the soybeans are being fertilized. If increases in these export crops materialize, fertilizer use would increase.

It is likely that the future will see changes in methods of fertilizer application, bringing greater efficiency in use as a response to higher prices. For example, when liquid fertilizer is sprayed directly on the leaves, it is used more efficiently by the plant. Twenty percent of all fertilizer is applied in liquid form now, but more is expected to be applied this way in the future. Applying fertilizer in irrigation water is also a more efficient method than application on the ground, although one drawback is the runoff of nutrients

TABLE 5-4 Changing Regional Use of Total Plant Nutrients in the United States, 1960, 1970, and 1979 (1000 metric tons plant nutrients)

	1960	1970	1979	1960 (percent of total)	1970 (percent of total)	1979 (percent of total)
New England	111	114	110	1.6	0.8	0.5
Middle Atlantic	513	662	747	7.6	4.5	3.7
South Atlantic	1,370	1,888	2,292	20.2	12.9	11.3
East-North Central	1,549	3,595	5,522	22.9	24.6	27.2
West-North Central	1,066	4,035	6,213	15.7	27.7	30.6
East-South Central	787	1,098	1,409	11.6	7.5	6.9
West-South Central	548	1,614	1,948	8.1	11.1	9.6
Mountain States	207	575	771	3.1	3.9	3.8
Pacific States	518	885	1,136	7.7	6.1	5.6
Others	103	112	172	1.5	0.9	0.8
TOTAL	6,772	14,578	20,320	100.0	100.0	100.0

SOURCE: Adapted from Hargett and Beray 1979.

in tailwaters. Applying fertilizer in the fall requires greater quantities applied more frequently because of the runoff and leaching that occurs during the winter. About 60 percent of all cropland receives only one application of fertilizer. There is general agreement that several small applications are agronomically more significant than a single large one. Also if smaller amounts are applied at one time, less runoff and leaching will occur. Aerial application of fertilizer is a practice likely to increase, particularly in areas where soil compaction from heavy equipment is a problem or where fields are sometimes very wet.

More than 450 million metric tons of animal waste was generated in feedlots in 1976. As costs of chemical fertilizers increase, manure will increase in importance as a fertilizer. Manure application decreases runoff, but it also increases nitrogen levels and organic materials in the runoff.

Pesticides

Information on pesticide use is generally inconsistent from year to year, overlapping and duplicative in categories, and incompletely reported. The only historical data available on which trends can be based are the USDA reports on farmers' use of pesticides. Estimates are that total use of pesticides on all crops increased 40 percent between 1971 and 1976 (USDA 1978). Herbicide use increased over 75 percent in the same period, mainly because of increased applications to major crops, particularly corn, cotton, and tobacco. Herbicides are being used primarily to reduce labor needed for weed control. Conservation tillage also necessitates the application of about twice as much herbicide but helps reduce soil erosion (USDA 1975).

Use of pesticides varies widely by crop. For example, in 1976 corn used nearly 95 thousand metric tons of herbicide, or more than 50 percent of all herbicides; cotton used about 30 thousand metric tons of insecticides, or 40 percent of all insecticides; and fruits and vegetables used almost 16 thousand metric tons of fungicides, or 81 percent of all fungicides.

Pesticide use also varies regionally (Table 5-5), in part because of regional differences where crops are grown. Southeast and Delta subregion states in 1976 used half of all insecticides, because these areas are heavy

TABLE 5-5 Quantities of Pesticides by Type of Pest Control, by Region in the United States in 1971 and 1976 (metric tons)

	Insecticide[a]		Herbicide[b]		Fungicide[c]	
	1971	1976	1971	1976	1971	1976
Northeast	2,488	1,179	5,389	5,841	4,362	2
North Central						
Lake States	1,937	2,359	16,650	19,976	1,120	1
Corn Belt	8,357	7,139	37,021	70,434	2,403	7
Northern Plains	3,422	4,995	12,806	19,604	244	
South						
Appalachian	4,521	4,331	5,692	14,425	6,377	589
Southeast	18,326	13,665	6,386	8,188	24,264	2,177
Delta States	14,626	15,291	21,553	15,387	603	78
Southern Plains	8,376	5,871	21,553	6,534	3,515	817
West						
Mountain	2,454	2,059	4,765	3,842	2,410	1
Pacific	5,464	2,213	45,785	5,366	23,489	--
TOTAL	69,971	59,103	167,112	169,591	68,788	3,672

[a]Does not include petroleum.
[b]Does include petroleum.
[c]Does not include sulfur.

SOURCE: Adapted from USDA 1978.

producers of cotton, soybeans, tobacco, and peanuts. In 1976, more than 50 percent of all herbicides was applied in the Corn Belt. And one third of all fungicides used in 1971 was applied in the Pacific region, where fruit and vegetable production is extensive. Regional variation is striking and should be considered carefully in analyzing impacts on habitat.

A large difference exists among crops in the percentage of acres receiving pesticides; i.e., nearly all cotton and fruit acreage receives pesticide treatment, whereas a small percentage of rangeland receives treatment.

The types of material used have changed over the past decade, partly in response to environmental regulation but also to offset resistance. There has been a marked shift away from organochloride insecticides to organophosphate and carbamate insecticides (USDA 1978). Greater use of broad spectrum chemicals has resulted in impacts on nontargeted species. Among the advantages of pesticides currently in use is that many of them are much more rapidly degradable even though the initial toxicity to fish and wildlife may be great.

Expenditures, in constant dollars, for pesticides during the last decade more than doubled while all farm expenditures rose only about 15 percent (USDA, Economics, Statistics, and Cooperatives Service 1981). Future rate of growth of farm pesticide use in the United States is expected to slow to about 1 percent per year. Actual manufacture and sale of these materials, however, will be greater because of nonagricultural use and production for export. Contributing to the slowdown in rate of use is the expanded practice of integrated pest management. Integrated pest management practices have perhaps the greatest potential for reducing pesticide use. Pheromones are used principally to monitor pest populations, but their use in direct control is still under study. Release of large numbers of sterile males has been used successfully in eradication programs, but appears to have little use in management programs. Release of insects that prey upon or parasitize pest species has been used effectively to reduce pest populations. An important feature of most biological controls is that they are often species specific, attacking or exerting their impact only on the undesirable species without harming others.

The increased demand for herbicides and other pesticides will more than offset reductions in use due to adoption of other pest control strategies. A small decline in rate of growth of pesticide use is anticipated, but total amounts will increase. It is also anticipated that the use of plant growth regulators will increase at a greater rate than the use of other agricultural chemicals because of their important role in preventing postharvest deterioration.

Organic Farming

There are different estimates of the potential for expanded use of organic agriculture. As with conservation tillage, there are various degrees of organic farming. It relies, insofar as possible, on crop rotations, residues, animal manures, legumes, green manures, off-farm organic wastes, mechanical cultivation, and biological pest controls. Limited use or, in some cases, no use of chemicals reduces or eliminates the possibility of environmental contamination from insecticides, fungicides, and herbicides, while reduced use of high-stability fertilizers minimizes contamination of ground water and runoff. A significant benefit in the form of decreased soil erosion results from the greatly reduced use of moldboard plowing and the use of cover crops in the rotations. On the other hand, totally organic systems can deplete soil fertility if no artificial materials are added. Various technologies associated with organic farming are expanding, but the data are inadequate to evaluate their potential impact (USDA 1980).

Technology and Mechanization

Continued improvements are expected in food, fiber, and feed cultivars. Selective breeding has increased the tolerance of various plants to cold, heat, drought, and salinity and has made it possible to expand areas where agriculture can be economical. Production is now possible in previously marginal areas, and multicropping can be done on some farms in regions where production possibilities are limited by short growing seasons, extreme temperatures, variable rainfall, and adverse soil and water conditions. Further increasing the tolerance of plants to salt is an extremely important advance in expanding production possibilities and in maintaining yields in irrigated regions, and genetic engineering will further broaden the possibilities for adapting particular plants to specific growing conditions.

Production efficiency can increase but probably not markedly in the next two decades. At some point in the future, however, several avenues of current research are likely to provide the scientific understanding essential for a major increase. Breakthroughs in photosynthetic efficiency, nutrient uptake efficiency, biological nitrogen fixation, genetic resistance to pests and diseases, and greater sophistication in manipulating hormones and their biochemical processes could revolutionize agriculture. A comparable array of possibilities exists for animal agriculture, with discoveries likely in improved breeding efficiency through shorter breeding cycles, feed conversion efficiencies, and disease control. Although such technological advancements would not eliminate the need for fertilizers and pesticides, significantly lower applications per hectare would be possible.

The cost of energy and concern about soil loss will affect the types of machinery adopted by agriculture in the future. Large machinery is not adaptable to small farms or contoured land. In designing tractors and other motorized machinery, the trend will be toward reducing the number of times the equipment must pass over the land. Weight reduction and fuel efficiency will also be important criteria. Improvements in efficiency, of course, will also increase production and, at the same time, help to protect and conserve our natural resources.

Cropping Systems

Future cropping systems can take several directions. One is intensive farm monoculture with possible double cropping or intercropping and continued regional specialization. Another is greater regional diversification through introduction of new crops or plant varieties where comparative regional advantages shift because of rising energy prices. A third possibility is individual farm diversification in the form of cash crops, forage, pasture, and livestock. It is likely that all three patterns will develop in the future, dependent primarily upon region and size of farm.

Monoculture will continue where there are economies of size, where alternative crops are limited, or where management skills must be specialized. Smaller farms are the most likely candidates for increased diversification to provide year-round employment for the operator and sufficient production to generate an adequate income. It is likely that relative changes in prices of production inputs will result in some regional diversification.

Cropping systems will not be adopted by farmers in the future simply on the basis of personal preference, but as a result of factors over which the individual farmer has little control (see Chapter 3). Market developments will play a large role, particularly the cost of borrowing money and the nature and amount of commodities demanded by importing countries. Public policies, too, will be important, especially as they relate to conservation and use of resources and agricultural chemicals. The cost of the energy needed to transport products to domestic markets will influence regional cropping patterns, and technological development will have a great influence on where crops can be produced and how they are processed and shipped.

RANGELAND MANAGEMENT PRACTICES

Both publicly owned and private rangelands will be more intensively managed as their increasing role in providing products for livestock places added pressure on the land. Grazing systems must be more carefully matched to site capabilities in numbers of animals, types and mixes of livestock grazed, and time of grazing; and grazing must be integrated with practices to increase production from rangelands if their carrying capacity is to be enlarged.

Estimates are that continuous grazing was practiced on 85 percent of rangelands in 1970, but the practice was expected to decrease (Development Planning and Research Associates 1978). For this to happen, restricted or part-time grazing must replace continuous grazing. Protecting the range from excessive and untimely grazing is important if the quality of the range is to be improved. Seeding of forage species on specific sites followed by careful management of the sites can make it possible to remove livestock periodically from a given rangeland. This integrated use of several grazing sites can increase overall productivity markedly.

Sites for rangeland improvements and the treatments to be used must be carefully selected. Removal of undesirable woody vegetation followed by seeding of desirable range plants should continue to be a popular range improvement practice. Brush will still be removed mainly by chaining--if fuel costs do not become excessive--and by strip application of herbicides. Carefully controlled burning will be used increasingly to remove woody vegetation, and the strategic use of seeding, fencing, and watering locations will improve the distribution of grazing.

Given the economics of range livestock production and the ownership pattern of public rangelands, it is unlikely that necessary improvements will be made to them without government financial assistance to private owners or the use of tax funds or subsidies to users.

FOREST MANAGEMENT PRACTICES

Forest management practices have varying impacts on soil, water, and wildlife resources. Much of the harvestable timber resource is in areas without roads, and roads are essential to timber harvesting. Most of the roads still to be constructed, at the rate of about 10,000 km per year, will be in the West. All permanent road construction is expected to be completed by 2030. Once built, the road network must be maintained, and both construction and maintenance have adverse effects on soil and water quantity and quality.

Seedbed preparation by means of blades, rakes, or gouges will be used on much of the land converted from hardwoods to softwoods in the South. These techniques cause serious erosion problems on southern hills and lead to loading of streams with sediment and nutrients.

Prescribed burning is used to prepare the seedbed or remove undesirable undergrowth and litter and is currently being practiced on about 5 million ha, primarily in the South (USDA, Forest Service 1976). The growth of legumes and other wildlife food may be stimulated by the use of prescribed burning. When controlled, it does not have a significant impact on soil or water resources, but it is likely to decline as a practice in some areas because of its effects on air quality as that is now controlled. The use of prescribed burning may increase, however, particularly in California and the South, because of developments in the art of smoke management (Komarek 1981).

The use of chemical herbicides is expected to increase as a means of removing undesirable hardwood or brush and weed species from softwood forests. In many areas, such as the coastal plain of the South, many treatments might be made over a period of 100 years to control the vegetation. These chemicals may be detrimental to many species of wildlife because of their effects on food plants (particularly legumes) and the insects that live on them.

Use of chemical fertilizers to stimulate timber growth is a practice likely to increase, particularly in the South where soils deficient in phosphate are common, and where wetlands are likely to be converted to timber production. The practice will probably lead to increased nutrient loading of streams.

Logs must be removed from the forest before they have market value, and their transport from stump to road has often had adverse impacts. Soils are sometimes heavily disturbed, increasing erosion even on fairly level sites. Some mitigation of these impacts will be accomplished in the future through more careful planning of harvests, which will involve better control of the size and shape of harvest units, proper location of cutting units, and better road placement. New equipment and techniques will also play a role. Helicopters and cables make it possible to remove logs from remote areas or steep slopes without major disruption of soils, soil loss, or damage to water. Where and when these techniques are adopted will depend on relative costs.

In the future, greater use of timber residue is expected. Of the approximately 20 million metric tons of logging residues generated annually, 50 percent is in the Pacific Coast forests. Roundwood chip production increased from nearly 70 thousand metric tons to nearly 2 million metric tons between 1968 and 1972. In the same period the use of utility logs doubled. The potential exists for further increases in residue recovery. Partial removal of forest residues reduces fire hazard and provides barriers against soil loss, but total removal increases the potential for soil loss and would contribute to nutrient loss.

There is a trend toward making use of smaller trees removed during thinning operations, and the practice will have increased by 2010. There will also be less waste of hardwoods as the technology develops to make better use of this range of species.

Clearcutting will increase in practice, particularly in the South, where shorter rotation periods (15 years for some species) are likely to be adopted. If done improperly, clearcutting can cause heavy sediment and nutrient loading. If done in small or irregular shaped areas, it can increase the diversity of wildlife habitat.

LITERATURE CITED

Anonymous. 1979. Estimates by Soil Conservation Service state agronomists of United States acreage farmed by no-till methods. Pages 4-5, No-Till Farmer, March 1979.

Bridges, J.D. 1979. Fertilizer trends 1979. National Fertilizer Development Center, Muscle Shoals, Ala.

Cosper, H.R. 1979. Soil taxonomy as a guide to economic feasibility of soil tillage systems in reducing nonpoint pollution. Natural Resources Economic Division; Economics, Statistics, and Cooperatives Service; U.S. Department of Agriculture; Washington, D.C.

Crosson, P.R., and S. Brubaker. 1982. Resource and environmental impacts of agriculture in the United States. Resources for the Future, Washington, D.C. (In press.)

Development Planning and Research Associates. 1978. Environmental implications of trends in agriculture and silviculture. Vol. II, Environmental effects of trends. USEPA 600 3 78 102. Dec. 226 pp. (Available from NTIS, No. PB-290 674, Springfield, Va.)

Hargett, N.L., and J.J. Beray. 1979. 1978 fertilizer summary data. National Fertilizer Development Center, Muscle Shoals, Ala.

Komarek, E.V. 1981. Current application of prescribed fire in key geographical areas, in Prescribed fire and smoke management symposium, Jan. 20, 1981. Withlacoochee State Forest, Fla.

U.S. Department of Agriculture. 1975. Farmers use of pesticides in 1971--extent of crop use. Ag. Econ. Rep. 268. Washington, D.C.

U.S. Department of Agriculture. 1978. Farmers use of pesticides in 1976. Ag. Econ. Rep. 418. Washington, D.C.

U.S. Department of Agriculture. 1980. Report and recommendations on organic farming. USDA Study Team on Organic Farming. Washington, D.C.

U.S. Department of Agriculture, Economics, Statistics, and Cooperatives Service. 1981. Farm pesticide economic evaluation. Ag. Econ. Rep. 464. Washington, D.C.

U.S. Department of Agriculture, Forest Service. 1976. Southern forestry smoke management guidebook. USDA For. Serv. Gen. Tech. Rep. SE-10. 140 pp.

U.S. Department of Agriculture, Soil Conservation Service. 1977. National resources inventories. Washington, D.C.

6
Impacts of Agricultural Trends on Cropland and Pasture Habitats

INTRODUCTION

Croplands, the most intensively managed of all agricultural lands and the most ubiquitous habitat type, are distinctly different from the other habitat types discussed in this report. Croplands are unnatural areas converted by man from natural rangelands, forests, or wetlands. Even though croplands are no longer pristine areas, however, all but the most intensively manipulated are capable of supporting some wildlife. With proper planning, these wildlife populations can be diverse and, in some instances, abundant.

Croplands and Pasturelands as Wildlife Habitat

On farmlands used primarily for crop and forage production, the basic components of a wildlife habitat--food, water, cover, and living space--must be present in appropriate proximity and abundance in order to have a balanced ecosystem that will support wildlife. The removal of any one component will result in serious degradation of the wildlife habitat. The conversion of forage land to row crop production, for example, results in the loss of the living space that many wildlife species require for reproduction. Even though the remaining components of the habitat are of the best quality, no new wildlife generations will be produced. Developing agricultural management systems that incorporate all of the required habitat components is the challenge facing those who desire a diverse, aesthetically pleasing, and healthy landscape in intensively farmed regions. Aquatic habitats on land used for agriculture are discussed in Chapters 9 through 11.

The utilization of prime agricultural lands for such uses as housing and industrial development will continue to result in the conversion of less productive lands to farmland and a further decrease in wildlife habitats. If this trend is to be minimized, an economically sound program to retain or improve current wildlife habitats will be required. Few agricultural management schemes are designed with any intention to maintain a habitat for wildlife. In most cases the components of a wildlife habitat occur by accident in areas that are difficult to till, that are too wet, or whose inclusion in fields devoted to row crops could not be achieved efficiently. The overall reduction in the number of farms, and the consequent increase in their size, also influences the availability of wildlife habitats. In some areas of the nation, demographic changes have altered farm practices. Smaller farms operated as a hobby or as a second vocation are, in some instances, beneficial to wildlife. Maximum production is not stressed on these farms, some small areas are not cultivated, and the cropping patterns are more mixed. All these characteristics enhance the habitat for wildlife. Human population shifts within the United States also influence how land areas are utilized and what areas remain for the use of resident and migratory wildlife. Net emigration from the northeastern states will alter land use patterns in that part of the nation, and as a result there may be some improvement in habitats through the abandonment of intensive cropping and the use of former farms for retirement homes. High immigration to the sunbelt, on the other hand, will reduce wildlife habitats in the West and the South (see Chapter 3).

Impacts of Intensive Agriculture on Wildlife Habitat

The agricultural system is driven by many forces: economic, social, political, and international. These forces have an impact on the availability, distribution, and quality of wildlife habitats. Federal laws and regulations heavily influence how land is utilized for crop production and pasture. These laws and regulations greatly affect the quantity and quality of wildlife habitats. Crop support programs and disaster payments, for example, make marginal agricultural areas suitable for exploitation. Federal funds available for drainage, clearing, and pasture improvement, which result in expansion of the areas devoted to agricultural production, also influence the amount of available wildlife habitat. The rising costs of fossil fuels, high interest rates, and reduced profit margins all dictate farming practices that are as efficient as possible. But efficient, clean farming is not conducive to the preservation of high-quality wildlife habitats. Economic considerations dictate not only ownership and cropping patterns but also the day-to-day management decisions that affect wildlife. Fall plowing is a good example of how wildlife habitats are reduced. Fall plowing not only severely reduces wildlife habitats but also increases erosion. As long as land use decisions are driven by economic considerations, there will be continued decreases in wildlife habitats throughout areas devoted to croplands and pasture.

Current and projected agricultural trends generally point to additional hardships for wildlife (see Chapter 4). This stems from a general view at all levels of management that wildlife is a by-product of the land instead of a crop and that wildlife can survive without any consideration of ecological principles. Wildlife as a crop capable of generating income for the landowner is therefore a concept that should be encouraged.

Although irrigation is expected to increase on farms east of the Mississippi River, it is not known how withdrawal of surface and subsurface waters will influence terrestrial wildlife. Some of the most valuable remaining wildlife habitats exist in riparian zones (zones that include the land, vegetation, and wildlife associated with bottomlands and river, stream, and lake banks). If increased irrigation requires more channelization or reduces the availability of water for riparian vegetation, these remaining wildlife habitats are likely to be seriously impaired (see Chapter 9).

Perhaps one of the greatest external costs of agriculture is soil erosion. Any decrease in potential land productivity results in lowered production of wildlife as well. Many of the other external costs of agriculture, such as water salinization, ground-water depletion, wetland drainage, and deforestation also have direct negative impacts on wildlife and fish. Soil erosion results in decreased land productivity as well as increased siltation of wetlands, streams, and rivers (see Chapter 4). Any reduction in soil erosion will therefore benefit wildlife in direct and indirect ways. Consideration of long-term benefits must be injected into management decision-making, either through subsidy payments or legal requirements.

Any increase in the amount of arable land devoted to crop and pasture and any increase in the intensity of agricultural land use will increase the number of conflicts pitting wildlife considered as pests against the production of agricultural commodities. As the costs of production increase, landowners become less and less tolerant of even minor losses to vertebrate and invertebrate animals and weeds. As these conflicts arise, there will be increased effort to control wildlife, ultimately by eliminating their habitats. The removal of marshlands, which serve as both breeding and roosting sites for blackbirds, results in the loss of habitat for a great diversity of other marsh-dwelling wildlife species. More intensive development of certain crops, such as sunflower seeds for oil and protein production, also brings about new conflicts between agricultural producers and wildlife. The expansion of croplands and pasturelands to more northern areas will result in other wildlife species being regarded as agricultural pests. As these problems are enhanced by more intense land management, and as reduction of wildlife habitats further concentrates the damage they cause to crops, producers will become even less sympathetic to retaining or providing wildlife habitats on or adjacent to their lands.

Various scenarios have been developed involving alternative choices in agricultural management practices (see Chapter 5). Some of these alternatives could benefit wildlife. Greater diversity in the kinds of crops planted on a regional basis would result in more diverse land use patterns and create alternative habitats for wildlife. If practices such as intercropping or double cropping resulted in more intensive use on smaller land areas, the remaining unused land could be developed for high-quality habitats. Whether this occurs will depend on economic and political decisions about exports of food and fiber and on farmers' decisions on land use. As a general rule, however, clean farming, larger fields, control of weed and insect pests, and more intensive cultivation are detrimental to wildlife habitats.

If rising energy prices compel less use of large equipment and more labor intensive practices, wildlife will benefit. Field sizes will be smaller, and there will be less potential destruction of such habitats as fencerows and lowland marshes. But if decisions are made that result in larger and larger equipment being used on larger and larger fields, there will be a great reduction in the diversity and numbers of wildlife species. The rationale for choosing between these alternatives, as diverse as they are, is not well understood and cannot be predicted. If greater wildlife habitat diversification could be brought about by economic or deliberate land use decisions, croplands and pasture farming could enhance wildlife habitats.

Ecological studies show that small and isolated habitats are susceptible to wide variation in emigration, immigration, and extirpation of wildlife species (Simberloff 1976). The preservation of wildlife habitats could be taken into account in crop and pasture management practices, integrated pest management programs, and land use decisions, but this will not happen until adequate scientific research is available to provide estimates of the costs and benefits of doing so, since economic decisions are paramount in agriculture. If expenditures on agricultural research increase by 7 percent each year, it is estimated that production increases 1.2 percent per year.

REGIONAL IMPACTS

The Northeast

The total amount of land devoted to intensive agricultural production in the Northeast is considerably less than in other areas of the nation. As a consequence, emerging trends in agriculture will not affect wildlife habitats substantially. If, for example, the current trend of reducing areas devoted to wheat and small grain production is reversed, increased production would reduce the amount of land that has become suitable for wildlife. There is a trend toward more intensive use of pasture and forage crops for beef cattle, dairy cattle, and sheep in the Northeast. Further increases will reduce the use of these lands by such species as deer, wild turkeys, and other wildlife. Some practices might improve wildlife habitats, such as the use of manure for fertilizer. High-intensity grazing, on the other hand, results in increased erosion and a reduction in riparian habitats. An increase in sorghum and corn lands would cause a general reduction in habitats. Soybean production reduces fertilizer use and provides summer food for some wildlife species. Reduced or conservation tillage is expected to increase in the Northeast, but its impact on wildlife is not yet known. There could be both beneficial and detrimental effects. Herbicides, insecticides, and fungicides and their degradation products could result in negative influences on soil organisms, terrestrial and aquatic wildlife, and fish.

Integrated pest management in the Northeast could have both beneficial and detrimental effects. If such management provides opportunities for intercropping or double cropping, the effect would be negative. If the result was less pesticide use, the effect could be beneficial.

The Northeast is unique because of its long history of suburban development and the use of small parcels of land for residences. Generally, these can be considered beneficial, since habitat diversity is enhanced. Small clearings are developed in forested areas, and agricultural land is taken out of production. The potential for these changes to disturb sensitive habitats for endangered species must be considered.

The application of fertilizers might enhance wildlife habitats if land is not used intensively for agriculture. The use of herbicides on croplands and pasture, however, is usually detrimental to wildlife habitats. High human density in the Northeast requires high rates of water use and reuse. Any increase in irrigation might cause diminished stream flows in the summer. The creation of water impoundments for water supplies could also adversely affect wildlife.

Areas that are already intensively managed for fruit and vegetable production have little value as wildlife habitats, and any increase in the use of acreage for these purposes will have a direct impact on wildlife. Confined (dry lot) dairy farms will also create local pollution problems.

The Northeast is also unique in that it is the major area in the United States affected by acid rain. How this environmental problem will influence agricultural trends and terrestrial wildlife is not yet understood, but its effects on aquatic systems have been documented, and a reduction in fish diversity and productivity is evident (Loucks 1980). If some species of wildlife are also highly sensitive to acid rain, serious changes in the structure of the ecosystem may occur. The use of lime in agriculture for acid soils may have a beneficial effect on wildlife that use croplands and pastures.

The Southeast

The land in the four states (Alabama, Florida, Georgia, and South Carolina) that make up the Southeast region is dominated by forests, which grow on 52 percent (26 million ha) of the land in the region. Much of the land devoted to agricultural crops (14 percent, or 7.1 million ha) is very intensively managed and is of little value as wildlife habitat. Georgia has the highest proportion of land in agriculture, about 46 percent of the total agricultural land in the region. Most of the irrigated acreage (688,000 ha) is in Florida and is devoted to vegetable and fruit production. As a result of rapid demographic change--Florida's population increased by about 7,500 people a week between 1966 and 1977--there has been a significant conversion of agricultural land to urban and industrial uses. About 2.7 million ha of land, about 5.4 percent of the total land area in the four states, has been converted. In Florida alone, 1.4 million ha of agricultural land has been developed, and in Georgia 567,000 ha. The direct impact of these land use changes on wildlife habitats is readily evident. Because of favorable climatic conditions, cropland is intensively used through double cropping and is of little value as wildlife habitat. As a result of both land conversion and the highly productive nature of the area, particularly Florida, there has been accelerated conversion of bottomland hardwoods to crops and pasture. Intensive use of water has also influenced wildlife habitats by reducing runoff and lowering water tables. In some areas this has resulted in intrusion of saline water from the ocean and bays, further altering habitats. These problems have influenced and will continue to influence such unique wildlife areas as the Everglades. The drainage of upland bogs (pocosins) for conversion to crop or pasturelands, although not very great in terms of total acreage, will seriously impoverish wildlife habitats in certain areas. The alteration of these highly diverse and productive areas will also change water drainage patterns and increase pollution by agricultural chemicals.

Intensified use of the 5.7 million ha of pastureland (11 percent) in the Southeast is dictated by increasing energy costs. Maximizing the production of forage and livestock will be brought about by the use of legumes and perennial grasses that need less water and fertilizer. More herbicides will be used for weed control, but more intensive management of forage and pasturelands, as with row crops and fruit, will be detrimental to wildlife. Further urban and industrial development will increase the rate of conversion of natural habitats to agricultural production and further diminish coastal and estuarine habitats. Row cropping in much of the Southeast has frequently been done on small, irregularly shaped fields, which was beneficial to wildlife because it increases land diversity. Now that double cropping is possible, however, these areas have become of less value to wildlife. Many of the lands used for agriculture in the Southeast are light and sandy, requiring irrigation and fertilization whose high costs dictate intensive management to achieve high rates of return. Because of the climate and intensive cropping, pest problems are more severe and require higher frequency of pesticide application, another management practice that is detrimental to wildlife.

Major agricultural trends in the Southeast in the next two decades will include further loss of wildlife habitats through the conversion of bottomlands and bogs to croplands, changes in wetland habitats as a result of irrigation, and increased use of herbicides and insecticides. The conversion of wild areas to pasture frequently leads to subsequent conversion of pasture to fruit or crop production. In some instances, however, high energy costs have forced the abandonment of pasture. The restoration of natural vegetation in these areas has been of benefit to wildlife.

Because the human impact on the land of the Southeast has been so rapid and so great, recommendations for the retention or development of wildlife habitats should be carried out immediately. Some land use planning programs are under way, but much more needs to be accomplished if wildlife is to remain an integral part of the environment of the Southeast.

The Appalachian States

The five Appalachian states (Kentucky, Tennessee, North Carolina, Virginia, and West Virginia) have extremely diverse land use and habitat types, ranging from coastal marshes to intensively managed croplands to hardwood forests in the mountains. About 17 percent of the total land area is devoted to agriculture, 56 percent to forest land, 15 percent to pastureland, and about 12 percent to other uses. Crop types and cropping patterns vary considerably, from large farm fields in the coastal areas of North Carolina to small irregularly shaped fields in the hills and valleys of the Appalachians to intensively cropped areas in western Kentucky and Tennessee. Major crops include cotton, tobacco, soybeans, sorghum, and corn. Over the last 6 to 10 years the number of farms in Appalachia has decreased about 4 percent per year. The total amount of land used for farming has decreased about 1 percent per year, but the area in cropland has increased by over 4 percent per year. Pastureland has decreased about 0.4 percent per year, and nonfederal forest areas have decreased about 1.4 percent per year. Pasturelands are more variable than croplands, and small semiwooded or lowland areas are often used for pasture. Some areas at higher elevations support small herds, and because of favorable rainfall some very intensive pasture and forage management programs are present in these areas. The benefits to wildlife from pasturelands depend on the intensity of grazing or mowing and the species of forage plants grown.

Most of the increases in cropland have resulted from the diversion of land previously devoted to other uses and from the clearing of forest lands and drainage of wetlands. In the decade 1969-1979, forest land in North Carolina decreased by 8.1 million ha. These land use changes are generally detrimental to wildlife populations, although they can also result in changes in the wildlife species present that may be enhanced if the new land use is not intensive, the fields are small, and the use of chemicals is limited. The reduction in forest areas in North Carolina has had a particularly strong impact on such forest-dwelling wildlife as black bear.

There has been a significant decline in the land planted in cotton in the Appalachian region with a reduction of nearly 52 percent between 1969 and 1979. This has been beneficial to wildlife because alternative uses (such as soybean production) require less extensive use of insecticides and the direct impact on wildlife is reduced. The substitution of alternative crops, however, has not materially improved the availability of wildlife habitats. One of the most dramatic increases in crop types has been in soybeans. Prior to 1960 this crop was of little significance in the region, but by 1979 it was the most important crop in terms of area. The total area devoted to soybean production increased about 120 percent, or about 1.5 million ha, between the years 1969 and 1979.

The state most affected was Kentucky, where soybean acreage increased from 200,000 ha to 700,000 ha between 1969 and 1979. Much of this land was formerly cotton land or forest and bottomlands. Generally, this change has had a negative influence on wildlife habitats and has greatly increased erosion. Some species, such as bobwhite quail, do use soybeans as a highly nutritious food source, but the removal of permanent grasslands, lowlands, and forested areas has generally had a detrimental effect on wildlife. Quail and rabbit populations have declined, both as a result of conversion of land to row crops as well as an increase in the intensity of pasture management, chiefly the monoculture of fescues. The increased intensity of grazing by domestic animals on both managed pasture and forested slopes has increased erosion problems, and the removal of hawthorn shrubs in many areas to increase the value of land for grazing has further reduced the quality of many potential wildlife sites. Grazing in or near forested areas subjects livestock to attacks from predators, and in 1980 West Virginia paid $41,000 for damages to livestock, primarily as a result of attacks by bears. Black bears also occasionally damage commercial beehives.

Field size has also increased in the Appalachian region, causing the removal of fencerows and other strips of vegetative cover between fields that previously served as wildlife habitats. Fall plowing, another practice with negative effects on wildlife, is also common. Conservation tillage is expected to increase in the region, however, and there may be some resultant benefits to wildlife in the form of additional winter food and cover. Drainage of upland bogs in North Carolina has been extensive, and only about 20 percent of the more than 890,000 ha of bogs in the state remain intact. These high-quality habitats are important to a number of wildlife species, particularly black bear. On the other hand, white-tailed deer have thrived in North Carolina, and crop damage from deer has been reported. In 1977 at least 1700 deer were killed by farmers under a permit system.

In the western part of the Appalachian region, about 37 percent of the bottomland hardwood in the lower Mississippi alluvial plain has been removed. In parts of western Tennessee the increased level of agricultural operations on upland areas has caused such severe erosion and siltation that by 1980 an estimated 32,000 ha of prime bottomland hardwoods had been destroyed by siltation and standing water. In the Obion-Forked Deer River Basin of western Tennessee the amount of cleared land increased by 24 percent from 1960 to 1971. Bottomland hardwoods decreased by 28 percent, while forested swamps and shrub swamps increased by 43 and 85 percent, respectively. Land clearing for row crop production (soybean area more than doubled in Tennessee) can have severe impacts on all types of habitats.

Federally supported drainage and channelization projects in Appalachia will further reduce wildlife habitats. In Tennessee alone, about 1200 km of streams and rivers are scheduled for channelization. Some benefit to wildlife results from the construction of farm ponds, however. About 340,000 ponds have been built in the region, creating nearly 81,000 ha of aquatic habitat. Pond edges, if they are not grazed by livestock, can provide habitats for a variety of wildlife species.

The area devoted to agriculture in the Appalachian region will continue to increase and to be intensively managed for row crop production. Fortunately, from the standpoint of maintenance of wildlife habitats, much of the region is heavily forested and too steep for modern agricultural methods.

The Lake States and the Corn Belt

The Lake States of Minnesota, Wisconsin, and Michigan and the Corn Belt states of Iowa, Missouri, Illinois, Indiana, and Ohio contain some of the most productive agricultural lands in the United States and are some of the most intensively used areas for farming. The high productivity of agricultural land in this region also makes it one of the most productive regions for wildlife as well. The area is extremely diverse; the northern areas are heavily forested, while the Corn Belt lands are intensively cropped. Some of the largest deer herds in the nation occur in the Lake States and are highly important to the economy of these states. The southern states of the region once had some of the largest pheasant and quail populations in the nation, but the loss of habitat through more intensive agricultural production and urban and industrial encroachment has reduced these populations in most of the Corn Belt states. About 47 percent of the land in the region is devoted to crops, 11 percent to pasture, and 23 percent to forests. The Lake States have slightly more than twice as much forested land as the Corn Belt, 35 percent as compared to 15 percent. About 4 percent of the cropland in this region was converted to other uses during the period 1967 and 1977.

The harmful effects of highly mechanized and more intensive agricultural production on wildlife have been evident in the region for nearly 30 years. Early in the century, however, agricultural production sometimes resulted in greater diversity. Prairie grouse, for instance, initially thrived as a result of agricultural development. Burger (1978) has presented a very well documented and well written review of these events in a chapter entitled "Agriculture and Wildlife" in the book Wildlife and America. Among other things, he cites wildlife losses on an area in Jasper County, Illinois, where prairie chickens were completely eliminated, bobwhite quail declined by 78 percent, and cottontail rabbits decreased by 96 percent between 1939 and 1974.

Erosion is a very serious problem in the Corn Belt and the Lake States. This loss of topsoil seriously affects crop production as well as the quality of wildlife habitats. The estimated soil loss for the total United States in 1975 was over 2.7 billion metric tons (3 billion tons), or about 20 metric tons (22 tons) per hectare. In Iowa alone, one of the most productive of the Corn Belt states, over 180 million metric tons (200 million tons) of soil is lost each year. This soil cannot be replaced for several generations (Brown 1981). Declines in agricultural production result from depleted topsoil, and any improvement of soil husbandry that reduced erosion would also improve wildlife habitats. Crop cover during the winter, retention of crop residues, reductions in grazing in riparian zones, and cessation of fall plowing would all serve to enhance wildlife habitats while conserving soil. Long-term impacts should be considered as well as short-term profits, even though the reduction of soil erosion to tolerable levels may cost up to 3 times the amount of the immediate economic benefits. These high costs prevent the average farmer or landowner from putting erosion control practices into effect. The choice is bankruptcy in the short term or continued mining of the soil until productivity declines and the land must be abandoned. Some kind of public intervention is necessary to reduce the intolerable levels of erosion that are occurring, not only in the Corn Belt but throughout the world.

There should be a decrease in the amount of erosion in the Corn Belt states as a result of an increase in reduced or no-till practices. Minimum tillage can maintain production while reducing tractor fuel use (Van Doren 1964, Schwab et al. 1970, Eckert 1979). Most of the lands suitable for these practices are corn, wheat, and soybean areas, which predominate in the Lake States and Corn Belt. Between 1978 and 1979, the amount of land in minimum or no tillage increased about 4 percent in the Corn Belt but decreased in the Lake States by about 0.5 percent. Iowa has the highest area in minimum tillage or no tillage, about 40 percent of the cropland; about 75 percent of the cropland in the state is suitable for this practice. Aside from the reduced erosion as a result of minimum tillage or no-till practices, an added benefit for wildlife would be the retention of cover on the land over the winter. About 51 percent of the active cropland in Iowa is plowed in the fall, thus eliminating winter cover and food. Even if double cropping was coupled with minimum tillage, this would result in a better winter habitat than bare soil. The land subject to reduced tillage is expected to increase by 50 percent by the year 2010.

One aspect of minimum tillage that has not been evaluated in terms of its effects on wildlife, however, is the increased use of fertilizers, herbicides, and insecticides. Half of the total amount of herbicide used in the United States is applied in the Corn Belt. Between 1971 and 1976 the total amount of herbicide applied to corn land more than doubled, and total pesticide use during that period increased by 40 percent. Although more short-lived organophosphorus insecticides are now being used, some effect on wildlife can be expected at the time of application. Furthermore, the runoff of these chemical compounds will increase despite the use of minimum tillage because pesticides are applied to the surface of the land and are not worked into the soil by plowing. Pesticide costs have more than doubled, so more efficient and timely use under integrated pest management (IPM) programs will be beneficial. Fertilizer use has also increased, and by 1990 the application of nitrogen fertilizers will include 98 percent of the total area planted in corn, 80 percent of that planted in wheat, and 25 percent of the land used to grow soybeans.

Improved technological developments will increase the amount of irrigated land in the Lake States and the Corn Belt. Land leveling assisted by lasers, better drainage systems, and advanced sprinkler and drip irrigation systems will be used to increase production and enhance double-cropping practices. Since irrigation is most suitable for large landholdings, wildlife habitats will be eliminated to permit these intensive management procedures. More fencerows and more small wooded areas will be removed for the installation of irrigation systems.

Diversification of some small farms will occur, but larger farms will continue to be single-crop farms raising corn, soybeans, or wheat. Improved harvesting equipment will reduce the amount of waste grain available to wildlife, but a reduction in fall plowing leading to more weed seeds for wildlife diets may balance out this detrimental effect.

In summary, wildlife habitats throughout the Lake States and Corn Belt will be reduced by a number of agricultural trends, including increased land drainage, improved land-leveling systems, larger fields, and reductions in fencerows and woodlots in order to increase irrigation. The value of riparian zones will be reduced by increased water use and increased livestock grazing. Coupled with this reduction in habitats will be increased pesticide use, especially herbicides. Some benefits may accrue to wildlife through the use of minimum tillage or no-till farming and a reduction in fall plowing. There is little information available concerning the prospects for integrating wildlife habitat management with modern agricultural practices, particularly from a cost-benefit standpoint. Unless this information can be developed, disseminated, and put into practice, either through subsidy payments or other economic incentives, the quantity and diversity of wildlife throughout the Lake States and Corn Belt will continue to decrease in the years ahead.

Delta States

Severe losses in wildlife habitats have occurred in the three Delta States of Arkansas, Mississippi, and Louisiana through increased land clearing for agricultural purposes. The total increase in cropland between 1937 and 1977 was nearly 50 percent, and the amount of land planted in soybeans increased more than 14 times during that period. The habitat type most heavily affected has been bottomland hardwoods; this area has decreased nearly 56 percent. About 23 percent of the total area of the Delta States is in cropland, and the percentage is increasing. About 14 percent of the land is pasture, 45 percent is forested (and is decreasing), about 1 percent is in rangeland, and the remaining 40 percent is in urban and industrial uses. During the period 1967-1977, about 29,000 ha of prime cropland was converted to other uses. Mississippi lost the most agricultural land during that period, nearly 29,000 ha per year. The total area devoted to irrigated crops has increased in Arkansas and Mississippi, but it has decreased in Louisiana.

During the 40-year period between 1937 and 1977, the percentage of bottomland hardwood decreased from 40 to 13 percent in Arkansas, 54 to 35 percent in Louisiana, and 37 to 19 percent in Mississippi. The rate of reduction has decreased in Arkansas and Mississippi but has increased in Louisiana. As in many other states, most of the remaining area valuable for wildlife habitats is along the riparian zones, including the alluvial plain of the Mississippi River. The three Delta States contain a total of 8.6 million ha of alluvial plain. These are not only important areas for many forms of resident wildlife; they are crucial as habitats for migratory birds using the Mississippi Flyway. Continued reduction of this very important type of habitat will have a serious impact on continental waterfowl populations.

The loss of habitats through the conversion of floodplain forests to agricultural lands is a serious loss to wildlife, and further effects will result from the high use of pesticides on many crops in this region. Slightly more than 3 million ha was planted in soybeans in 1977, and this acreage is increasing each year. Total pesticide use on soybeans averages about 12 kg/ha; the approximate total use of pesticides on soybeans in the Delta states is about 36 million kg per year. In 1980 alone, Louisiana used 2.7 million kg of pesticides to protect its cotton crops. Some of these compounds enter the ecosystem, where they accumulate and have subsequent detrimental effects on wildlife. The development of newer, less persistent, and better-targeted specific compounds will reduce this hazard. The increased use of fertilizers will also affect runoff water, and the conversion of land has increased the rate of siltation and further reduced high-quality habitats for aquatic wildlife and fish. Because of favorable climate and rainfall, the Delta States region will continue to be heavily affected by increased agricultural development, and only a concerted effort will result in the retention of minimal wildlife habitats.

The Northern Plains

This region of the United States is and will continue to be one of the areas most heavily utilized for agriculture. Soil and climatic factors ensure the suitability of virtually all of the region for cropping or grazing. Over half of the land available for agriculture is cropland in North Dakota, South Dakota, Nebraska, and Kansas, and much of it is also grazed at some time of the year. Nearly 45 percent of the land available is in pastureland and rangeland. Forests cover only about 1 percent of the total land area of the region, but they are very important as wildlife habitat.

About 11 percent of the cropland in the region is irrigated, ranging from about 33 percent in Nebraska to only about 0.2 percent in North Dakota. Irrigation is increasing as dryland cropland and rangeland are being converted to row crops. Field and farm size has increased in this region, as has the leasing of land. All of these developments have negative impacts on wildlife because of losses of edge, cover, and vegetative diversity. Leasing usually results in giving precedence to short-term returns over long-term land needs. The conversion of prime agricultural lands to other uses has also occurred, about 45,000 ha of cropland having been converted between the years 1967 and 1977.

More intensive use of cropland is expected in the form of double cropping on irrigated land and increased grazing on pastureland, rangeland, and crop residues. As a result of management decisions, high equipment costs, and climatic factors, most farmers in the region will continue to concentrate on the production of one or two crops. The risks of one-crop or two-crop dependency have been reduced by price supports and crop insurance.

The initial increases in irrigated lands in the region improved wildlife habitats by making food crops available in more areas, but more intensive irrigation and utilization of water resources will be a detriment to wildlife as water tables drop and stream flows are reduced. Lined ditches, conduits, and vegetation control will adversely affect wildlife habitats.

Corn and wheat will remain important, but in some areas sorghum may replace corn. This may benefit wildlife because less intensive chemical control is required to raise sorghum. Improved strains of hard winter wheat may permit conversion from spring wheat, thus providing winter cover and reducing winter erosion. This may also improve nesting habitats for some species of wildlife. Increased production of sunflower seeds in the Dakotas will provide high-quality summer cover and fall food for wildlife, but no winter food or cover. The expansion of sunflower acreage, however, will depend on the development of disease- and pest-resistant strains. Crop and crop residues will continue to be heavily grazed by livestock. All of these uses have negative effects on wildlife habitats. Feedlot operations are increasing in some areas, and shifts to the production of more feed and ensilage will reduce cover and food for wildlife.

As long as energy costs and crop prices maintain a stable relationship to one another, the high cost of energy will not influence the effects of agriculture on wildlife habitats in the Northern Plains. But if energy costs increase appreciably, wildlife would benefit. Less productive areas could not then be intensively cropped.

Southern Plains

Perhaps the greatest impact of agricultural trends on wildlife habitats is in the Southern Plains region (Oklahoma and Texas), due to the clearance of land for livestock production and the rapid withdrawal of ground water for irrigation. Once land is cleared for livestock, the likelihood that it will be diverted to row crops is much greater, frequently because this shift is subsidized by federal programs.

Extensive irrigation in the western part of the Southern Plains has led to the depletion of ground-water reserves. In some areas of western Texas and Oklahoma, mining of ground water accounts for 50 to 78 percent of annual consumption for agriculture. In addition, irrigation has increased both the salinity and the alkalinity of soils and runoff water. In these areas the most important remaining wildlife habitat is riparian, where the diversity of bird species may be 7 times greater than that found in grassland and pastures (Tubbs 1980).

Of the nearly 86 million ha of land in the Southern Plains, about 25 percent is agricultural land. As in other areas of the nation, conversion of agricultural lands to other uses has been rather substantial. In the period 1967 to 1977, about 1 million ha was converted, and it is projected that before the year 2000 another 769,000 ha will be lost. About 3.6 million ha of cropland has been converted to pasture, largely as a result of the high cost of water and its reduced availability. Some of this conversion from crop to pastureland was beneficial to wildlife. Of the total land area of the Southern Plains, about 9.4 percent could be converted to pastureland, rangeland, and forest land. Pastureland and rangeland increased nearly 8.5 million ha between 1967 and 1977 in the Southern Plains. This has caused major changes in species diversity and numbers of wildlife. Some species increase with the advent of grazing (mountain plover, horned lark), while others decrease (western meadowlark, lark bunting). Even gullying and erosion provide habitats for some species (rock wren, rough-winged swallow) (Ryder 1980).

The large increase in pastureland and rangeland is a consequence of increased international demand for U.S. exports of meat and meat products. As the developing countries increase their earning power, meat consumption also increases. Federal programs have also helped to encourage a shift toward placing more and more land in pasture and range. As energy costs for feed grains increase, thus raising grain prices, there will be more demand for grazing to maintain meat production. Wildlife predation on sheep has been a problem in some areas, and the methods and costs of control have not been satisfactory.

The conversion of natural areas to range, then to crops, and then back to pasture or range, has both beneficial and deleterious effects on wildlife. Stable vegetative systems are not permitted to develop, meaning that wild animal species that benefit from early successional stages are favored.

There will be some expansion of cotton areas in eastern Texas where rainfall is adequate, but high rates of pesticide use on cotton plants would have detrimental impacts on wildlife. There has been a decrease in the land area planted in rice in Texas, largely because of higher energy costs and higher pesticide use. The development of new genetic strains of various crops that are more drought-resistant will permit more intensive cropping on a larger land area in the Southern Plains. All of these practices, such as the mining of ground water, greater use of surface waters for irrigation, and large increases in pastureland and rangeland, have a detrimental influence on wildlife. In some areas of Texas, wildlife has become an income-producing crop, particularly through the commercial sale of deer-hunting privileges. Areas that are managed for deer also support many other forms of wildlife. As water becomes more expensive and less available and as energy and pesticide costs rise, more areas may provide adequate economic returns through efforts to combine agricultural and wildlife management objectives.

The Mountain Region

Eight states make up the Mountain region (Arizona, Colorado, Idaho, Montana, Nevada, New Mexico, Utah, and Wyoming), which has a great diversity of agricultural pursuits and wildlife habitats. Much of the remaining wildlands of the continental United States occur in this region. As in the other regions of the nation, high energy costs currently influence agricultural management decisions, which are made almost exclusively on a cost-benefit basis. Consideration of wildlife habitats must therefore be put on an economic basis. Much of the high-quality cropland in the region is irrigated for alfalfa, corn, barley, wheat, oats, sugar beets, and vegetables. Dryland areas primarily produce wheat, although some land is devoted to raising millet, sorghum, corn, oats, and barley. There is every indication that an intensification of agriculture will occur in the Mountain region. Urbanization is causing the conversion of agricultural lands to nonagricultural purposes, as is the discovery and exploitation of large blocks of land containing coal and oil shale. These changes are resulting in lower quality lands for agricultural crops. These lands were once used as wildlife habitats. As demand for water increases and as it becomes more expensive, all irrigated lands will be used more intensively. Irrigation demands will also reduce reservoir and stream-pond riparian zones, further reducing habitats. Increased intensity of grazing on managed pasture will be the rule, and there will be increased use of crop residues for grazing, further reducing the quality of both food and cover for wildlife.

The grazing of crop residues on both irrigated and dryland areas influences both resident and migratory wildlife species. Increased intensity of grazing also reduces the quality of riparian zones for wildlife purposes. Conversion of native vegetation to either dryland crops or irrigated lands frequently leads to wildlife damage.

Conservation tillage will increase primarily on dryland crop sites and may be beneficial to wildlife. Irrigated lands are so intensively managed that little minimum tillage will occur. The effect of increased herbicide use is unknown, but the propensity to use herbicides to control undesirable plants throughout the area, not only on cropland, will reduce what little wildlife habitat remains on these areas. The development of irrigated lands in the past benefited some wildlife species because some areas were too wet and water ponded in other areas (see Chapter 9). These small areas offered good habitat for many species. But as water supplies become more limited, newer and more efficient irrigation methods will cause a reduction in these small habitat areas. Some wildlife populations will therefore be seriously affected. Farm sizes will also increase as a result of ownership changes, and even small vegetable, orchard, and truck garden areas will be used more intensively. Old homesteads, fencerows, and shelterbelts will disappear. Although their total area is not great, these small units have provided high-quality habitat sites for a variety of species.

Some ground-nesting birds could benefit as conservation tillage follows the depletion of ground water. Crops will change from corn, pinto beans, and sugar beets to grain sorghums and rye pastures. Genetic engineering is expected to produce new varieties of winter wheat that will become biennially grown monocultures. The raising of proso millets will also increase on dryland and on sagebrush lands at higher elevations. Integrated pest control will lead to chemicals that are less dangerous to human beings, but these toxic substances will still affect wildlife. Increased use of herbicides will have a greater effect through the destruction of habitats than through direct toxic effects on wildlife. More intensive management will require greater control of all noxious weeds.

Although higher energy costs will result in the abandonment of some areas of low or marginal productivity in the Mountain region, the expected increase in demand for export grains will increase prices, once again making these lands economically suitable for row crop production. The extent to which crops or crop residues will be used to produce forms of fuel is unknown, but fewer residues would reduce food and cover and ultimately reduce wildlife productivity and species diversity.

If wildlife habitats are to be retained in the Mountain region as a part of agriculture, monetary incentives must be offered to landowners so that present agricultural practices can be altered. Changes in the Food and Agricultural Act of 1977 have been suggested to provide a means to preserve wildlife habitats in the Mountain region. (The Food and Agricultural Act of 1981 was passed while this report was in press.)

The Pacific Region

The Pacific region (excluding Alaska and Hawaii) has some unique agricultural characteristics. Although only about 11 percent of the area is in cropland, about half of that cropland is irrigated, and the region produces more fruits and vegetables than any other part of the country. Crop patterns are highly variable, from the dryland wheat farms of the Palouse area of Washington and Oregon to the highly fertile valleys of California, where irrigated crops are predominant. Because of the high productivity and fertility of the region, most of the agricultural lands have few wildlife habitats, and those that remain are being eliminated as land costs and the availability of water become greater problems. High productivity in many of these areas also means high pesticide use, further complicating the lives of wildlife. Large migrations of birds move up and down the Pacific Flyway, increasing the depredation of crops as well as wildlife losses to pesticides. The extensive use and reuse of water also increases pollution problems and the concentration of pollutants in water runoff (see Chapter 9). Because of the high value of most of the Pacific cropland, very little is converted to other uses. Between 1973 and 1977, for example, there was a conversion of about 14,000 ha of agricultural land in California to urban use, causing a net loss in the amount devoted to agriculture.

Water is a critical factor in agriculture throughout the Pacific region, particularly in California. Many of the agricultural crops provide food and habitats for migratory waterfowl and other wetland birds. Changes in technology, such as improved strains of rice that permit double cropping and laser leveling that allows more even applications and withdrawals of water, greatly reduce the value of these agricultural lands for wildlife. There has, however, been a great increase in the planting of corn in the valleys and delta region of California, and this has attracted large numbers of waterfowl. On some farms the land is plowed immediately following the corn harvest and then planted in barley or wheat. Other farmers have found that leasing lands for waterfowl hunting may be equally productive economically, and only an annual crop is planted. It should be noted that the increased use of irrigation and the reduction in natural marshes has led to a change in the species of waterfowl using these areas.

Throughout the region, four major impacts of agriculture are affecting wildlife habitats. These are loss of habitats through clean farming, loss of riparian habitat through improved water management and high-grazing intensity, increased water demands, and urbanization. In Washington, there has been some reduction in clean farming as a result of minimum tillage practices, and in these areas there has been an improvement in wildlife habitats. This has not occurred in California and Oregon, however. The loss of riparian zones is critical because in many areas these are the only remaining sites suitable for wildlife cover during most of the year. These areas are being reduced in size by clean farming practices and by improved water management methods. In addition, higher energy costs have made small hydroelectric projects practical, and the construction of these dam sites further reduces riparian zones that once offered optimum wildlife habitats. Increased numbers of human beings will also increase the need for water and further restrict the availability of the "wastewater" that was so important in maintaining small, high-quality habitat areas. Seepage from canals once created excellent habitat areas in many arid locations, but as these canals are lined or conduits are installed these sources of water are no longer available, and the habitat units are lost.

Changes in crops and cropping patterns are also resulting in a reduction of wildlife habitats. Conversion from pastureland to cropland, or conversion of grain crops to more intensively managed crops, such as fruits and vegetables, reduces the value of these lands for wildlife.

High net gains in the human population of the Pacific region will have severe impacts on wildlife habitats (see Chapter 3). This loss will occur through the displacement of agriculture by urban construction and the loss of habitats in natural areas converted to housing developments. These developments also result in increased water and energy use, which also have a direct and negative impact on wildlife habitats.

The Pacific region is highly productive of both agricultural products and wildlife. For many species the retention of habitats in association with agriculture is critical. This is particularly true for many species of migratory birds. There is a great need to develop programs that will permit the continued existence of wildlife habitats in conjunction with agricultural production. Without such positive action, there will be a great impoverishment of the environment for both wildlife and the human population.

RESEARCH NEEDS

- Determine through cost-benefit analyses which combinations of plant species and agricultural practices yield increased returns to producers while maintaining or improving habitats for wildlife.
- Further investigate the direct and indirect effects of various pesticides on wildlife and focus on the development of crop varieties most resistant to pests requiring the application of harmful chemicals.
- Determine the minimum sizes and complexity of habitats for various species of resident wildlife and develop food and cover plants that may enhance habitat carrying capacity or reduce the area required to sustain populations.
- Determine the various effects of livestock grazing intensity, timing, and patterns on wildlife and wildlife habitats.
- Establish methods for the collection and retrieval of faunal data so that changes in populations and habitats can be documented and evaluated.
- Determine the effects of soil erosion on wildlife habitats and evaluate changes in agricultural productivity as a result of erosion.
- Determine the impacts of international markets on land use and the consequent effects on wildlife habitats.
- Evaluate the responses of wildlife to cropland- and pastureland-use changes: abandonment, clearing, changes from row crops to pasture and back again, and time sequences.

• Determine the possible impacts of crops and crop residues used for biofuel production on wildlife and wildlife habitats.

LITERATURE CITED

Brown, L. 1981. Eroding the base of civilization. Environ. Prot. Agency J. 7(4):10-11; 40-41.

Burger, G.V. 1978. Agriculture and wildlife. Pages 89-107 in H.P. Brokaw, ed., Wildlife and America. Council on Environmental Quality, Washington, D.C.

Eckert, D.J. 1979. Agronomic tips. C-8, Sept. Ohio State University Department of Agronomy, Columbus.

Loucks, O.L. 1980. Acid rain: living resource implications and management needs. Trans. North Am. Wildl. Nat. Resour. Conf. 45:24-37.

Ryder, R.A. 1980. Effects of grazing on bird habitats. Pages 51-66 in Management of western forests and grasslands for nongame birds. U.S. For. Serv. Tech. Rep. INT 86.

Schwab, G.O., G.S. Taylor, and A.C. Waldron. 1970. Measure of pollutants in agricultural drainage. Ohio Rep. 55(4):87-89. Wooster, Ohio.

Simberloff, D. 1976. Experimental zoogeography of islands: effects of island size. Ecology 57(4):629-648.

Tubbs, A.A. 1980. Riparian bird communities of the Great Plains. Pages 419-433 in Management of western forests and grasslands for nongame birds. U.S. For. Serv. Tech. Rep. INT 86.

Van Doren, D.M., Jr. 1964. Research report on tillage systems. Ohio Rep. 49(6):83-84. Wooster, Ohio.

7
Impacts of Agricultural Trends on Forest Wildlife Habitats

THE FOREST RESOURCE

Forests occupy about 251 million ha (619 million acres), or roughly one quarter, of the total land area in the 48 contiguous states (American Forest Institute 1979). Forest lands are widely distributed and are a predominant land use in most of the states east of the Mississippi River as well as those on the Pacific Coast. Some central states, on the other hand, such as North and South Dakota, Nebraska, and Kansas, are only 2 or 3 percent forested. Most of the southern states are more than 50 percent forested. In New England, New Hampshire and Maine are 90 percent forested.

Forests are classified as either commercial or noncommercial. Commercial forests are defined as areas available for timber production and capable of yielding 1.40 m^3/ha/year (20 ft^3/acre/year) from natural stands. About three quarters of the total forests in the country, or 193 million ha (476 million acres), are classified as commercial forests (Table 7-1).

About 17 percent of the commercial forest land (33 million ha) is located in national forests, where wildlife must be given equal consideration with timber and other values. Slightly less than 10 percent of the commercial forest land (17 million ha) is in other public ownership, either federal, state, or municipal. High fiber production is the primary goal on about 14 percent of the commercial forest lands (28 million ha) owned by private companies. Industrial forests are more intensively managed than those in other ownerships. More than half of the forest land (114 million ha) available for wood production is privately owned, chiefly in woodlots of 40 ha (100 acres) or less. The goals of

TABLE 7-1 Distribution and Ownership of Forest Land in the 48 Contiguous States (1000 hectares)

	Total Land	Total Forest	Percent Forested	Commercial	Ownership of Commercial			
					National Forest	Other Public	Forest Industry	Other Private
North								
New England	16,317	13,159	81	12,561	286	466	4,009	7,800
Mid-Atlantic	35,319	21,000	60	19,527	542	1,855	1,156	15,944
Lake States	84,253	21,574	26	20,244	2,297	5,701	1,709	10,537
Central	118,111	17,508	15	16,830	974	532	326	14,997
South	206,864	83,864	41	76,315	4,438	2,749	14,480	54,649
Pacific	82,715	37,809	46	23,757	10,112	3,277	5,001	5,367
Rocky Mountain	224,672	55,788	25	23,395	14,756	2,726	849	5,063
TOTAL	768,251	250,702	27	192,629	33,405	17,336	27,530	114,357
					17%	9%	14%	60%

SOURCE: Adapted from American Forest Institute 1979.

these owners vary, and they often give priority to values other than fiber production.

The remaining forest--58 million ha (143 million acres) of noncommercial forest land--includes wilderness areas, national parks, and other lands withdrawn from timber use by statute or administrative regulation. Most of these areas are utilized by many species of wildlife. Large parts of the remaining habitats for large birds and mammals are in wilderness and other places rarely used for human purposes.

Soils, climate, and topography are the environmental variables that determine the composition, productivity, and succession of a forest. Forests are diverse. The Society of American Foresters recognizes 156 separate forest types, ranging from dense stands of Douglas fir in the humid Pacific Northwest to cypress swamps in the Southeast and oak-hickory ridges along the Appalachians.

The regenerative ability of the forests allows humans to modify forest ecosystems often without eliminating them. The result of natural forces and man-caused alterations is a complex array of constantly changing forest communities, utilized to varying degrees by an equally diverse wild fauna that includes about 1500 vertebrate and many more invertebrate species.

FORESTS AS WILDLIFE HABITAT

From the arid Southwest to the humid coasts, there is an almost endless variety of forest communities. Each provides a different mixture of food, cover, water, and other conditions needed for wildlife survival. Some forests support a rich abundance of wildlife; others support only a few species. Marked differences in the richness of the animal fauna are even apparent in adjacent forest areas. What makes a forest more or less attractive to wildlife?

At the risk of oversimplifying the complex interaction between an animal and its environment, one answer is variety in the forest community. Many field studies during the past three decades support the ecological theory that highly stratified communities contain a greater assortment of microhabitats and niches and thus have the richest variety of animal life. Recent studies further contributing to our understanding of the relationship of forest structures to wildlife are reviewed by Thomas et al. (1975). Fish habitats affected by forestry practices are discussed in Chapters 9 through 11.

Horizontal stratification and vertical layering in ecological communities are important aspects in structural diversity. Whenever soil types, moisture, topography, aspect, or other abiotic gradients change, plant communities also vary. Species composition, growth form, nutritive value, and other characteristics differ. The result is an interspersion of vegetative types across a landscape in response to natural variations in environmental factors, including man-caused disturbances. The resulting edges, where the boundaries of two or more kinds of plant communities meet, are especially attractive to wildlife.

Interspersion of resources is important to wildlife. The requirements for each species must be available within its normal living area. For example, Gullion (1970) has identified three forest types, plus openings in the forest, that are necessary for ruffed grouse. Since a grouse may spend its entire life in an area of less than 20 ha (50 acres), interspersion of the required vegetative types must occur in that relatively small area. Large mammalian predators that wander over several square kilometers require greater vegetative variety than the small mosaics of plant types needed by grouse, but the principle is the same.

Harris et al. (1979) state that "Forest structural diversity is the primary determinant of wildlife species and abundance." Their description of forest structure further illustrates the concept:

> Forest structure, in turn, has several important dimensions. The vertical aspect is measured by parameters such as foliage height diversity. The horizontal aspect includes the concepts of interspersion, edge, juxtaposition, patchiness and landscape heterogeneity. Additional aspects of forest structural diversity include the abundance of live wood versus dead wood, differences between hardwood and softwood tree form, and the nature and size of mast (nuts, berries and seeds) produced. It is largely because of these factors that hardwood forests almost universally possess nearly double the wildlife density of coniferous forests (see Thomas et al. 1975 for literature review).

A bare site is quickly invaded by grasses and forbs, which are soon replaced by shrubs, sprouts, and tree seedlings. The process is repeated as one plant community

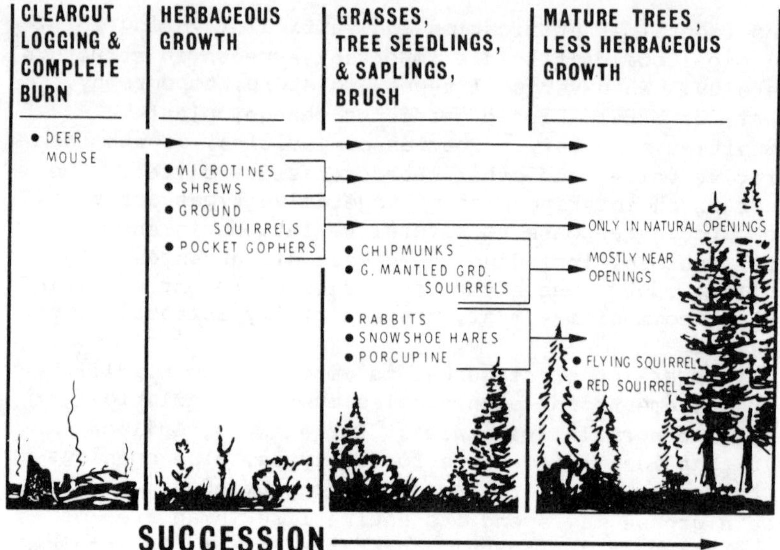

FIGURE 7-1 Response of some mammals to successional stages following clearcut logging and burning. SOURCE: Ream and Gruell 1980.

replaces another until a more stable, mature stage is reached. Wildlife responds to these changes in forest succession (Figure 7-1). Deer seek the new plant growth in recently logged or burned places. Some species, such as the endangered Kirtland's warbler, have very specific needs. This bird nests on the ground in stands of jack pine 5 to 20 years old and thus is restricted not only to a single tree species but also to an early seral stage that is caused by forest fires.

Forest structure is a convenient and meaningful measure of the relative value of forests for wildlife and of the impacts of agricultural and forestry practices. In general, whenever large-scale disturbances simplify plant community structure, fewer species of amphibians, reptiles, birds, and mammals can be expected to appear.

The application of the concept of forest diversity to wildlife habitats has been discussed by Evans (1974) for public forests in Missouri, by Siderits (1975) for Superior National Forest, and more recently by others for several other national forests where attempts are being made to increase habitat diversity (Evans 1978, Thomas 1979, Smith et al. 1981, Mealey and Horn 1981).

IMPACTS OF FORESTRY PRACTICES ON WILDLIFE HABITATS

Expanding tree nurseries, growing networks of permanent forest roads, and new timber mill construction clearly signal a strong trend toward more intensive forest management over the next several decades. On tens of thousands of hectares of the best forest land, stands of trees are being cultivated more intensively. New techniques are being applied to grow the greatest volume of high-quality wood in the shortest time permitted by current technology and economics.

The rapid expansion in the cultivation and harvesting of preferred species is in great contrast to the laissez-faire exploitation typical in the past, when timber harvesting took precedence over the regeneration of new stands. By World War II, better timber cropping practices were becoming more common in some of the larger industrial forests, but "timber mining" was still prevalent on smaller private holdings (Dana 1956). Natural forest succession following logging (and often fire) would eventually produce another tree crop, if one could wait a half-century or more.

Populations of deer, elk, hare, and other herbivores rose to new highs after logging but subsided when the succulent new forage grew out of reach. This boom-and-bust cycle for many preferred game species was repeated across the country wherever forests were exploited. By contrast, carefully planned forest management that gives consideration to wildlife can provide a mix of vegetative types arranged in varied geometric patterns that can yield an even flow of timber products as well as more stable wildlife habitats.

Forestry and agricultural trends, and associated land management practices, have variable effects on wildlife habitats, depending upon the geographic area, forest type, and species of wildlife present. Tables 7-2, 7-3, and 7-4 summarize some of the impacts resulting from forestry trends and highlight the variability in their impacts on wildlife and wildlife habitats. It is apparent that such practices as clearcutting are beneficial in providing habitats attractive to many species but may reduce the numbers of other species. Each habitat resulting from a particular silvicultural practice has a characteristic group of animal species. In the long run, overall forest management programs will exert a more controlling influence on wildlife habitats than any single practice. There has been little research

TABLE 7-2 Some Examples of the Impact of Site Preparation and Plantations on Wildlife Habitat

	Area	Impact	Reference
Site Preparation: burning chipping drainage tilling fertilization herbicides	Southeast	Increase in nutrient export.	Swank and Douglas 1974
		Rate of succession > 50%. Negative impacts proportional to intensity of site disturbance.	Harris and Smith 1978
		An increase in available soil nutrients.	Haines and Pritchett 1965
		Decreased game food plants.	Hebb 1971
		Quail food plants declined drastically after third year.	Brunswig and Johnson 1972
		Each succeeding process of site preparation exacerbates the impact on wildlife.	Harris and Smith 1978
		Increased site preparation accelerated pine overstory and shrub midstory.	White et al. 1975

Plantations: single species even-age, sometimes nonnative species	Northeast	A large variety of animals fulfill some of their requirements in plantations, but intermediate state with closed canopy and no understory is a "biological desert" for wildlife.	Bailey and Alexander 1960
	Southeast	As much as 75% of rotation is in dense pines.	Harris 1980
		Quickly lose value to wildlife adapted to early successional stages. Have fewer birds and mammals of all species in contrast to natural stands because of canopy closure, reduced understory, reduced vertical stratification, litter buildup, all reducing wildlife food and cover.	Harris and Smith 1978
		Quail populations reach near zero by age 5 in unburned plantations.	Brunswig and Johnson 1972

TABLE 7-3 Some Impacts of Forest Harvesting Practices on Wildlife Habitat

	Area	Impact	Reference
Even-age management, clearcutting	Southeast	Cuts provide good deer forage, quickly eliminated by overbrowsing on small (<20 ha) cuts. Large cuts become dense and unattractive to deer.	Harlow and Downing 1969
		Deer obtained over twice as much crude protein and digestible dry matter in clearcut as in uncut areas.	Regelin et al. 1974
		Initial reduction in breeding bird species diversity and number of birds. Increase in 3-, 7-, and 12-year cuts--peak 7 years.	Conner and Adkisson 1975
		Many clearcuts may fragment habitat to degree that none of the stands are large enough to fulfill species food and cover requirements.	Harris and Smith 1978
	Northeast	Decrease in gray squirrels; small clearcuts best.	Nixon et al. 1980a
		Minor effect on small mammals.	Krull 1970
	Southwest	Clearcuts 8 to 16 ha (20 to 40 acres) in spruce-fir and ponderosa pine increased forage and deer and elk use.	Reynolds 1966, 1969

Even-age management, clearcutting (continued)	Rocky Mountains and general	Increases snow depth and wind; reduces cover; increases animal damage; simplifies ecosystem.	Pengelly 1972
	Pacific Northwest	Bird populations increase and reach peak 3 to 6 years after cutting.	Hagar 1960
		Clearcutting in Douglas fir creates openings distributed in patchwork fashion that offer range of optimum habitat for wildlife.	Hooven 1973
	General	Long rotations enhance habitat for more bird species than short rotations regardless of harvest system used in even-age management.	Crawford and Titterington 1979
		Summarizes studies highlighting beneficial aspects to big game, small mammals, and birds. In general more diverse habitats provided for greater number of species.	Resler 1972
		Number and density of birds and mammals often greater after clearcutting than before.	Several authors--summarized by Harris and Smith 1978

TABLE 7-3 (continued)

	Area	Impact	Reference
Uneven-age management, selective cutting	Northeast	Vertical development maximized. Produces continuous cover of many ages and heights. Bird populations remain more stable. Not many standing dead trees.	Titterington et al. 1979
		Removal of 37% to 55% basal area (without cull tree removal) had no effect on survival, reproduction, or density of gray squirrels.	Nixon et al. 1980b
	Southeast	Thinning increased bird diversity by stimulating understory growth.	Hooper 1967
	Pacific Northwest	Decrease in edges; lack variety of successional stages; old snags and large trees lacking; forest diversity lacking.	Hall and Thomas 1979
Variable harvests removing, 25%, 50%, 75%, and 100% of merchantable volume on individual areas. One natural area control.	Northeast (Northern hardwoods)	Number of species and diversity indices for songbirds were higher in logged areas and were positively correlated with increased logging intensity.	Webb et al. 1977

TABLE 7-4 Some Impacts of Grazing on Forest Wildlife and Their Habitats

	Impact	Reference
Northeast	Breeding birds 4 times more abundant on ungrazed compared with grazed area.	Dambach 1944
	Reduced tree and shrub bird nesters; bird populations rose 35% to 40% when grazing was eliminated.	Good and Dambach 1943
	Regeneration is depressed. Soil erosion increases and water quality is lowered. Wildlife habitat significantly depreciated through loss of understory vegetation and fallen mast.	USDA 1978
Southeast	Reduced tree growth, damage to ground cover.	Wahlenberg 1937
Rocky Mountains	Songbird/raptor use increased in enclosures protected from grazing.	Duff 1979
Pacific Coast	Moderate grazing maintains habitat for California quail in humid areas where brush or tree growth is dense.	Leopold 1977
Overview	Alter species competition, delay normal succession. Great variability in the effect from area to area.	Ryder 1980

on the impacts of specific programs over a period of several decades, however.

It is impossible to assess, habitat by habitat or species by species, every kind of impact. However, some definite trends in forest management changes that will affect the quality and quantity of wildlife habitats are apparent (see Chapter 4).

Telescoping Plant Succession

Practices that speed the establishment of a new stand, accelerate tree growth, and shorten the rotation period compress some seral stages. Although grasses, forbs, and shrubs quickly invade newly exposed sites, potential crop trees may not appear for several years without human intervention.

Artificial regeneration is faster as seedlings from genetically superior stock are planted on prepared sites, and the seedlings are spaced to accommodate mechanical harvesting when they mature. Site preparation may include burning or chipping the residues of earlier logging, removing stumps, providing for drainage, mechanically tilling the soil, applying fertilizer, and using herbicides. These techniques may be applied singly or in combination. As the markets for fuelwood and silvichemicals grow, it is likely that complete utilization of the tree, including stump and roots, will further intensify site changes. The removal of forest residues and stumps will have a serious impact on forest soil, the environment, and natural biota.

When natural regeneration occurs, grasses, forbs, and shrubs dominate the site for several years, and the production of forage for herbivores is greatly increased. Deer, rabbits, some types of mice, and a rich assortment of birds respond. When the site is cultivated and planted, however, fast-growing conifers soon shade out lesser vegetation, and shrubs or hardwood tree sprouts are killed with herbicides if they compete seriously with the conifers. The period when wildlife can use the early successional stages of vegetation is thus decreased by half or more. In general, the more intensive the site preparation techniques used, the shorter the period when the early seral stage is available to wildlife. In areas where large sites are devoted to plantation forestry, wildlife that need the very early seral stages will decrease unless adequate habitat areas are provided. On a few intensively managed forests where the timing, spacing, size, shape, and overall pattern is planned, the interspersion of seral stages beneficial to many kinds of wildlife is provided for.

Shorter rotation of forests decreases the proportion of old tree growth. Southern pines grown for pulpwood sometimes are harvested in as little as 25 to 30 years. The silviculture of Douglas fir in the Northwest is based on clearcut plantation management, with rotations as short as 50 years. Wildlife species that depend upon older trees during part of their life will therefore decline as management intensifies. Other wildlife species requiring younger trees may benefit, however. In the Pacific Northwest, shortening the rotation period from 80 to 100 years to 50 years is reported to have doubled the capacity of forests to support black-tailed deer. Several other species of herbivores have increased dramatically wherever large quantities of new vegetation have become available following logging.

Examples of wildlife that need older trees include the spotted owl in the Pacific Northwest. This owl lives in mature conifer stands and is threatened in California and Oregon because of increasingly short rotation and the consequent disappearance of old growth forests. The red-cockaded woodpecker in the South is another "old growth species" that requires mature trees, chiefly longleaf pines 80 or more years old, as sites for its nesting cavities. The holes made in the live wood by this woodpecker eventually are used by several other cavity dwellers that do not make their own tree holes. Across northern New England and the Lake States, white-tailed deer seek old growth conifer stands for protection during the winter.

Saving stands of old growth spruce, fir, and white cedar will become increasingly difficult as landowners intensify their forestry operations and shorten the rotation period. In Maine, 350 areas where deer spend the winter have been classified as protection districts where cutting trees is regulated by the state to maintain sufficient overhead shelter for wintering deer. Such land use regulations are often temporary, however, and are not likely to be adequate to protect special habitats.

Even relatively small clumps of older trees can be important to wildlife. In the Southwest, suitable roosting sites for wild turkeys consist of a group of a dozen or more ponderosa pines, 0.6 m (2 ft) in average diameter and 24 m (80 ft) tall. Large ponderosa pines with high-density interlocking crowns serve as nesting habitats for Abert's squirrels. Bald eagles also prefer nests in large old trees.

Maintaining older trees in units large enough to benefit species that depend upon mature stands will become more difficult as the demand for wood increases. Conflicts between government agencies and landowners may occur because of the economic value of large trees and also because mature trees can be lost because of insect infestations or blown down by high winds.

Streamside zones where complete removal of trees is prohibited will, in addition to maintaining water quality, become increasingly important as places where older trees can be maintained for the benefit of many species of wildlife.

Changing Forest Diversity

Site preparation in tree plantations reduces or eliminates stumps, snags, and ground litter, and the trees themselves form dense canopies that reduce differences in the height of foliage by casting shade that eliminates lower vegetative layers. There are fewer forage- and mast-producing plants because of an emphasis on conifers, and variations in vegetation types and the resulting edges are masked because of site preparation. Finally, stands are harvested at relatively young ages, before older seral stages develop.

The loss of tree snags for hole-nesting mammals and birds becomes an acute problem wherever intensive forestry is practiced. Old snags are eliminated, and quick rotation designed to produce maximum economic returns does not allow time for the development of new snags.

Although intensive forestry practices tend to reduce heterogeneity, the interspersion of various age classes of forest communities can be enhanced by planning the spacing, timing, and configuration of reforestation and size of harvesting operations. Conifer plantations may not support as many kinds of wildlife as hardwoods or mixed woods, but conifer plantations scattered among poor quality second-growth hardwoods can enhance the value of a region for wildlife. Plantations with variable-sized units can improve edges, provide additional shelter, and attract new wildlife species.

The key to accenting the positive effects of plantations is careful planning appropriate to local conditions.

Once the trees in regenerating stands have grown beyond the early stages, thinning reduces competition and favors the eventual crop trees. Slow-growing, diseased, and poorly formed trees are removed. But thinning can also enhance structural diversity and improve the habitat for some types of wildlife by stimulating growth of the understory. In some forest types the benefits of this practice to wildlife are short-lived, since one objective of intensive management is to maintain crown closure and reduce competitive crown overlap. In other types of forests, such as ponderosa pine forests in the Southwest, the benefits of thinning last longer and can greatly increase understory production (Reynolds 1962). Understory forage response is variable and is related to site quality, residual crown density, overstory composition, and the successional stage of the stand (Zeedyk and Evans 1975).

Forest modification can range from "light" (uneven-aged silviculture) to "heavy" (clearcutting followed by site preparation and planting) (Crawford and Titterington 1979). Between these extremes there are many degrees of cutting. The effects on wildlife habitats differ along the continuum. The practices most beneficial to wildlife habitats may not always be easily defined but are likely to be somewhere between the extremes for most forests.

The selection of a harvesting system is governed in part by its influence on the regeneration of the next stand. For many forest types, clearcutting is recommended for successful natural regeneration. It is also the method employed when a plantation system of regeneration is used.

The size, shape, and positioning of clearcuts and timing of clearcutting influence the interspersion of age classes, the amount of edge available, and the overall horizontal diversity of the area. Vertical diversity within stands is minimized by clearcutting, but horizontal diversity can be enhanced except where large clearcuts are made close to each other.

The clearcutting of scattered small blocks of trees is recommended to improve wildlife habitats for grouse, woodcock, deer, and other species that use regenerating stands. Songbirds and small mammals usually respond quickly to this practice. Clearcuts of more than 20 ha (50 acres) are not well used by some kinds of wildlife, however, and when adjacent to each other they create large expanses of even-age stands that are not desirable.

Under even-aged management, harvests are made at intervals to remove selected trees or groups that have reached merchantable size. Uneven-aged management for most species of trees maintains a forest in the later stages of succession, and shade-tolerant trees are favored. Vertical diversity is increased, while horizontal diversity decreases (Zeedyk and Evans 1975).

Clearcutting or even-aged management will increase as forest management intensifies, especially on industrial forests. Uneven-aged management will be practiced on some private lands for aesthetic reasons and in some of the northern hardwoods, where the species tolerant of shade such as sugar maple and yellow birch are favored.

A third option, sometimes referred to as exploitation, occurs when a landowner decides to liquidate a timber resource without regard to the future of the area. All merchantable material is removed, and "the exploited forest normally develops a distinctive two-storied condition of scattered, nonmerchantable relics overtopping an even-age understory" (Zeedyk and Evans 1975).

Exploitation logging is reported to be the most common practice on private nonindustrial forests throughout the country and poses a major challenge. Heavy "opportunistic cutting," at best poor forestry, probably contributes to very long rotation periods and is probably detrimental to wildlife species requiring early successional stages.

Conversion of Hardwood Sites to Conifers

Clearing hardwoods from a site and replacing them with conifers will accelerate, especially in the South and in varying degrees in the Northeast and the Lake States. In a recent summary, the National Forest Products Association (1980) indicates that about 14 million ha (35 million acres) of hardwoods can be converted to pine, chiefly in the East, on sites where the growth rates of pine can produce an incremental rate of return of at least 10 percent after taxes. While not made as a projection, this information does indicate the potential magnitude of conversion. There are, of course, additional millions of hectares of hardwoods that may be converted if economic conditions make it profitable.

Wherever hardwoods are converted to conifers on a large scale, wildlife habitats are seriously reduced, since hardwood forests support a greater diversity and abundance of wildlife than do conifers. Structurally simplified plantations of a single species cannot support the wildlife characteristic of more diverse stands. Furthermore, conversion usually occurs on the most fertile sites, where the forage is more nutritious to wildlife. In the pine regions of the South, the conversion of hardwoods to conifers represents a shift from a habitat type that is declining to one that is already quite common.

Greater Access

Intensive management requires improved access to forests. Hence road systems to forest lands will continue to expand, with mixed consequences for wildlife. The opportunity for human beings to enjoy the recreational values of wildlife will be enlarged and there will be greater flexibility in management operations, thus improving coordination of timber-wildlife management programs. But increased access will also intensify conflict between landowners and recreational users, increase poaching, and significantly reduce the quality of the recreational experiences being sought.

Increase in Forest Pest Problem

Even-aged forests containing single species of trees are more vulnerable to damage from wildlife, insects, and disease. Deer, elk, moose, hare, rabbits, porcupines, squirrels, mice, and some birds feed upon seeds, shoots, or buds. Young plantations of firs are particularly vulnerable to animal damage. Hence animal damage will increase. Animal damage will also be severe if hardwoods are planted on a larger scale to serve as biomass for energy production.

Outbreaks of insects have caused major changes in forests over large areas, with harmful impacts on wildlife species. Although some silvicultural practices are being used that may lessen insect attacks, several decades will pass before such practices are applied on a scale large enough to appreciably reduce the problem. Large-scale spraying of chemicals to control insects will continue to threaten forest ecosystems. Shorter rotation strategies in some forest types will be effective in reducing insect attacks but will contribute further to the removal of older trees needed by some species of wildlife.

IMPACT OF GRAZING ON FOREST LANDS

Grazing by livestock is generally considered detrimental to wildlife habitats in most hardwoods, riparian habitats, and in places where the livestock disturb the surface sufficiently to compact root systems or increase erosion. Deterioration of wildlife habitats from erosion is common and often severe. The soil loss from grazed woodlands in northwestern Missouri, for example, is as high as 31.3 metric tons per hectare per year (14 tons per acre per year). Woodland protected from grazing has an average soil loss of less than 1.1 metric tons per hectare per year (0.5 tons per acre per year) (USDA 1978).

In some areas, however, grazing in dense woody vegetation may create or maintain openings and edges that benefit wildlife. Controlled grazing also is compatible with timber and wildlife in some conifer forests in the West, Southwest, and South, where abundant forage production occurs naturally under sparse tree growth. In most of the midwestern states, where hardwood forests are a minor land use scattered throughout agricultural areas, one third to three quarters of all woodland is grazed. The ability of these woodlands to provide habitats for wildlife is greatly reduced because of the loss of understory vegetation and mast.

Ryder (1980) has provided a comprehensive review of the effects of grazing on bird habitats. Grazing may eliminate some plants, alter species composition, modify plant growth form, delay normal succession, or shift the community to an earlier seral stage. Ground and shrub layers are modified or eliminated in forests, to the detriment of species that forage or seek cover in the lower strata. All in all, forest structural diversity is reduced. Ryder (1980) also notes that the effects of grazing vary from area to area and concludes that grazing can be a powerful tool.

The pressures to provide more land for grazing are great. Open range laws are still prevalent, and in some regions grazing is a traditional use of forest land. Competition for food between livestock and wildlife and habitat destruction from overgrazing are common. Although grazing in federally owned areas presumably is better controlled, in an effort to increase grazing allotments for private users, grazing in one national forest in 1981 was destroying an understory of hawthorn shrubs, which provides important brood habitat for turkeys and ruffed grouse, in an effort to increase grazing allotments for private users.

Damage to riparian zones because of grazing is widespread, frequently in areas where narrow belts of flood plain forest are the only tree cover. Because riparian habitats have unique value for wildlife, some authors refer to them as endangered and in need of immediate protection from overgrazing. There is every indication that overgrazing will increase on private lands, leading to further deterioration of wildlife habitats. Better control of grazing on both private and public lands is needed and long overdue.

LOSS OF FOREST LAND

Conversion of forest land to cropland or to urban-related uses, such as roads or reservoirs, will cause further loss of wildlife habitats. Overall, a 5 percent decrease in forest land by 2010 is projected. Clearing for cropland will be much higher locally, with marked reductions in wildlife. Some of the forests that will be lost are among the most productive and valuable for both wildlife and wood products.

The most significant decline in wildlife habitats will result from the continued conversion of bottomland hardwoods to cropland in the Mississippi alluvial plain. In 1937 there was an estimated 4.8 million ha (11.8 million acres) of bottomland hardwoods in the lower Mississippi area. About 2.1 million ha (5.2 million acres) remained in 1978. Projections to 1995 indicate that another 0.5 million ha (1.3 million acres) will be lost. Soybeans is the main crop replacing bottomland forests. Soybean production is stimulated by "the export advantage provided by PL 480 (Food for Peace Program)" and the ability of soybeans to tolerate poorer soils (MacDonald et al. 1979).

Important losses of bottomland hardwoods have also occurred because of poor agricultural practices. In Tennessee an estimated 32,400 ha (80,000 acres) of bottomland hardwoods has been killed during the past half-century by siltation and by standing water dammed up by silt and debris.

Smaller losses of bottomlands will occur in most other parts of the South. In the heavily forested Ozarks, sizable areas of upland hardwoods will be cleared for pasture to accommodate rising demands for forage for livestock. Existing tax incentives will also continue to encourage the conversion of woodlands to agricultural uses. Biologists throughout much of the South and in the central states believe that conversion of woodlands to other uses is a major problem in the loss or degradation of forest wildlife habitats.

MITIGATING THE LOSS OF WILDLIFE HABITATS

Although periodic small-scale disturbance of woodlands is beneficial to maintaining a variety of habitats, the application of intensive forestry practices over large areas will gradually erode the utility of forests for wildlife. Combined with the continued loss of forests to other uses and the degradation of habitats from grazing, erosion, and other causes, the impacts of intensive forestry on wildlife will be severe locally.

Technology is available for accenting the positive influences of forest management and mitigating adverse impacts. Methods for meeting both timber and wildlife needs are being tested in some public areas, chiefly national forests, where management for multiple purposes is required by law. Progress has been slow, however, and additional commitments will be needed to implement the programs described in planning documents.

Some consideration of wildlife needs is being incorporated into industrial forestry activities, partly for the sake of public relations and in a few cases because of income from leasing land for hunting. There is little planned wildlife habitat management in private nonindustrial forests, however, since modifying the silvicultural or harvesting operations or retaining the special habitats needed by some wildlife species can be costly to landowners.

It is unrealistic to expect landowners to alter their forest management operations on a scale large enough to significantly benefit wildlife without financial incentives. Despite personal interest in wildlife, few landowners can afford to make the trade-offs required. Ways must be developed to provide a financial incentive to landowners for maintaining wildlife habitats. This would be no different, in principle, from the many incentive programs already in operation for many other forestry and agricultural practices.

The demand for softwoods by 2030 is expected to increase by 58 percent; for hardwoods the increase is expected to be 207 percent. This wood will come from both public and private lands, but farmers and other private owners are expected to provide the largest part of the increase (USDA 1980). The National Forest Products Association (1980) estimates that output from small owners must increase nearly 100 percent to meet anticipated demands within the next 50 years.

The problem of low timber productivity from the private nonindustrial sector is receiving increasing attention by the Society of American Foresters, the American Forest Institute, the National Forest Products Association (NFPA), and others. Short owner tenure, inadequate investment tax credits, the inability to acquire needed technical help, and the wide range of individual reasons for owning woodlands all hinder better management practices.

The NFPA private woodland program (National Forest Products Association 1980) includes 19 proposals that would:

(1) enhance the economic climate for forestry investments;
(2) provide for adequate technical assistance and support services to landowners; and
(3) familiarize landowners with the attractiveness of forestry investments and of the technical and financial help available to them.

Assistance programs will probably expand and have an increasing influence on forest use. Differential taxes, more moderate estate taxes, loan programs, and more readily available technical services are among the most likely incentives.

While such programs may encourage better management for fiber production, they can also stimulate the application of technology to mitigate the loss of other forest values, including wildlife habitats. Existing programs offer a framework for incorporating financial incentives to landowners for saving or enhancing habitats that otherwise would continue to be degraded or lost.

Current barometers of public attitudes about natural resources indicate that the public has greater interest in resource management than ever before (Vaux 1980).

That interest is expressed in part by debate about land management practices. Clearcutting is a recent example. It is also manifested in increased land use regulation. In the case of forests, such regulation has included mandates for multiple-use management in federal areas, and some states have adopted specific forest practices acts.

Recent public surveys also indicate high interest in wildlife resources and public willingness to pay for the protection of wildlife habitats. In one survey, for example, 76 percent of the respondents agreed with the statement, "Cutting trees for lumber and paper should be done in ways that help wildlife even if this results in higher lumber prices" (Kellert 1979). The responses to several other statements in the same survey also indicated a strong public desire to protect wildlife habitats.

CONFLICTING GOVERNMENTAL PROGRAMS

Scores of current federal and state activities have an impact on wildlife habitats in forests. They range from cost-sharing practices for brush control (which sometimes means control of tree reproduction) to the purchase and conversion of forests to croplands, the creation of reservoirs in wooded draws, subsidized drainage and channelization projects that destroy riparian forests, FHA loans that permit land development without the benefit of a comprehensive plan, and others. Too often, these and similar incentive programs are detrimental to wildlife or to other natural resource values.

A critical review of land management programs is urgently needed to assess their impact on the total ecosystem and to identify the long-range consequences of the ecological trade-offs encouraged by various kinds of governmental support. Some existing measures clearly are counterproductive. What government has wrought is a piecemeal approach that provides landowners with incentives for single-purpose and conflicting objectives that all too frequently cause serious and irreversible damage to the land.

OUTLOOK

During coming decades the importance of forests for wildlife habitats will increase because of more intensive use of nonforested land and also because of greater public concern about wildlife resources. Silvicultural practices used to increase wood production often will aid in maintaining a diversity of wildlife habitats, but wherever such practices as site preparation and intensive cultivation are applied over large areas, or where grazing and other uses reduce forest diversity, the ability of woodlands to support a variety of wildlife species will be reduced.

The future of forest wildlife on federal lands will be governed by law and by the effectiveness of multiple-use management of the land. While regulation will play a role in safeguarding special areas for wildlife on private lands, strong economic incentives must be provided if the public desires to maintain and enhance suitable habitats. The increasing demand for forest products, new efforts to develop incentive programs for private landowners, and a strong public willingness to maintain wildlife habitats provide an excellent opportunity for adopting new approaches that integrate wildlife protection with sound forest management.

RESEARCH NEEDS

- Research must be expanded and accelerated to determine and evaluate the response of wildlife populations to forestry management practices. This research should be focused on intensive forestry practices and in regions where such practices are likely to expand.
- More information is needed regarding the attitudes and needs of owners of forest lands, especially private nonindustrial owners. Without such information, wildlife conservation programs may not be responsive to needs and will not be implemented.
- More study is needed of the economic trade-offs (cost-benefit analyses) of integrating forestry and wildlife concerns in planning. In these studies, methods of providing income to landowners for meaningful habitat preservation or enhancement should not be overlooked.
- Research is needed to compare the public acceptability and economics of alternative means of promoting habitat management. Comparison of private incentive programs and land use regulations would be valuable.

LITERATURE CITED

American Forest Institute. 1979. Forest facts and figures. Rev. ed. American Forest Institute, Washington, D.C. 14 pp.

Bailey, J.A., and M.M. Alexander. 1960. Use of closed conifer plantations by wildlife. N.Y. Fish Game J. 7:130-148.

Brunswig, N.L., and A.S. Johnson. 1972. Bobwhite quail foods and quail populations on pine plantations in the Georgia piedmont during the first seven years following site preparation. Proc. Southeastern Assoc. Game Fish Comm. 26:96-107.

Conner, R.N., and C.S. Adkisson. 1975. Effects of clearcutting on the diversity of breeding birds. J. For. 73:781-785.

Crawford, H.S., and R.W. Titterington. 1979. Effects of silvicultural practices on bird communities in upland spruce-fir stands. Pages 110-119 in Proceedings of workshop on management of northcentral and northeastern forest for nongame birds. U.S. For. Serv. Gen. Tech. Rep. NC-51.

Dambach, C.A. 1944. A ten-year ecological study of adjoining grazed and ungrazed woodlands in northwestern Ohio. Ecol. Monogr. 14:256-270.

Dana, S.T. 1956. Forest and range policy. McGraw-Hill, New York. 455 pp.

Duff, D.A. 1979. Riparian habitat recovery on Big Creek, Rich County, Utah. Pages 91-92 in O.B. Cope, ed. Forum-grazing and riparian stream ecosystems. Trout Unlimited, Denver, Colo.

Evans, K.E. 1978. Forest management opportunities for songbirds. Trans. North Am. Wildl. Nat. Resour. Conf. 43:69-77.

Evans, R.D. 1974. Wildlife habitat management program: a concept of diversity for the public forests of Missouri. Pages 73-83 in Timber-wildlife management symposium. Mo. Acad. Sci. Occas. Pap. 3. 131 pp.

Good, E.E., and C.A. Dambach. 1943. Effect of land use practices on breeding bird populations in Ohio. J. Wildl. Manage. 7:291-297.

Gullion, G.W. 1970. Factors influencing ruffed grouse populations. Trans. North Am. Wildl. Nat. Resour. Conf. 35:93-105.

Hagar, D.C. 1960. The interrelationships of logging, birds, and timber regeneration in the Douglas fir region of northwestern California. Ecology 41:116-125.

Haines, L.W., and W.L. Pritchett. 1965. The effects of site preparation on the availability of soil nutrients and on slash pine growth. Proc. Soil Crop Soc. Fla. 25:356-374.

Hall, F.C., and J.W. Thomas. 1979. Silvicultural options. Pages 128-147 in J.W. Thomas, ed., Wildlife habitats in managed forests--the Blue Mountains of Oregon and Washington. U.S. For. Serv. Agric. Handbk. No. 553. 512 pp.

Harlow, R.F., and R.L. Downing. 1969. The effects of size and intensity of cuts on production and utilization of some deer foods in southern Appalachians. Trans. Northeast Sect. Wildl. Soc. 26:45-55.

Harris, L.D. 1980. Forest and wildlife dynamics in the southeast. Trans. North Am. Wildl. Nat. Resour. Conf. 43:307-322.

Harris, L.D., and W.H. Smith. 1978. Relations of forest practices to non-timber resources and adjacent ecosystems. Pages 28-53 in T. Tappen, Productivity on prepared sites. USDA, Forest Service New Orleans, La.

Harris, L.D., D.H. Hirth, and W.R. Marion. 1979. Development of silvicultural systems for wildlife. Proc. Annu. La. State Univ. For. Symp. 28:65-81.

Hebb, E.A. 1971. Site preparation decreases game food plants in Florida sandhills. J. Wildl. Manage. 35:155-162.

Hooper, R.G. 1967. The influence of habitat disturbance on bird populations. M.S. thesis, Virginia Polytechnic Institute and State University, Blacksburg. 132 pp.

Hooven, E.F. 1973. A wildlife brief for the clearcut logging of Douglas fir. J. For. 71:210-214.

Kellert, S.R. 1979. Public attitudes toward critical wildlife and natural habitat issues. Phase I. USDI, Fish and Wildlife Service, Washington, D.C. 138 pp.

Krull, J.N. 1970. Small mammal populations in cut and uncut northern hardwood forests. N.Y. Fish Game J. 17:128-130.

Leopold, A.S. 1977. The California quail. University of California Press, Berkeley. 281 pp.

MacDonald, P.O., W.E. Frayer, and J.R. Clauser. 1979. Documentation, chronology, and future projections of bottomland hardwood habitat loss in the lower Mississippi alluvial plain. Vol. 1, Basic report. HRB Singer, Inc., State College, Pa. 133 pp.

Mealey, S.P., and J.R. Horn. 1981. Integrating wildlife habitat objectives into the forest plan. Trans. North Am. Wildl. Nat. Resour. Conf. Vol. 46.

National Forest Products Association. 1980. America grows on trees. Washington, D.C. 63 pp.

Nixon, C.M., M.W. McClain, and R.W. Donohoe. 1980a. Effects of clearcutting on gray squirrels. J. Wildl. Manage. 44:403-412.

Nixon, C.M., S.P. Haver, and L.P. Hansen. 1980b. Initial response of squirrels to forest changes associated with selection cutting. Wildl. Soc. Bull. 8:298-306.

Pengelly, W.L. 1972. Clearcutting: detrimental aspects for wildlife resources. J. Soil Water Conserv. 27:255-258.

Ream, C.H., and G.E. Gruell. 1980. Influences of harvesting and residue treatments on small mammals and implications for forest management. Pages 455-467 <u>in</u> Symposium proceedings: environmental consequences for timber harvesting. U.S. For. Serv. Intermount. For. Range Exp. Stn. Gen. Tech. Rep. INT-90.

Regelin, W.L., O.C. Wallmo, J. Nagy, and D.R. Dietz. 1974. Effect of logging on forage values for deer in Colorado. J. For. 72:282-285.

Resler, R.A. 1972. Clearcutting: beneficial aspects for wildlife resources. J. Soil Water Conserv. 27:250-254.

Reynolds, H.G. 1962. Effect of logging on understory vegetation and deer use in a ponderosa pine forest of Arizona. U.S. For. Serv. Rocky Mount. For. Range Exp. Stn. Res. Note 80. Fort Collins, Colo. 7 pp.

Reynolds, H.G. 1966. Use of a ponderosa pine forest in Arizona by deer, elk, and cattle. U.S. For. Serv. Rocky Mount. For. Range Exp. Stn. Res. Note 63. Fort Collins, Colo. 7 pp.

Reynolds, H.G. 1969. Aspen grove use by deer, elk and cattle. U.S. For. Serv. Rocky Mount. For. Range Exp. Stn. Res. Note 138. Fort Collins, Colo. 4 pp.

Ryder, R.A. 1980. Effects of grazing on bird habitats. Pages 51-66 <u>in</u> Workshop proceedings: management of western forests and grasslands for nongame birds. U.S. For. Serv. Intermount. For. Range Exp. Stn. Gen. Tech. Rep. INT-86. Ogden, Utah. 535 pp.

Siderits, K. 1975. Forest diversity: approach to forest wildlife management. For. Chron. 51:99-103.

Smith, T.M., H.H. Shugart, and D.C. West. 1981. Use of forest simulation models to integrate timber harvest and nongame bird habitat. Trans. North Am. Wildl. Nat. Resour. Conf. Vol. 46.

Swank, W.T., and J.E. Douglas. 1974. Stream flow greatly reduced by converting deciduous hardwood stands to pine. Science 185:857-859.

Thomas, J.W., ed., 1979. Wildlife habitats in managed forests--the Blue Mountains of Oregon and Washington. U.S. For. Serv. Agric. Handbk. No. 553. 512 pp.

Thomas, J.W., G.L. Crouch, R.S. Bumstead, and L.D. Bryant. 1975. Silvicultural options and habitat values in coniferous forests. Pages 272-287 in Proceedings of symposium on management of forest and range habitats for nongame birds. U.S. For. Serv. Gen. Tech. Rep. WO-1. Washington, D.C. 343 pp.

Titterington, R.W., H.S. Crawford, and B.N. Burgason. 1979. Songbird responses to commercial clear-cutting in Maine spruce-fir forests. J. Wildl. Manage. 43:602-609.

U.S. Department of Agriculture. 1978. Missouri resources appraisal 1978. Soil Conservation Service, Columbia, Mo.

U.S. Department of Agriculture. 1980. An assessment of the forest and range land situation in the United States. U.S. For. Serv. FS-345 631 pp.

Vaux, H.J. 1980. The expanding urban influence. Pages 17-18 in Town meeting forestry--issues for the 1980's. Proc. Soc. Am. For. 320 pp.

Wahlenberg, W.G. 1937. Pasturing woodland in relation to southern forestry. J. For. 35:550-556.

Webb, W.L., D.F. Behrend, and B. Saisorn. 1977. Effect of logging on songbird populations in a northern hardwood forest. Wildl. Monogr. 55. 35 pp.

White, L.D., L.D. Harris, J.E. Johnson, and D.G. Milchaunas. 1975. Impact of site preparation on flatwoods wildlife habitat. Proc. Southeastern Assoc. Game Fish Comm. 29:347-353.

Zeedyk, W.D., and K.E. Evans. 1975. Silvicultural options and habitat values of deciduous forests. Pages 115-127 in Proceedings of symposium on management of forest and range habitats for nongame birds. U.S. For. Serv. Gen. Tech. Rep. WO-1. Washington, D.C. 343 pp.

8 Impacts of Agricultural Trends on Western Rangeland Habitats

THE RANGELAND RESOURCE

"Rangeland is land on which the potential natural vegetation is predominantly grasses, grass-like plants, forbs, or shrubs; including land revegetated naturally or artificially that is managed like native vegetation" (USDA, Forest Service 1979).

A huge part of the United States is made up of rangeland, whose uses and resources figure prominently in the economic and social welfare of the country as well as being the driving forces in local and regional economies. Rangelands, together with forest lands, are also the most productive and largest habitats for wildlife in the United States because they are managed less intensively than other kinds of ecosystems.

For the purpose of briefly describing the major rangeland types or ecosystems in the 17 contiguous western states, we have leaned heavily on two documents: Description of the Ecoregions of the United States (Bailey 1978) and An Assessment of the Forest and Range Land Situation in the United States (USDA, Forest Service 1980). These contain the most up-to-date statistical data available on rangelands. Data on wildlife distribution and numbers, as reflected by harvest statistics, were obtained from Schweitzer et al. (1980).

Of the more than 688 million ha (1.7 billion acres) of forest land, rangeland, and water areas in the United States, some 332 million ha (820 million acres) is classed as rangeland (including both native and exotic plant species) (Table 8-1). More than 99 percent of the rangeland is located in the 17 western states, i.e., those states on or west of the 100th meridian. Furthermore, rangeland comprises more than 50 percent of the

TABLE 8-1 Area and Ecosystems Represented in Rangelands of the 17 Western States (1000 hectares)

	Hectares of Rangeland	Percent of Land Area of State in Rangeland	Percent of Rangeland in Private Ownership	Major Ecosystems or Rangeland Types
Pacific				
Oregon	9,034	36	41	Tundra
Washington	3,195	19	79	Mountain meadow
California	17,418	43	41	Alpine grassland Desert shrub Sagebrush Annual grassland
Mountain				
Arizona	18,280	62	54	Sagebrush
Colorado	11,259	42	69	Mountain meadow
Idaho	9,550	45	31	Tundra
Montana	21,584	57	79	Alpine grassland
New Mexico	19,719	63	69	Desert grassland
Nevada	23,022	79	8	Pinyon-juniper
Utah	12,020	52	22	Chaparral-mountain shrub
Wyoming	18,979	76	56	Plains grassland
Southern Plains				
Texas	37,070	55	99	Plains grassland
Oklahoma	3,764	21	98	Prairie Scrub savanna Pinyon-juniper Desert grassland
Northern Plains				
Kansas	6,588	31	99	
Nebraska	9,824	49	98	Tallgrass, midgrass, and shortgrass prairies
North Dakota	4,976	28	88	
South Dakota	9,469	48	93	
TOTAL	235,752[a]	60	63	

[a] Total area of rangeland in the 17 contiguous western states, Alaska, and Hawaii is 814,975.4 acres.

SOURCE: Data from USDA, Forest Service 1980, Table 2.3; and Bailey 1978.

land area of eight states: Alaska, Arizona, Montana, Nevada, New Mexico, Texas, Utah, and Wyoming. The federal government owns over 54 percent of the rangelands, and the agencies charged with administering and managing the greater part of this land are the U.S. Forest Service of the Department of Agriculture, the Bureau of Land Management (BLM), the U.S. Fish and Wildlife Service, the National Park Service of the Department of the Interior, and the Department of Defense, which owns many military reservations. The Forest Service and the BLM are by far the two largest administrators of public lands. Thus these two have had a major impact through the years on how and for what purposes the rangelands have been used.

Ranges are used for animal agriculture and for products obtained from management of the land for reasons related to their physical properties. Rangelands are ordinarily fertile lands, but in many places they are steep or precipitous and their soils are too thin, rocky, or saline for cultivation (Stoddart and Smith 1955). Precipitation is usually inadequate, either in amount or seasonal distribution, to ensure dependable production of row crops. Rangelands are more suited, physically and ecologically, to growing forage plants in extensive systems that can be efficiently managed for and harvested by grazing and browsing herbivores, be they domestic or wild. Moreover, the plant communities in these areas control the precipitation runoff that provides water in these semiarid and arid lands. In addition, rangelands serve as water catchments that recharge aquifers and river systems from which water is drawn, often many hundreds of miles from its source.

Rangeland Wildlife Resources

Wildlife is one of the great resources of the western United States. As objects of sport hunting and nonconsumptive uses, wildlife attracts many visitors to the region and is of great interest to the local residents as well. The fauna is particularly rich in large ungulates, carnivores, rodents, and lagomorphs. Table 8-2 lists harvests of large mammals and upland game birds in the 17 western states in 1975, with estimates of the percentages of these animals taken on public lands (Schweitzer et al. 1980). Many species of grouse, other upland game birds, and waterfowl occur there.

TABLE 8-2 Western States Big Game and Game Bird Harvest, 1975, and Expected 1985 Percentage of 1975 Harvest; Number of Users and Percentage of Harvest That Occurred on Public Land in 1975

TABLE 8-2a Pacific Coast States

	Washington				Oregon			
	Harvest		Users		Harvest		Users	
Species	1975	1985(%)	1975	% Public	1975	1985(%)	1975	% Public
Antelope	<10	0	0	50	730	105	1,580	90
Elk	5,500	100	104,000	80	10,700	110	69,200	80
Roosevelt elk	5,400	105	--	--	3,830	115	36,100	60
Mountain lion	210	100	2,700	90	20	200	100	90
Wild turkey	130	100	1,520	20	20	200	300	90
Black-tailed deer	235,000	110	--	--	46,300	125	153,000	70
Mule deer	16,800	120	--	--	32,000	200	118,000	70
White-tailed deer	8,300	110	--	--	200	110	--	60
Mountain goat	270	90	874	100	<10	0	--	100
Bighorn sheep	10	300	23	100	10	200	--	100
Black bear	3,820	100	23,700	60	1,600	105	15,000	80
Chukar partridge	173,000	110	36,500	20	113,000	125	20,800	70
Common snipe	35,800	100	7,500	30	--	--	--	--
Sage grouse	1,040	90	2,700	20	2,000	100	1,500	70
Band-tailed pigeon	83,000	100	18,100	20	62,000	150	10,500	60
Hungarian partridge	63,200	110	24,500	10	15,400	100	5,100	50
Ring-necked pheasant	434,000	70	99,500	10	172,000	150	58,700	10
Mourning dove	250,000	100	26,000	20	182,000	100	17,700	50

TABLE 8-2a (continued)

Species	California			
	Harvest		Users	
	1975	1985(%)	1975	% Public
Antelope	310	110	375	100
Elk	50	100	50	100
Roosevelt elk	--	--	--	--
Mountain lion	10	0	--	--
Wild turkey	2,500	125	10,000	0
Black-tailed deer	--	--	--	--
Mule deer	66,000	175	390,000	70
White-tailed deer	--	--	--	--
Mountain goat	--	--	--	--
Bighorn sheep	<10	0	--	--
Black bear	600	100	30,000	90
Chukar partridge	--	--	--	--
Common snipe	103,950	100	--	--
Sage grouse	--	--	--	--
Band-tailed pigeon	111,300	125	22,500	50
Hungarian partridge	--	--	--	--
Ring-necked pheasant	560,000	125	190,000	--
Mourning dove	--	--	--	--

TABLE 8-2b Mountain States

	Wyoming				Montana			
	Harvest		Users		Harvest		Users	
Species	1975	1985(%)	1975	% Public	1975	1985(%)	1975	% Public
Moose	1,500	87	1,900	80	500	137	760	70
Antelope	55,000	71	64,000	60	17,300	147	25,000	30
Elk	17,000	109	46,000	100	14,600	109	90,700	70
Mountain lion	10	--	8	50	80	105	406	90
Wild turkey	1,800	167	4,100	20	940	109	2,665	90
Mule deer	5,800	119	89,000	60	49,000	119	111,900	40
White-tailed deer	15,000	100	22,000	10	28,500	153	65,700	40
Mountain goat	<10	100	4	100	250	145	500	90
Bighorn sheep	100	150	350	100	100	202	750	90
Black bear	250	130	2,500	100	1,300	132	8,000	60
Brown bear	<10	160	--	--	10	115	790	90
Chukar partridge	14,000	100	3,000	20	800	137	48,900	10
Ruffed grouse	7,000	130	2,000	90	47,400	129	32,700	90
Sage grouse	49,000	122	12,000	70	45,000	109	31,600	30
Blue grouse	9,000	144	3,000	90	49,000	124	32,700	90
Little brown crane	10	--	48	--	--	--	--	--
Sharp-tailed grouse	2,300	213	920	50	87,700	125	316,000	30
Hungarian partridge	6,000	100	2,000	20	56,500	110	489,000	10
Ring-necked pheasant	27,000	70	11,000	--	58,600	126	48,900	30
Mourning dove	43,000	--	4,000	70	--	--	--	--
Gambel's quail	--	--	--	--	--	--	--	--

TABLE 8-2b (continued)

Species	Colorado				Nevada			
	Harvest		Users		Harvest		Users	
	1975	1985(%)	1975	% Public	1975	1985(%)	1975	% Public
Moose	--	--	--	--	--	--	--	--
Antelope	3,100	177	4,400	40	220	92	398	80
Elk	24,000	108	131,700	100	10	333	10	100
Mountain lion	50	192	185	100	90	80	--	--
Wild turkey	440	488	1,340	30	--	--	--	--
Mule deer	55,300	171	155,500	80	7,250	234	34,121	90
White-tailed deer	200	125	--	--	--	--	--	--
Mountain goat	20	444	20	100	--	133	--	90
Bighorn sheep	40	986	170	100	30	177	54	100
Black bear	56	117	11,200	80	--	--	--	--
Brown bear	--	--	--	--	--	--	--	--
Chukar partridge	1,720	--	668	100	130,000	154	13,940	90
Ruffed grouse	--	--	--	--	--	--	--	100
Sage grouse	10,500	83	6,481	100	17,730	113	7,887	90
Blue grouse	40,800	132	15,985	80	2,170	185	1,427	100
Little brown crane	--	--	--	--	--	--	--	80
Sharp-tailed grouse	1,450	61	1,033	100	--	--	--	--
Hungarian partridge	--	--	--	--	4,700	128	1,238	80
Ring-necked pheasant	105,620	69	59,300	20	--	--	--	--
Mourning dove	688,000	118	41,000	40	140,640	--	12,429	90
Gambel's quail	3,000	93	1,000	40	51,000	196	6,169	90

Species	Utah				Idaho			
	Harvest		Users		Harvest		Users	
	1975	1985(%)	1975	% Public	1975	1985(%)	1975	% Public
Moose	43,180	100	15,580	60	125,200	132	23,800	70
Antelope	23,470	110	--	--	--	--	--	--
Elk	19,560	100	13,831	70	57,700	134	27,400	70
Mountain lion	32,640	110	--	--	--	--	--	--
Wild turkey	--	--	--	--	--	--	--	--
Mule deer	150	100	150	--	3,000	333	27,400	40
White-tailed deer	6,350	150	3,676	30	68,400	123	19,500	40
Mountain goat	154,220	166	78,949	20	268,900	75	78,900	30
Bighorn sheep	341,630	100	34,231	30	246,800	111	24,500	20
Black bear	5,700	100	--	--	--	--	--	--
Brown bear	20	300	25	100	100	145	100	70
Chukar partridge	190	110	245	100	1,200	127	2,000	80
Ruffed grouse	2,630	115	19,946	100	8,600	111	94,100	80
Sage grouse	190	110	363	100	140	107	400	90
Blue grouse	10	450	137	80	20	406	300	80
Little brown crane	53,310	188	196,431	100	33,000	124	238,600	80
Sharp-tailed grouse	--	--	--	--	7,400	108	238,600	60
Hungarian partridge	--	--	--	100	100	132	300	100
Ring-necked pheasant	--	500	5	100	30	183	100	100
Mourning dove	20	100	165	100	2,300	130	12,700	100
Gambel's quail	--	--	--	--	<10	--	--	100

TABLE 8-2c Southwest and South Central States

Species	Arizona				New Mexico			
	Harvest		Users		Harvest		Users	
	1975	1985(%)	1975	% Public	1975	1985(%)	1975	% Public
Antelope	690	108	1,278	90	1,610	125	2,697	50
Elk	1,480	100	8,189	100	1,810	100	7,146	80
Javelina	4,520	133	22,273	90	40	200	186	80
Mountain lion	230	100	5,129	90	40	200	120	90
Wild turkey	730	205	12,285	100	2,630	120	22,381	90
Mule deer	10,840	150	67,750	90	--	--	--	--
White-tailed deer	2,660	170	15,250	90	--	--	--	--
Bighorn sheep	40	--	60	--	<10	200	16	100
Black bear	220	100	7,087	90	370	--	11,226	70
Barbary sheep	--	--	--	--	50	400	155	70
Little brown crane	--	--	--	--	1,770	97	1,092	50
Ring-necked pheasant	--	--	--	--	7,340	85	7,216	20
White-winged dove	475,100	100	59,425	30	--	--	--	--
Band-tailed pigeon	3,470	144	860	100	1,430	120	824	80
Blue grouse	360	139	386	100	2,530	105	1,488	90

Species	Oklahoma Harvest 1975	Oklahoma Harvest 1985(%)	Oklahoma Users 1975	Oklahoma Users % Public	Texas Harvest 1975	Texas Harvest 1985(%)	Texas Users 1975	Texas Users % Public
Antelope	--	--	--	--	580	--	--	--
Elk	--	--	--	--	10	--	--	--
Javelina	--	--	--	--	--	--	--	--
Mountain lion	--	--	--	--	--	--	--	--
Wild turkey	4,725,100	136	--	--	15,870	--	125,684	--
Mule deer	--	--	--	--	11,070	--	--	--
White-tailed deer	--	173	--	--	348,950	--	--	--
Bighorn sheep	--	--	--	--	--	--	--	--
Black bear	--	60	--	--	--	--	--	--
Barbary sheep	--	--	--	--	100	--	--	--
Little brown crane	--	--	--	--	6,100	--	--	--
Ring-necked pheasant	1,761,700	--	596,984	--	20,000	--	--	--
White-winged dove	--	--	--	--	120,000	--	--	--
Band-tailed pigeon	--	--	--	--	--	--	--	--
Blue grouse	--	--	--	--	--	--	--	--

TABLE 8-2d Great Plains States

Species	Kansas				Nebraska			
	Harvest		Users		Harvest		Users	
	1975	1985(%)	1975	% Public	1975	1985(%)	1975	% Public
Antelope	80	276	80	--	1,470	100	1,945	20
Wild turkey	130	162	367	20	1,700	150	4,345	30
Mule deer	1,100	122	3,221	0	8,070	100	17,656	10
White-tailed deer	4,390	122	12,886	0	9,560	100	19,123	10
Bighorn sheep	--	--	--	--	--	--	--	--
Common snipe	--	--	--	--	2,000	100	--	--
Ring-necked pheasant	596,000	66	141,100	--	576,960	105	117,500	--
Bobwhite quail	2,152,250	88	148,200	--	351,690	100	58,130	--
Sharp-tailed quail	--	--	--	--	37,650	100	11,373	4C
Prairie chicken	16,000	87	17,100	--	8,260	100	2,496	--
Mourning dove	1,448,000	127	86,000	--	840,000	--	50,000	10

Species	North Dakota				South Dakota			
	Harvest		Users		Harvest		Users	
	1975	1985(%)	1975	% Public	1975	1985(%)	1975	% Public
Antelope	1,550	100	2,000	40	6,200	150	1,945	20
Wild turkey	150	433	300	30	1,810	259	5,449	100
Mule deer	3,500	110	6,300	50	12,470	100	22,886	50
White-tailed deer	26,000	125	36,600	10	22,170	100	40,687	50
Bighorn sheep	10	250	12	60	--	5	--	--
Common snipe	--	--	--	--	2,010	--	552	--
Ring-necked pheasant	75,000	105	31,000	30	1,113,000	31	147,754	10
Bobwhite quail	--	--	--	--	--	--	--	--
Sharp-tailed quail	151,000	85	41,000	30	--	--	--	--
Prairie chicken	--	--	--	--	--	--	--	--
Mourning dove	--	--	--	--	--	--	--	--

SOURCE: Data gathered to prepare Schweitzer et al. 1980.

The sheer number of species that make up the fauna of any particular ecological subdivision precludes any discussion of them here on a species-by-species basis. In the Blue Mountains of Oregon and Washington alone, for example, there are 378 species of vertebrates (Thomas et al. 1979a).

Differences in the vertebrate fauna among plant communities can be quite pronounced. In the Blue Mountains, for instance, 129 species reproduce and 148 species feed in the conifer communities, compared to 69 and 93, respectively, in lodgepole pine areas. However, many of these are the same species. When the fauna of, say, the grass-forb and mature mixed-conifer successional stages are compared, substantial differences are found--32 reproducing and 99 feeding in the grass-forb stage versus 115 and 136, respectively, in the mature forest stage. Moreover, there is little species overlap between these successional stages (Thomas et al. 1979b).

Mineral Resources on Rangelands

The rangelands are a source of mineral wealth even now not totally charted. About 40 percent of the coal that may be needed in the next two or three centuries in the United States is found in the West, and the oil shale reserves there are potentially greater than the oil reserves of the entire Arabian peninsula (Box 1977). The western rangelands and forests also are ecosystems that receive very large amounts of solar energy. Thus they produce substantial vegetation, without which lumbering, grazing, and recreation economies could not prosper.

Condition of Western Rangelands

The present condition of the western rangelands for grazing herbivores is generally conceded to be decidely inferior to what it was when domestic livestock were first introduced (Wagner 1976, Box et al. 1977, Box 1978). The Homestead Acts of 1862, 1909, 1912, and 1916 provided for the settlement of western lands, but it was not until the Taylor Grazing Act of 1934 that regulations to control grazing on public lands were instituted. By that time, most of the degradation and deterioration in productivity had occurred. It was estimated that about 85 percent of the rangelands had been severely depleted by 1935 (U.S. Senate 1936). In a careful examination of the uses of public lands for grazing, Box (1978) developed a method for classifying the condition of these lands. These data suggest that improvements occurred between 1936 and 1966, but that most of the improvement was in lands classified as "fair" or "poor or bad."

	Percent in Range Condition Class		
	Good or Excellent	Fair	Poor or Bad
1936	16	26	58
1966	18	49	33

Although these data deal with public lands in the western states, a similar trend has appeared on private lands. There are, of course, many areas that are exceptions to general conditions on both public and private lands, but it seems safe to say that management of grazing lands in the West lags far behind the biological and technological practices used on other kinds of agricultural lands. In many cases, advanced practices have been developed but have not yet been adopted by producers because of economic constraints or the influence of tradition. Federal subsidies for range improvement practices, such as vegetation management (brush control and reseeding) and water development and conservation (pond construction and control of woody plants that transpire water) have not stopped range deterioration. Rangelands have been overgrazed by several kinds of domestic livestock and game, invaded by noxious species of plants that compete with more desirable forms for space and water, depleted of wildlife with cultural or commercial value, and eroded because of denudation of the vegetative cover. All of these factors have conspired to reduce rangeland productivity.

Brush species have replaced many of the grass and other desirable forage species on 81 million ha (200 million acres) of rangeland in the southwestern area of the United States alone (National Association of Conservation Districts 1979), and over 77 percent of all nonfederal rangelands need some kind of conservation treatment.

Rangelands as Wildlife Habitat

The value assigned to rangelands normally refers to their value for domestic livestock and may not reflect their value as wildlife habitat. Wildlife managers have not developed systems for rating wildlife habitats in rangelands, but this is essential where multiple uses of lands are to be practiced. Some species of wildlife are benefited by ranges judged to be in less desirable condition because these species utilize plants in lower successional or seral stages. Other species of wildlife may require plant communities that have achieved their ecological climax, and thus ranges degraded for livestock are also degraded for these species of wildlife. Nevertheless, rangeland classifications are generalities that require further elaboration for each species of herbivore.

White-tailed deer, for example, an extremely abundant and commercially important species in the Edwards Plateau and Rio Grande Plains of Texas, are far more numerous today than when livestock first grazed in those areas. Since deer seek habitats with woody cover, and since brush has invaded the grasslands and savannas of central and west central Texas, the habitat has been degraded for cattle but improved for deer.

In general, however, it can be said that ranges that have been maltreated for decades are degraded of almost any value. Losses of the basic resources of soil, water, and desirable vegetation are the causes of this ultimate effect.

The report of a committee on setting priorities for research in rangelands (Soil Science Society of America 1981) identified some of the unique problems of rangeland management:

1. Range management decisions are difficult because of lack of knowledge of the interdependence among the multiple uses of the range ecosystem, and lack of climatic and economic data and analysis.
2. Competing biologic components reduce productivity.
3. Water shortage limits productivity.
4. Our knowledge of nutrient cycling in relation to soil-plant interactions, soil fertility, water supply, and animal performance and production is inadequate.
5. Our knowledge of optimum livestock breeds and crosses and wildlife species for various ecosystems and management systems is lacking.

This lack of information is the chief constraint in maximizing the productivity of rangelands for livestock, but the absence of information on developing strategies for managing wildlife and livestock on the same lands is far greater. Funds for wildlife research and management have always received the lowest priority in governmental organizations, and the private sector is seldom willing to put resources into research that has little market value. As Evans (1981) states in his incisive review of the problem:

> . . . there are approximately 2,100 vertebrate species occurring in North America. Ornithologists are in reasonable agreement that 650 species of birds are known to breed in North America. The numbers of subspecies and ecotypes [sic] of wildlife are even greater. In contrast, there are only three classes of domestic livestock: beef cattle, sheep and goats. Even if monies for research had been proportionately distributed between livestock and their wild coinhabitants, the wildlife manager's job would be more complex, but in fact a greatly disproportionate sum has been directed toward livestock.

AGRICULTURAL TRENDS

Human Populations in the West

The human populations of the western states have shown a marked increase since 1970 (see Chapter 3). The number of people in the southwestern states of Arizona and New Mexico, for example, increased approximately 44 percent from 1970 to 1980 (U.S. Department of Commerce, Bureau of the Census 1981a,b). The states of Colorado, Kansas, Montana, Nebraska, North Dakota, Oklahoma, South Dakota, and Texas had a combined average population increase of approximately 21 percent for the same period, while even more notable increases occurred in Nevada (63.5 percent), Arizona (53.0 percent), and Wyoming (41.5 percent). Collectively, the Great Plains, Southwest, and Pacific Coast states showed a gain of approximately 22.4 percent, or 11,787,136 people, from 1970 to 1980. In comparison, the total U.S. population increased by only 11 percent (U.S. Department of Commerce, Bureau of the Census 1981a).

The West is also experiencing a "back-to-the-country" movement. Rural homes at densities much higher than those found earlier are springing up across the West, especially in valleys. High land prices are causing many ranchers to subdivide and sell their lands.

Current projections for the year 2000 show the populations of Arizona and New Mexico increasing another 24 percent and the Great Plains states another 25 percent. The combined average increase predicted for all the western states, including California, Idaho, Nevada, Oregon, Utah, and Washington, is approximately 24 percent (U.S. Water Resources Council 1981), or nearly 15.5 million residents.

In addition to continuing increases in the population of the West, wildlife habitats in the rangelands will be affected by increases in the cost of energy, continuing efforts to safeguard the environment from degradation and exploitation, and the need to produce food and fiber for a larger population. These factors will affect land use patterns, agricultural practices, and the pace of technological change.

The primary result of these changes will be an intensification of the uses of both public and private rangelands. More intensive use of rangelands, however, may result in reductions in flora and faunal diversity. Species diversity among various groups of vertebrates, including lizards (Pianka 1967) and rodents (Rosenzweig and Winakur 1969), has been associated with habitat heterogeneity. Various studies have shown bird variety to be associated with differences in foliage height and volume, percentage of cover, and diversity of plant species (Balda 1975). Among rangeland game birds, sharp-tailed grouse require a diverse habitat (Sisson 1976). A habitat that provides thermal and escape cover is important to mule deer (Leckenby et al. 1981), pronghorn antelope (Kindschy et al. 1982), and elk (Thomas and Toweill 1982).

The projected increases in human populations in the United States and the world mean that the need for more food and fiber for domestic uses and for export will increase. Agricultural export commodities, including beef and dairy products, are also becoming more important in world politics as a way of influencing foreign policy decisions. It is a foregone conclusion that U.S. exports of cereal grains, beef, mutton, cotton, wool, and mohair will increase. Conflicts over whether to use rangeland for food and fiber production or for human settlements are bound to increase.

In addition, citizens are using public lands for more purposes and in greater numbers than ever before, and this trend is likely to continue. The public lands, which were the domain of the timber man, the rancher, and the miner during the country's first 150 years, are being claimed by other segments of society for parks, wilderness areas, campsites and trails, and other kinds of recreational use. This is zoning for highest use, or for multiple use. The Federal Land Policy and Management Act of 1976 identified wildlife as one of the major uses of BLM lands. As a result, wildlife and its habitats will now have to receive attention in federal land management plans. Differing from past practice, the present orientation of BLM and the Forest Service is to give consideration to all species of vertebrates, not just game species.

The uses of cereal grains for feeding cattle and other domestic livestock, especially in feedlot operations, will decrease. More cereal grains will be used directly as food in North America per capita than ever before, and less will be used for animal production. Thus more cattle will be stocked and fed on rangelands. Grades of meat, especially beef, will have to be revised to reflect the fact that the meat comes from range-produced and grass-finished carcasses. Red meat will thus be leaner, and carcasses will be lighter. Energy-efficient systems of producing livestock products will have to be found if these products are to compete in the marketplace with other forms of protein, including those from plants, poultry, and fish. Economics will be the driving force in changing meat production practices, and higher energy costs will be the largest consideration in decisions on these changes.

Intensified management of rangelands will take several forms. One will be an increase in the rates at which all kinds of domestic livestock are stocked. Projections of the demand for grazing land by the year 2030 show that increases of 36 percent will occur in the Rocky Mountains, 61 percent in the Great Plains, and 38 percent in the Pacific Coast (USDA, Forest Service 1980, data adapted from Table 5.13). These projections include forests and rangelands in both public and private lands.

Further range improvement practices and grazing systems will favor domestic livestock. This is not a new trend; rather, it has been the standard practice throughout history in practically all U.S. grazing areas. In some areas of the West, however, such as Texas, where commercial systems of producing and marketing white-tailed deer and other game species have been highly developed, more attention will be given to wildlife in management plans.

A shift in the kinds of livestock being raised also will occur, particularly in arid areas and on rangelands with a variety of herbaceous and woody plant materials. Sheep and goats will replace cattle in some overused and low-productive ranges, and they will be stocked along with cattle in other areas so as to make fuller use of the various kinds of forage.

Increased consideration will have to be given to recreational activities (camping, hiking, snowmobiling, skiing, fishing, hunting, nature study, etc.). A total of 566,399,000 recreation visitor days was recorded at federal recreation areas in 1977 (USDA, Forest Service 1980, data from Table 3.5). Some widely dispersed recreational activities are projected to increase as much as 140 percent (snow and ice activities) and 106 percent (water-based activities) by the year 2030. A great part of this increase will take place in the western states.

Wherever possible, extensively managed lands--both rangelands and forests--that are convertible to croplands will be converted. The amount of land involved will probably not be large--5 percent in the case of forests--but this conversion to croplands and losses through urbanization will take a significant bite out of rangelands. Water, a critical item in the western states, will be a cause of increasing conflict as human populations, mining for coal and other hydrocarbons, and water-dependent industries all increase (see Chapter 4).

The dividing up of valleys into small holdings, many of which are fenced, is removing valuable winter range for big game as well as productive forage-producing land used by livestock. The remaining rangelands will thus receive more intensive use by all classes of herbivores, both wild and domestic, and the impacts will be greater than the actual loss in acreage might suggest. Lands in valleys are among the most productive range sites, and the loss of these lands represents a loss to productivity that will greatly exceed the proportionate loss of acreage.

There has been a proliferation of laws, and regulations issued pursuant to those laws, governing the management of public and, to a lesser extent, private rangelands. These laws were promulgated to correct perceived detrimental aspects of land management or to set policy for the management of land, particularly that owned or managed by the federal government (Thomas 1979a,b).

The application of some of these laws and regulations has resulted in a tangle of biopolitical problems and exercises in analytical overkill that is detrimental to land management. Overspecification of practices and legal constraints can lead to unjustified alterations in land management practices or the development of analytical processes and procedures that are far too complex and expensive for generalized use. Two examples follow.

Several land use plans and environmental impact statements of the Bureau of Land Management have been successfully challenged in court on the basis of inadequate inventory data. As a result of these challenges, BLM has developed a highly detailed, multi-resource inventory procedure referred to as SVIM (Soil-Vegetative Inventory Method) (USDI, Bureau of Land Management 1975). The amount of money and effort required to carry out such procedures, and the huge amounts of data generated, may satisfy the requirements of the law as interpreted by the courts, but they exceed common-sense requirements (Pearson and Thomas 1980).

The U.S. Forest Service is required by the National Forest Management Act and pursuant regulations to regenerate a forest stand on federal land within 5 years of harvest. This constraint has created pressure to restrict common management practices, such as seeding regeneration areas. These actions, singly or in combination, may be economically or ecologically irrational, but they are carried out to comply with the law.

A thorough review of the laws and regulations governing land management is needed to ensure that the laws are not causing more problems and costs than the problems they were created to correct.

The Net Result

The net effect of an intensification of the use of rangelands will be a loss in acreage and in the quality of wildlife habitats for practically all species. While it is perhaps improper to generalize about total effects on wildlife, the lessons learned from losses of habitat on more intensively managed lands lead to the generalization. Prime agricultural lands in the Midwest, for example, have lost most of their productivity for wildlife because they have been intensively used to grow agricultural products. On the other hand, one can be more optimistic when observing areas where wildlife production is intensively managed. On the whole, however, intensive use and high human population density mean elimination of habitats for many kinds of wildlife.

To maintain wildlife habitats in rangelands, multiple use has been a commonly accepted policy in the public domain and is becoming increasingly so through economic and social values being expressed by society. This approach was aptly expressed in the preface to Chapter 4, "Influence of Land Management on Wildlife," in the NRC study Land Use and Wildlife Resources (National Research Council 1970):

> . . . Over the past century, the elaboration of land-use concepts and the development of policy guidelines have accompanied the intensification of management. The growing expectation that every area can yield more products and services through applied technology than through single-purpose exploitation has raised issues with which land managers were not earlier concerned. It became evident that benefits of several kinds might be obtained through a recognition of the diverse values that any particular land type might provide for various segments of the population. That the general public has an interest and a responsibility in effecting and perpetuating sound management policies for all natural resources has been inherent in the conservation idea from its beginning.

REGIONAL TRENDS AND IMPACTS

The Great Plains and Southwest Regions

Land forms, climate, water resources, soils, and vegetation (plant communities) in the Great Plains and Southwest regions make them somewhat similar ecologically and thus in their agricultural production systems. For the most part the ecosystems consist of arid and semiarid lands with high evaporation-precipitation ratios. They offer complex and often fragile habitats of grasslands, deserts, and shrub lands inhabited by diverse avian and mammalian faunas, some of which are extremely important in sport hunting. Cattle, sheep, and goats are used in combination grazing systems or stocked alone. Big game is often abundant on rangelands in these regions, and a wealth of nongame species also live there. Most of the highly productive arable land has been converted to row crop farming, and the grains and forages produced are used as feed supplements for livestock. Drought is one of the climatic extremes in these areas and can be expected once every 7 years.

Depletion of ground water in the Ogallala Aquifer, rising energy costs, and competition for grain for exports, for more use in human foods, and perhaps for the production of ethanol will dictate greater reliance by livestock on rangeland forage. These trends dictate more efficient utilization of all forms of vegetation involved in primary production on rangelands.

Higher production of livestock per unit of area may in part be accomplished by using mixed stock, namely cattle and sheep, and by converting rangeland vegetation to a form, probably grasses, that can be used by a single type of livestock. This implies improved grazing systems, increased control of noxious range plants, increased development of tame pastures, and development of more combination farming-ranching operations.

Brush Management

Management of ranges invaded by brush is the primary problem in livestock production over much of the southwestern deserts, savanna systems, and southern portions of the Great Plains. At the same time, these woody species provide the kinds of habitats required by certain browsing species but have eliminated other forms of wildlife. The net effect of invasion by brush in such areas as the Edwards Plateau, the Rio Grande Plains, and the high and rolling plains of Texas, has been positive. Deer and turkey populations have increased dramatically over those in more pristine times, and some species of wildlife have become important in financial terms to both individual ranchers and regional economies.

Management of brush for the most desired species of livestock and wildlife is a worthy goal, and removal of much of the brush would assist in achieving that goal. In 1963, when the last survey was made, over 82 percent of the 107,900 acres of grasslands and noncommercial forests in Texas had been invaded to varying degrees by brush (Smith and Rechenthin 1964). The primary invading species are mesquite, various species of juniper, several kinds of cacti, several kinds of acacia, sand sagebrush, creosote bush, tarbush, whitebrush, yucca, and many others.

Control of woody species by mechanical methods, such as cabling, chaining, root plowing, roller chopping, discing, and grubbing, has been widely practiced in plant communities in the Southwest and elsewhere for many years. Mechanical practices are energy-expensive, however, and current trends in energy costs suggest that they will be used less in future years. Nonetheless, mechanical techniques can be used more selectively than chemicals in patterning clearings and brush to form a mosaic that benefits both livestock and wildlife. Strips, blocks, and contour clearings are geometric patterns often used. Special attention to habitats on ridges, in bottomlands, along stringers and creeks, in headers of canyons and draws, and to specific plants can compensate for losses in the total amount of brush. But there are no universal prescriptions for brush management. Management must be site-specific, and trained resource specialists are needed to make recommendations on the best approaches.

The total acreage currently under chemical treatment may not increase dramatically, but the improved effectiveness of herbicides and the integration of herbicides and mechanical methods with fire (Scifres 1979) should result in more cost-effective control with significantly less regrowth. Several products on the market are very effective against many species of broad-leaved plants. This makes them undesirable agents, since they destroy noxious plants as well as many plants that benefit both livestock and wildlife. Land clearing can be particularly detrimental to many wildlife species when accompanied by the establishment of introduced grasses (Kiel 1976).

Chemical control of brush in mixed brush communities usually results in an increase in livestock forage. Three years after *Prosopis*-*Acacia* rangeland in southeast Texas was sprayed with a mixture of 2,4,5-T and Picloram, for example, forage growth increased twofold per inch of rainfall (Scifres et al. 1977). Given this kind of return, harm to wildlife habitats is often ignored by ranchers.

Some examples of target species and treatments now under way serve to make the point. About 20,000 ha of Harvard oak, a woody species attractive to lesser prairie chickens (Taylor and Guthery 1980), quail (Jackson 1969), and mule deer was being treated in the High Plains of Texas in 1981 with Tebuthiuron (Russell Pettitt, Texas Tech University, personal communication, 1981). Mesquite, labeled the most noxious plant of all woody species in the Southwest because of its vigorous competition for space and water, covers about 23 million ha in Texas alone (Smith and Rechenthin 1964). The seeds of this species are extremely important food for deer, furbearers, turkeys, and quail, however, and the removal of mesquite from 90 percent of a pasture in west Texas negatively affected late winter quail populations (Davis 1979). Brush provides bobwhite quail with a secure area for daytime resting (Guthery 1980); herbaceous cover alone, no matter how tall, cannot compensate for a lack of high-grade woody cover (Jackson 1969).

Sagebrush in the Northern Plains, sandsage, yucca, and tree cholla in parts of Texas, New Mexico, Colorado, Kansas, and Oklahoma, and eastern red cedar in the tallgrass areas of Kansas are examples of brush targets on livestock ranges in the Great Plains. Sage grouse, however, are dependent on a sagebrush-dominated environment (Braun et al. 1977), while sandsage grasslands provide habitats for bobwhites (Snyder 1978), scaled quail (Hoffman 1965), and lesser prairie chickens (Taylor and Guthery 1980). Yucca and tree cholla are also important components of scaled quail habitats (Schemnitz 1961, Hoffman 1965, Stormer 1981).

Brush control that reduces vegetative diversity and eliminates browse on large areas negatively affects pronghorn antelope. The ensuing grassland is of limited value to pronghorn antelope (Reeker 1969), especially when it covers large acreages (Yoakum 1980). For pronghorn antelope, three considerations must be taken into account: (1) the site of the brush control project should be limited to less than 400 ha; (2) 5 to 20 percent of the browse canopy should be retained; and (3) winter ranges and spring fawning areas should not be included (Autenrieth 1978).

Control of pinyon-juniper by mechanical methods has been widespread in Arizona, New Mexico, Utah, and other western states. When clearings are large (i.e., of sizes approaching clearcutting of very large timber tracts in the mountains), wildlife habitat is destroyed temporarily, if not permanently. Studies at Ft. Bayard, New Mexico (Short et al. 1977) showed that clearings of large areas of pinyon-juniper woodland resulted in decreased use by deer and elk. Conversion of chaparral to grass has been widespread in the shrub lands of Arizona, California, and elsewhere in the West. Such conversions also deplete shrubs on which deer feed (McCulloch 1972).

Conversion to Cropland

In Kansas, center-pivot sprinkler systems permit the irrigation of lands formerly uneconomical or technically impossible to farm (Waddell 1977). Sand prairies south of the Arkansas River are disappearing at an average rate of 5 percent per year (Waddell and Hanzlick 1978).

Conversion of sandy rangeland to farmland is also occurring in Texas, Colorado, New Mexico, and Nebraska (Taylor and Guthery 1980, Russell Pettitt, Texas Tech University, personal communication, 1981). The amount converted in Texas may increase because the water table is relatively high (Taylor and Guthery 1980).

In the region above the Ogallala Aquifer south of South Dakota, the amount of land under cultivation is expected to increase by 2020. Most of this increase will result from the conversion of rangeland to cropland in western Nebraska because of the availability of irrigation water. It is projected that the 7.8 million acre-ft irrigated in 1977 in Nebraska will increase to about 13.2 million acre-ft in 2020 (Grubb and Higgins 1981). Ground water offers great potential for agricultural development in the Sand Hills of Nebraska (Keech and Bentall 1971), and conversion of range to row and hay crops through the use of center-pivot sprinkler irrigation is now in progress in the Sand Hills. This will affect sharp-tailed grouse and greater prairie chickens (Sisson 1976). Habitat loss through conversion of rangeland to cropland is expected to reduce the Kansas population of chickens to 9500 birds (a loss of 7500) by 1983 (Waddell 1977). In Colorado, center-pivot irrigation may soon eliminate the remnant populations of lesser chickens near Holly (Taylor and Guthery 1980). However, enough habitat remains in public ownership within the lesser prairie chicken's range to maintain the species (Taylor and Guthery 1980).

The impact of the conversion of sandy rangelands to farmlands depends upon the type of crop planted and the extent of the conversion. Conversion to cotton in the southern Great Plains would represent a severe loss for wildlife, but limited conversion to grain might be beneficial to upland game birds by providing a source of food and by increasing habitat diversity. The Sand Hills of west Texas, where 63 to 95 percent of the land is in native rangeland and the balance is in grain, provides a better habitat for the lesser prairie chicken than areas of 100 percent native rangeland. Areas where the range in native vegetation is less than 63 percent, however, are not capable of sustaining chicken populations (Crawford and Bolen 1976).

The fate of sandy lands following the depletion of ground water for the irrigation of crops is a matter of concern. Conversion back to rangeland will require irrigation, spraying, and mulching to stabilize fragile sandy sites. Unless such measures are implemented, desertification may become a reality in such areas.

Tame Pastures

Increased use of tame pastures throughout the Great Plains and high precipitation areas of the Southwest is expected. Efforts will be made to balance seasonal forage supplies by using these improved pastures. Grasses and legumes that are drought resistant and more productive will be made available through plant breeding. In localized areas, forage plants are being irrigated. If energy costs permit, this practice will continue. Improved pastures are most likely to be concentrated on the most productive sites, such as riparian zones, which are frequently also key wildlife habitats. The development of drought-resistant legumes is likely to supplant the fertilization of grasses, a practice being performed on some ranges. Stocking rates can be increased by about 50 percent on nitrogen-fertilized ranges of Kansas (Launchbaugh and Owensby 1978). High costs will serve to restrict fertilization to mixed and tallgrass regions, and to localized areas with natural subterranean irrigation.

The conversion of rangelands to tame pasture, and range improvement practices that promote grassland climaxes, may have their most damaging effects on wildlife through the loss of abundance and diversity of forbs. Forbs make up about 60 percent of the winter diet of bobwhite quail in west Texas (Jackson 1969) and 16 percent of the annual diet of wild turkeys (Litton 1977). In southeastern New Mexico, forbs constitute about 30 percent of the annual diet of scaled quail (Davis et al. 1975). Forbs made up 22 percent of the annual diet of pronghorn antelope in a study of a four-state area (Yoakum 1958), and of 788 kinds of plants reported eaten by mule deer, 484 were forbs (Kufeld et al. 1973).

For songbirds, grasslands are best when their composition is varied. Several species and growth forms of grass, intermingled with different species of forbs, provide diversity for many species (Burger 1973, Sprunt 1975). However, Buttery and Shields (1975) reported that reseeding, particularly with native plant species, is largely beneficial to songbird habitats because it changes succession to one more nearly resembling climax communities, thus replacing subclimax bird species with those more closely resembling climax species.

Grazing Systems

More intensive forms of grazing of all kinds of ranges by livestock, especially systems that rotate livestock among several ranges or pastures throughout the year, will increase in the Southwest and Great Plains. The ecological attributes that make rotation especially suitable in the Southwest and Great Plains regions are drier climates, lower biomass production, and instability of plant communities due to vagaries of weather patterns.

Rotation grazing systems have wide appeal, but some of the more intensive forms have not been evaluated for their value to wildlife. In some rotation grazing systems, range plants are allowed to mature before grazing occurs, thereby providing food and cover for many kinds of wildlife. However, new types of intensive grazing systems that are modifications of rest-rotation systems are now being initiated. With respect to high-intensity-low-frequency grazing systems (HILF systems), where the vegetation is grazed by large numbers of livestock (sometimes at twice the average number appropriate for continuous grazing of the range site) in very short periods (3 to 7 days) in short rotation cycles (seven to ten pastures), very little can yet be said of their potential usefulness for wildlife. The usefulness of the vegetation may be damaged for many kinds of wildlife, but it may be increased for other kinds of wildlife. The primary concerns are forbs and shrubs. Unlike grasses, which grow from or near the base of the plant and can be cropped close, forbs and shrubs grow from terminal buds and apical meristems. Livestock can crop these plants so closely that they are either destroyed or hedged so closely that their productivity is greatly reduced. These systems of grazing, of course, can be modified to accommodate wildlife. Intensity of use is the key.

Grazing systems of this kind can be as damaging to wildlife habitats as overstocking in yearlong continuous grazing systems.

Mixed Livestock Grazing

Grazing by sheep will probably increase, especially on ranges that have been overgrazed by cattle. The diets of sheep are more catholic than those of cattle, and in many ecotypes sheep can be used in combination with cattle. In a study of the incomes of western cattle and sheep ranches, Gray (1971) reported that sheep ranches are found from California to Texas and that net incomes per animal unit were greater for sheep than for cattle primarily because production costs tended to be lower. As escalating costs reduce ranch incomes, it seems safe to predict that livestock production systems will favor the animals that offer the highest return.

The angora goat population in the United States is centered in west and west central Texas. This activity, along with sheep raising in the Mountain States, will increase as raw materials (petroleum products) used in the manufacture of synthetic fibers become more costly.

Under a mixed grazing regime, habitats are likely to be reduced owing to more complete utilization of forage. This may affect nongame wildlife and small game by reducing escape and nesting cover. Sheep may directly compete for food with wildlife, especially big game. A significant dietary overlap between pronghorn antelope and sheep has been demonstrated (Buechner 1947, 1950; Yoakum 1975). Sheep also compete with mule deer (Smith 1961, Patton and Jones 1977) and white-tailed deer (McMahan 1964) for forage. However, compatibility among range animals is related to the number of animals using the same range and the condition of the forage (Yoakum 1975).

Sheep-proof (net) fences can be a major obstacle for pronghorns attempting to procure food or water or to escape from deep snow (Yoakum 1980). Sheep-proof fences, in other words, can be death traps for some forms of wildlife (Buechner 1950, Yoakum 1975).

When properly used, fire is an effective grassland management tool (Scifres 1980). An important use of fire in rangelands is to control shrubs (kill nonsprouting shrubs or trees, reduce cover of sprouting shrubs, reduce density of cactus, and remove dead logs or standing stems). Burning can also be used to increase forage production, increase the palatability of herbage, and control unwanted grasses (Wright 1978). Because it is energy efficient and cost-effective, prescribed burning of rangeland will be increasingly used in the future as range managers gain experience in using it. Whitson (1980) estimated per acre costs of burning in the Edwards Plateau of Texas at $2.02 (518 ha) to $5.37 (65 ha). The degree to which fire is used as a management tool will vary among grassland types. Fire has few uses in shortgrass prairie, but it has greater utility in mixed and tallgrass prairie (Wright 1978, Wright and Bailey 1980). Similarly, fire may be detrimental to black grama rangelands of the semidesert grass-shrub type of the Southwest but could be used as a management tool on reclaimed range in good condition (Wright 1980).

Controlled burning has been long recognized as a tool of wildlife management. Since fire is a means of reversing or maintaining plant succession, species of lower seral stages are benefited the most. Rangeland wildlife that can be aided by fire include the bobwhite quail (Miller 1963), mourning dove (Southiere and Bolen 1972), sharp-tailed grouse (Ammann 1963, Vogl 1967, Kirsch and Kruse 1973), greater prairie chicken (Vogl 1967, Westemeier 1972), Attwater's prairie chicken (Lehman 1965, Chamrad and Dodd 1972), and white-tailed deer (Armstrong 1980). However, the degree of either a positive or negative response is dependent on a large number of factors, including the timing and intensity of the burn, soil moisture conditions prior to and following the fire, the size of the area burned, the spatial pattern of the burn, the sprouting habits of woody plants present, the tolerance of the various plant species to fire, and the condition of the preburn habitat with respect to the requirements of the wildlife present. Hence it is difficult to define specific impacts.

The response of subclimax wildlife species to fire would most likely be positive in the higher precipitation areas of the prairie parkland and tallgrass prairie provinces (Bailey 1978) and decrease with declines in precipitation and woody cover in the mixed and shortgrass prairies and semidesert regions farther west. In any case, large-scale burning conducted without regard to habitat values that results in increased grass at the expense of floristic and spatial heterogeneity and reductions in the quality and quantity of essential cover and forb foods will negatively affect the habitats of most wildlife species. As with other range management tools, the key is the integration of wildlife habitat objectives with the use of fire--for example, by leaving woody motts for cover and providing several seral stages of postburn vegetation (Bock et al. 1976).

Riparian Zones

Riparian habitats are special or high-use habitats desired by many elements of society for particular purposes. They are often the focal or key elements in the habitats of many kinds of wildlife. In the Southwest they have been subjected to intensive brush control to promote water conservation and to provide grazing for livestock. In some areas, wild herds of horses and burros are especially damaging to riparian habitats, but the Wild Horse and Burro Act (PL 92-195) directs BLM to protect these animals. In the northern Great Plains, woody communities in riparian zones are declining (Severson and Boldt 1977; Boldt et al. 1978, 1979), primarily owing to concentrated livestock use (Sisson 1976, Severson and Boldt 1977). Likewise, cottonwood ecosystems in northeastern Colorado are declining owing to several biological and physical factors including grazing and water management practices (Crouch 1979).

Johnson (1979) reported that riparian communities are the most neglected and poorly understood among the various ecosystems, and damage to them caused by livestock grazing and irrigation projects has done irreparable harm to wildlife habitats. Less than 15 percent of the original riparian habitat remains in Arizona (McNatt et al. 1980). In a region known for its aridity and fragility, loss of riparian vegetation impoverishes the landscape and those that use it. In the northern Great Plains, loss of woody draws negatively affects sharp-tailed grouse, deer, and many nongame birds (Severson and Boldt 1977).

Commercialization of Recreation

Unless the larger mammals, mainly deer, elk, antelope, and sheep, can compete in the marketplace with livestock, it appears likely that much of the rangeland habitat will be degraded for wildlife use. In Texas there is a market for many species of wildlife because there are few public lands available to hunters and most private lands are protected by laws against trespassing. Hundreds of thousands of hectares on rangelands in Texas are leased for hunting each year, at prices ranging up to $10 per acre (Burger and Teer 1982). Big game, upland game birds, and migratory waterfowl are hunted on these lands, as are exotic animals (Teer 1975). Although there are no current estimates of the income obtained by ranchers from leasing land, the income exceeds that gained from the sale of domestic livestock in a great many cases. In 1977, a hunting lease cost an average $224 for the season, and it is estimated that 45 percent of the hunters paid such leasing fees (L.B. Merrill and R.E. Whitson, Texas A&M University, personal communication). Hunters paid landowners in Texas $108 million for leases in 1971 (Berger 1974), and the average cost has increased twofold or threefold since then.

Rangelands are obvious places for game hunting and other recreational activities, which are steadily increasing. Eventually there will be pressures to use public rangelands for these purposes, which will then have to be considered in land use and budget decisions. The federal government is ethically and economically justified in requiring the payment of a fee for access to public rangelands. The users-pay concept has validity in public land management, and use of this concept by managers will surely increase.

The Pacific Northwest and Rocky Mountain Regions

The Pacific Northwest and Rocky Mountain regions have much greater diversity in climate, soils, topography, and vegetation than the arid and semiarid regions of the western United States. Very low amounts of precipitation characterize the cold deserts and the rain shadows of high mountains, while precipitation falls in large amounts in the rain forests of the coast. Vegetation communities include annual and desert grasslands, chaparral, shrub lands, shortgrass and midgrass prairies, and a great array of forest communities.

Livestock grazing is the predominant form of rangeland use. Although lumbering is the primary industry in the forest lands, grazing by cattle and sheep is important there also. Most of the level and productive lands are privately owned, and ranchers very often have access to public lands, which are used as integral parts of their ranching operations. Water rights and access to public lands are extremely valuable assets, and their value is reflected in the prices charged in sales of private holdings.

The two regions are well known for their great herds of big game, including elk, deer, moose, mountain sheep, and wild goats. They are perhaps the most-used vacation-lands in North America because of their scenic grandeur and natural beauty. They contain many wilderness areas and parks of great interest to recreationists and society generally.

Conflicts among user groups are intense, and they are increasing. Since mineral, oil, lumbering, livestock, wildlife, recreational, and environmental interests all vie for control of resources in the two regions, the administration and management of public and private lands are quite complex. The Sagebrush Rebellion, a name given to the attempt by some individuals and groups to have the federal government divest itself of public lands by selling them or giving over their management to the states, has been a fervent issue in the late 1970s and early 1980s. The matter is still being debated.

Intensified Livestock Production

By the year 2000, cereal grains will probably become so important as human foods that we may not be able to afford to feed as much to fatten livestock. More red meat will thus have to be produced on rangelands alone. Many livestock feedlots in the Columbian Basin of Washington have already gone out of business. As the use of rangelands for cattle and sheep production grows more intensive, it will have an increasing effect on wildlife habitats in the regions (USDA, Forest Service 1979).

Large numbers of domestic livestock feeding on the range for longer periods of time will inevitably reduce the forage available for big game species. Range used by big game in winter, for example, is frequently summer range for livestock. Even though cattle and sheep and elk (Leege et al. 1977) are primarily grass eaters, while deer (Hosley 1956, Urness 1981, Wallmo and Regelin 1981) and pronghorn antelope (Yoakum 1958) consume more forbs and browse, at times both domestic and wild herbivores eat the same foods. This is especially true in spring throughout most of their shared range.

The land use planning process for public rangelands has emphasized the allocation of animal-unit-months

(AUMs) of grazing between domestic and wild ungulates on higher elevation summer and spring-fall ranges. But the numbers of wild ungulates, particularly elk, have increased rather substantially in certain areas. These animals are said to be causing severe damage on private lands at lower elevations, where they spend the winter. The states and the Forest Service are being pressed by increasing numbers of landowners and ranchers to reduce wild ungulate numbers (Peek et al. 1982).

Meanwhile, some of the larger private timber companies are beginning to lease their lands for livestock grazing. Since tree rotation cycles in the regions east of the Cascades are 50 years or more, the inclination of the companies to seek additional income from the land is understandable.

Even though intensified use by livestock will generally reduce the value of forested habitats for wildlife, there are some opportunities to alleviate negative impacts. For example, livestock grazing can be directed to control the growth of some vegetation species, such as tall shrubs, to keep them within reach of deer and elk (Hedrick et al. 1981). Likewise, an understanding of the dietary overlap between livestock and wild ungulates can be used to relieve grazing pressure on plants used by both. Heavy livestock grazing may be needed to keep the regrowth of introduced plants (e.g., crested wheatgrass) palatable to deer (Leckenby et al. 1981).

In summary, wildlife habitat conditions will suffer because of intensive rangeland practices in the decades ahead, but these effects can and should be alleviated by thoughtful management.

Conversion to Croplands

In the Pacific Northwest (Idaho, Washington, Oregon, and northern California) there has been an increase in the conversion of rangelands into croplands through irrigation and dry-land farming methods. Although the amount of water available for irrigation will diminish because of demand from industrial and domestic users, more land area will be irrigated through more efficient irrigation methods. Dry-land farming will increase further because of the development of drought-resistant varieties of cereal grains and minimal tillage techniques.

In BLM's Boise District, 36,000 of the district's over 2.3 million ha was transferred to private ownership through the Desert Land Entry Act during the 1970s. An additional 81,000 ha is being considered for transferral during the 1980s. These lands are being sought by private owners mainly for irrigated agricultural uses. Roughly 15 to 20 percent of the Boise District can be converted to irrigated cropland (Michael Kochart, Bureau of Land Management, Boise, Idaho, personal communication). In the entire state of Idaho between 1947 and 1962, 1900 applications for land transfer were filed under provisions of the Desert Land Entry Act. Since 1962, 4200 applications have been filed.

The amount of acreage to be irrigated in the district will not be impressive compared to the whole. However, the areas to be converted are apt to be the best of what is available--riparian zones or zones adjacent to such areas, i.e., winter range for mule and black-tailed deer, elk, and pronghorn antelope (Wallmo 1981, Thomas and Toweill 1982, Kindschy et al. 1982). The increase in vegetation caused by irrigation will attract some wildlife, particularly deer and elk, which will be treated by ranchers as pests. The amount of investment needed to bring such lands into agriculture is quite high on a per hectare basis, and tolerance of damage to crops by wildlife is apt to be correspondingly low. Thus negative effects will extend to many more animals than might be expected from the amount of acreage involved. Other areas critical for particular species, such as the Idaho Birds of Prey Natural Area, are also likely to suffer encroachment through conversion to agriculture. In such cases the agricultural operation will result in the introduction of pesticides, herbicides, and fertilizers into what is now a relatively "clean" environment, and adversely affect wildlife stocks.

Revegetation and Brush Control

Seeding to grasses generally reduces the heterogeneity of an area and produces a more uniform vegetative cover. Such sites are not usually productive of food for wildlife, especially small mammals and birds (Reynolds and Trost 1980). On the dry canyon escarpments of the Snake, Salmon, and Clearwater Rivers of northern Idaho, however, crested wheatgrass provides spring food for chukar partridges because it is the first to produce new growth in early spring.

High desert steppes are in generally poor condition and make poor grazing land, but there is a trend toward intensified management in the form of sagebrush-juniper control, with or without conversion to crested wheatgrass (Heady and Bartolome 1977). Lands that can be irrigated are being converted to croplands.

High desert steppes are structurally quite simple, even when occupied by forb-grass, shrub (largely sagebrush), and tree (largely juniper) layers. Intensified management tends to remove (temporarily) sagebrush and juniper. This further simplifies structure and reduces the wildlife species associated with sagebrush and tree cover (Maser et al. 1981). This impact is particularly apparent when combined with the planting of grasses, and most graphic when crested wheatgrass is used (Reynolds and Trost 1980).

The exact relationship between wildlife and crested wheatgrass seedings is not well understood, but few wildlife species are expected to benefit. Among birds, only horned larks and long-billed curlews have been identified as nesting in crested wheatgrass seedings. Pronghorn antelope may benefit from a reduction in sagebrush-juniper, with or without seedings, in certain areas (Kindschy et al. 1982).

Much of the conversion of native rangelands of the Northwest has been to crested wheatgrass, a step toward more beef production. Livestock numbers tripled in Idaho between 1950 and 1975, mainly because of range improvements on private lands (brush control, seeding, and water development) (Sharp and Sanders 1978).

A decline in the use of herbicides is predicted for the region. Some herbicide formulations are extremely toxic to fish, and their application along streams also reduces shade, thereby increasing water temperature. Proper herbicide use (applied at the right time and in the right amount) can reduce low-value browse and promote high-quality forage for big game species, particularly elk, pronghorn antelope, and mule deer (Scotter 1980).

Fire will increasingly be used to manage undesirable brush species. Fire in sagebrush can reduce thick stands and increase the edge effect, because flames do not carry well in thinner stands (Neuenschwander 1980). A mosaic of burned and unburned areas is thus created that benefits forage production for livestock and yet retains wildlife food and cover.

Forest Grazing

Livestock grazing occurs on a significant portion of federal forested lands and in the Northwest and is destined to increase. For example, 58 percent of the Forest Service lands in Idaho are grazed (Sharp and Sanders 1978). The Multiple Use and Sustained Yield Act and the BLM Organic Act are intended to ensure that both wildlife and domestic animals, among other uses, will be supported.

The planting of grasses and forbs for forage production will decrease, where not needed for erosion control, to hold down competition with trees, prevent grazing damage to trees, or both. Damage to forest crops by ungulates--domestic or wild--will be less tolerated. Simultaneously, pressures are developing for increased grazing on public lands (USDA, Forest Service 1979). Private timber companies are turning to grazing leases as a means to increase revenues.

Recent forestry legislation and economic pressures (increasing long-term demand and decreasing land base) have combined to produce a trend toward intensification of land use practices for both forage and wood production in forests east of the Cascades. Such intensification is oriented toward increased production of livestock and timber. Timber harvests will therefore occur at relatively young ages; i.e., old growth forests will become increasingly rare. The planting of selected seeds or seedlings will increase, as will more intensive site preparation (Thomas 1979a).

In land use planning on public lands, there is a conflict between desired increases in the production of timber and livestock and maintenance of deer, elk, fish, and cavity nesters (for example, see USDA, Forest Service 1980 and USDI, Bureau of Land Management 1981). Intensified management is the result of rapidly increasing density of roads, which in turn increases human access and disturbance (Peek and Hieb 1976). A reliance on relatively small even-aged forests is increasing structural diversity between stands but decreasing the diversity within stands (Thomas 1979b). More intensive grazing systems are being installed. General range condition seems to be steady or declining, and in general ranges are classed as "poor" or "fair."

Red meat production is considered an appropriate product from forest-grassland areas and is apt to receive increased emphasis (USDA, Forest Service 1980), but this trend will come under greater opposition as being contrary to forestry and wildlife interests. Conflicts will increase, but in the end the losers are likely to be deer and elk.

OUTLOOK

The intensification of land management practices to enhance production of domestic livestock, wood fiber, and other agricultural products will have generally adverse impacts on wildlife. If wildlife is to be maintained in numbers desired by society, it will be essential to intensify wildlife management and research. No longer will it be sufficient to permit wildlife to be a chance by-product of other circumstances.

The most important step is to make sure that all land management plans and research include consideration of wildlife values. Without this step, the loss in the quantity and quality of wildlife habitats will continue at its present alarming rate. This is a trend that can be reversed only with planning.

As in the management of agricultural products, the management of wildlife habitats must be directed at the species most desired. The notion that wildlife can be preserved or favored through the management of other resources is not demonstrated by history or supported by ecological theory. "Good range management," "good forestry practices," and "conservation agriculture" are pious phrases that have been costly to wildlife habitats.

Without question, however, the desires of private landowners must be considered in decisions about how the rangelands and woodlands are to be used. Very few Americans, especially those in the West, support zoning on private lands, but the bulk of public opinion also seems to be that the public lands are no longer the private domain of the West or of special interest groups. It is now generally held that public lands everywhere are the property of all the people of the United States.

Because the public is asking for things other than food and fiber from both private and public lands, intensified management to preserve wildlife habitats is justified. The trend toward commercialization of recreation, be it hunting, fishing, skiing, hiking, or camping, is giving wildlife habitats a place in the market and a chance to compete with other forms of land use. On public lands, management for wildlife as well as other uses is mandated by governmental laws and regulations, and enforcement of laws and regulations requiring multiple use of resources has gained momentum in the past decade. Management strategies may involve setting priorities for the highest or best use; however, there are few land forms or ecological types that cannot produce more than a single product.

The case for combining domestic livestock with wildlife protection is no longer questioned. Livestock grazing can be thought of as a tool in wildlife management that, when properly applied, can have a synergistic effect on the production of both wildlife and livestock. However, key habitats--such as riparian zones and winter ranges (usually valleys and lower slopes)--should be considered to be of essential value to wildlife. They have disproportionate importance in relation to their size because they meet seasonal requirements not available otherwise. They should therefore be protected from intensive livestock grazing, and wherever possible, other areas (such as clearcuts and tree plantations) should be made available to livestock to relieve pressures on key wildlife habitats.

The regulations and laws governing the uses of public lands should be examined with a view to clarifying responsibilities, removing inequities among user groups, and ridding the system of overly restrictive rules. The federal government manages the land, the states control the wildlife, and the livestock producers own the livestock (Council for Agricultural Science and Technology 1975). To protect these basic resources while using them wisely is a goal that has different dimensions and definitions. It seems propitious to accept the Jeffersonian doctrine that the federal government should be involved only in those things that the states or individuals cannot do for themselves. Clearly, the federal government must continue to administer public lands, but with firmer, more efficient, and more equitable management.

The setting of priorities for production on private lands is done largely on the basis of economics and land productivity. These concepts are appropriate for public lands as well. For example, it is difficult to raise sheep and goats in areas where coyotes and other large predators are not controlled. These lands may be zoned for sheep ranches and the predators removed. On the other hand, domestic animals that are vulnerable to predation may be barred from areas where particular wildlife species need protection. The losses occurring to ranchers from the build-up of migratory hoofed mammals on winter ranges is another example. Ranchers in such situations pay for a result that encroaches on their incomes. In some manner, an equitable solution must be found.

The concept that users should pay for specific rights should be promoted on both private and public lands. Wildlife is a commodity that is beginning to be traded, admittedly in a number of currencies. However, ranches, timber companies, and other agricultural industries are beginning to lease their lands for recreational purposes. In some cases, the income from such dispersed activities is higher than that from other land uses. Texas has the beginnings of a commercial hunting system, and this concept is now spreading in various forms throughout the United States.

Parks and equivalent preserves are not sufficient to save habitats for wildlife in the amounts and for the purposes desired by society as a whole. For a more detailed analysis of social benefits, see Burt and Brever (1971), Finsterbusch (1980), and Richards (1980). Nonconsumptive uses are the main uses in such areas. Hunters and fishermen make up a large segment of outdoor recreationists, and recreational opportunities should be allowed on private lands and on public lands other than parks and other preserves. Thus the trend toward charging fees for wildlife production will have to increase if wildlife habitats are to be protected or developed. It is not feasible or acceptable to most land managers to allot resources to a wildlife crop on which there is no economic return, or to allocate resources that might be used to produce more marketable products such as livestock.

The users-pay concept should also be extended to public lands. There are as strong ethical and biological reasons for charging fees for dispersed recreation, including hunting and fishing, as there are for charging entry fees to national parks and for ski-lift tickets, camp sites, and other amenities. Fund allocations for the management of wildlife on public lands have been among the lowest in both federal and state budgets. A users-pay system would provide needed additional funds.

Moreover, one or another potential product may be ruled out on biological, social, or economic grounds. Cost-benefit considerations, although they may constitute a bitter pill to those who favor some uses, are the currency of most decisions. Nonetheless, those making decisions about land use allocations and production systems should be wary of any pressure group, be it agricultural, environmental, or industrial.

With the steadily increasing population abroad, the United States faces some decisions on how it will exploit its natural resources for political, economic, and altruistic purposes abroad. Should we deplete renewable and nonrenewable resources to "feed a hungry world"? Should we intensify production systems at the expense of values that our society sees as part of its heritage? These are questions that must and will be debated during the next decade. Policymakers in and out of government must be organized to address these larger issues, which will have the largest impacts on preserving and enhancing wildlife habitats.

RESEARCH NEEDS

- Determine the impacts of various livestock grazing systems on wildlife populations and wildlife habitats. Many kinds of grazing systems are being initiated with the view of increasing livestock production. These systems are usually of a rest-rotation type, but some are designed for intensive grazing for short periods, and the potential for damaging dicots (shrubs and forbs) as wildlife food and cover plants may be very great.
- Develop chemical herbicides that are more selective for target species of plants. Chemicals that are being used in range improvement work are usually broad-spectrum agents. These agents destroy many plants valuable not only in the wildlife habitat but also to livestock. A great need exists to develop chemicals for individual species or groups of species.
- Determine the sizes, configurations, and vegetative composition of wildlife habitat areas to be protected in range improvement programs. In removal of noxious species of plants, mainly woody species, wildlife habitat is often destroyed because information on wildlife needs for specific kinds, amounts, and shapes of brush tracts to be left is not well known. Research to determine these parameters for various species of wildlife is a high priority because much rangeland in the western states has been invaded by woody species that are considered undesirable for livestock production but that have considerable wildlife values.

• Investigate methods of restoring wildlife habitats through the planting of seeds and nursery stock. Many rangeland sites have been destroyed as wildlife habitat through intensive range improvements and overgrazing. To restore these habitats, plantings of woody species and other plants may be required. A need exists to determine management of various cultivars of value to wildlife. There is also an increasing need to plant various kinds of woody and herbaceous materials on lands that have been mined for coal and other minerals. At present, only certain kinds of forages (coastal Bermuda, for example) of little value to wildlife are being used in land reclamation.

• Determine the social and economic parameters that are involved in initiating a users-pay system for recreation and other uses of both public and private lands. Hunting, recreation, and other outdoor uses of wildlands are being given to society by private landowners and by the U.S. government. Consequently, there is little impetus for the landowner to allocate resources for wildlife management. It seems important that users pay for what they receive, and that landowners and land operators be rewarded for their production--whether it be wheat or wildlife. Human dimensions in wildlife management are of increasing interest to resource agencies, and to investigate the problems in charging for recreation would seem to be important in this day and time.

LITERATURE CITED

Ammann, G.A. 1963. Status and management of sharp-tailed grouse in Michigan. J. Wildl. Manage. 27:802-809.

Armstrong, W.E. 1980. Impact of prescribed burning on wildlife. Pages 22-26 in L.D. White, ed., Prescribed range burning in the Edwards Plateau of Texas: proceedings of a symposium. Texas Agricultural Extension Service, College Station.

Autenrieth, R., ed. 1978. Guideline for the management of pronghorn antelope. Pages 473-576 in Proceedings of the eighth biennial pronghorn antelope workshop. Alberta Department of Recreation, Parks, and Wildlife, Jasper, Alberta, Canada. 526 pp.

Bailey, R.G. 1978. Description of the ecoregions of the United States. USDA, Forest Service. Government Printing Office, Washington, D.C. 77 pp.

Balda, R.P. 1975. Vegetation structure and breeding bird diversity. Pages 59-80 in Proceedings of symposium on management of forest and range habitats for nongame birds. U.S. For. Ser. Gen. Tech. Rep. WO-1. Washington, D.C. 343 pp.

Berger, M.E. 1974. Texas hunters: characteristics, opinions, and facility preferences. Ph.D. dissertation. Texas A&M University, College Station. 131 pp.

Bock, G.H., C.E. Bock, and J.R. McKnight. 1976. A study of the effects of grassland fires at the research ranch in southeastern Arizona. J. Ariz. Acad. Sci. 11:49-57.

Boldt, C.E., D.W. Uresk, and K.E. Severson. 1978. Riparian woodlands in jeopardy on Northern High Plains. Pages 184-189 in National symposium on strategies for protection and management of floodplain wetlands and other riparian ecosystems, Atlanta, Ga.

Boldt, C.E., D.W. Uresk, and K.E. Severson. 1979. Riparian woodland enclaves in the prairie draws of the Northern High Plains: a look at problems, a search for solutions. Pages 31-32 in Riparian and wetland habitats of the Great Plains: proceedings of the 31st annual meeting. Great Plains Agric. Counc. Publ. No. 91f. Rocky Mountain Forest and Range Experiment Station, Fort Collins, Colo. 88 pp.

Box, T.W. 1977. The past, present, and future of grazing on public lands. Rangeman's J. 4:167-169.

Box, T.W. 1978. The arid lands revisited: 100 years after John Wesley Powell. 57th Annual Faculty Honor Lecture. Utah State University, Logan. 30 pp.

Box, T.W., D.D. Dwyer, and F.H. Wagner. 1977. The past, present, and future of grazing on the public range and its management. Council on Environmental Quality, Washington, D.C. 56 pp.

Braun, C.E., T. Britt, and R.O. Wallested. 1977. Guidelines for maintenance of sage grouse habitats. Wildl. Soc. Bull. 5:99-106.

Buechner, H.K. 1947. Range use of the pronghorn antelope in western Texas. Trans. North Am. Wildl. Nat. Resour. Conf. 12:185-192.

Buechner, H.K. 1950. Life history, ecology and range use of the pronghorn antelope in Trans-Pecos, Texas. Am. Midl. Natur. 43:257-354.

Burger, G.V. 1973. Practical wildlife management. Winchester Press, New York. 218 pp.

Burger, G.V., and J.G. Teer. 1982. Economic and socioeconomic issues influencing wildlife management on private lands. Symposium, wildlife management on private lands, Milwaukee. Wisconsin Chapter, The Wildlife Society. (In press.)

Burt, O.R., and D. Brever. 1971. Estimation of net social benefits from outdoor recreation. Econometrica 39(5):813-827.

Buttery, R.F., and P.W. Shields. 1975. Range management practices and bird habitat values. Pages 183-189 _in_ Proceedings of symposium on management of forest and range habitats for nongame birds. U.S. For. Serv. Gen. Tech. Rep. WO-1. Washington, D.C. 343 pp.

Chamrad, A.D., and J.D. Dodd. 1972. Prescribed burning and grazing for prairie chicken habitat manipulation in the Texas coastal prairie. Proc. Tall Timbers Fire Ecol. Conf. 12:257-276.

Council for Agricultural Science and Technology. 1975. Multiple use of public lands in the seventeen western states. Counc. Agric. Sci. Tech. Rep. 45. Ames, Iowa. 36 pp.

Crawford, J.A., and E.G. Bolen. 1976. Effects of land use on lesser prairie chickens in Texas. J. Wildl. Manage. 40:96-104.

Crouch, G.L. 1979. Changes in the vegetation complex of a cottonwood ecosystem on the South Platte River. Pages 19-22 _in_ Riparian and wetland habitats of the Great Plains: proceedings of the 31st annual meeting. Great Plains Agricultural Counc. Publ. 91, Rocky Mountain Forest and Range Experiment Station, Fort Collins, Colo. 88 pp.

Davis, B.D. 1979. The effects of brush control on quail populations. Tex. Parks Wildl. Dep. FA Rep. Serv. No. 19. Austin. 126 pp.

Davis, C.A., R.C. Barkley, and W.C. Haussamen. 1975. Scaled quail foods in southeastern New Mexico. J. Wildl. Manage. 39:496-502.

Evans, W. 1981. Impacts of grazing intensity and specialized grazing systems on faunal composition and productivity. Draft report, Committee on Developing Strategies for Rangelands Management, National Research Council. National Academy of Sciences, Washington, D.C.

Finsterbusch, K. 1980. Understanding social impacts. Sage, Beverly Hills, Calif.

Gray, J.R. 1971. Organization, costs, and incomes of western cattle and sheep ranches. Bull. 587, New Mexico Agricultural Experiment Station. 56 pp.

Grubb, H.W., and G.F. Higgins. 1981. The High Plains Ogallala study: a status report. Unpublished. 14th Annual Meeting, Water, Inc., Lubbock, Tex., Feb. 21, 1981. Texas Department of Water Resources, Austin. 21 pp. plus figures.

Guthery, F.S. 1980. Bobwhite and brush control. Rangelands 2:202-204.

Heady, H.F., and J. Bartolome. 1977. The Vale rangeland rehabilitation program: the desert repaired in southeastern Oregon. Resour. Bull. PNW-70. USDA, Forest Service, Pacific Northwest Forest and Range Experiment Station, Portland, Ore. 139 pp.

Hedrick, D.W., J.A. Young, J.A.B. McArthur, and R.F. Keniston. 1981. Effects of forest and grazing practices on mixed coniferous forests of northeastern Oregon. Oreg. Agric. Exp. Stn. Tech. Bull. 103. 24 pp.

Hoffman, D.M. 1965. The scaled quail in Colorado: range, population status, harvest. Colo. Game Fish Parks Dep. Tech. Publ. 18. Denver. 47 pp.

Hosley, N.W. 1956. Management of the white-tailed deer and its environment. Pages 187-260 in Walter P. Taylor, ed., The deer of North America. Stackpole, Harrisburg, Pa., and Wildlife Management Institute, Washington, D.C.

Jackson, A.S. 1969. A handbook for bobwhite quail management in the West Texas Rolling Plains. Tex. Parks Wildl. Dep. Bull. 48. Austin. 77 pp.

Johnson, R.R. 1979. The lower Colorado: a western system. Pages 41-55 in Strategies for protection and management of floodplain wetlands and other riparian ecosystems. U.S. For. Serv. Gen. Tech. Rep. WO-12. 410 pp.

Keech, C.F., and R. Bentall. 1971. Dunes on the plains. Univ. Neb. Conserv. Surv. Div. Resour. Rep. 4. 18 pp.

Kiel, W.H., Jr. 1976. Bobwhite quail population characteristics and management implications in south Texas. Trans. North Am. Wildl. Nat. Resour. Conf. 41:407-420.

Kindschy, R.R., J. Yoakum, and C. Sundstrom. 1982. Wildlife habitats in managed rangelands--the Great Basin of southeastern Oregon: pronghorns. Oreg. Parks Wildl. Gen. Tech. Rep. Pacific Northwest Forest and Range Experiment Station, Portland. (In press.)

Kirsch, L.M., and A.D. Kruse. 1973. Prairie fires and wildlife. Proc. Tall Timbers Fire Ecol. Conf. 12:283-303.

Kufeld, R.C., D.C. Wallmo, and C. Feddema. 1973. Foods of the Rocky Mountain mule deer. USDA, Forest Service, Rocky Mountain Forest and Range Experiment Station, Fort Collins, Colo. 31 pp.

Launchbaugh, J.L., and C.E. Owensby. 1978. Kansas rangelands: their management based on a half century of research. Kan. Agric. Exp. Stn. Bull. 622. Manhattan. 56 pp.

Leckenby, D.L., D.P. Sheehy, C.H. Nellis, R.J. Scherzinger, I.D. Luman, W. Elmore, J. Lemos, L. Doughty, and C.E. Trainer. 1981. Mule deer <u>in</u> J.W. Thomas and C. Maser, eds., Wildlife habitat data in managed rangelands--the Great Basin of southeastern Oregon. USDA, Forest Service, Pacific Northwest Forest and Range Experiment Station, Portland, Ore. (In press.)

Leege, T.A., J.R. Nelson, and J.W. Thomas. 1977. Food habitats and diet quality of North American elk. Pages 221-241 <u>in</u> Handbook series in nutrition and food, section G: diets, culture media, food supplements. Vol. 1, Diets for mammals. Edited by M. Rechcigl, Jr. CRC Press, Cleveland, Ohio.

Lehman, V.W. 1965. Fire in the range of Attwater's prairie chicken. Proc. Tall Timbers Fire Ecol. Conf. 4:127-143.

Litton, G.W. 1977. Food habits of the Rio Grande turkey in the Permian Basin of Texas. Tex. Parks Wildl. Dep. Tech. Ser. No. 18. Austin. 22 pp.

Maser, C., J.W. Thomas, and R.G. Anderson. 1981. Wildlife habitats in managed rangelands--the Great Basin of southeastern Oregon: the relationship of terrestrial vertebrates to plant communities and their structural conditions. PNW Gen. Tech. Rep., USDA, Forest Service, Pacific Northwest Forest and Range Experiment Station, Portland, Ore. (In press.)

McCulloch, C.Y. 1972. Deer foods and brush control in southern Arizona. J. Ariz. Acad. Sci. 7:113-119.

McMahan, C.A. 1964. Comparative food habits of deer and three classes of livestock. J. Wildl. Manage. 28:798-808.

McNatt, R.M., R.J. Hallock, and A.W. Anderson. 1980. Riparian habitat and instream flow studies of Lower Verde River: Fort McDowell Reservation, Arizona. U.S. Fish and Wildlife Service, Albuquerque, N. Mex. 111 pp.

Miller, H.A. 1963. Use of fire in wildlife management. Proc. Tall Timbers Fire Ecol. Conf. 2:19-30.

National Association of Conservation Districts. 1979. Pasture and range improvement report. National Association of Soil and Water Conservation Districts, Ankeney, Iowa. 38 pp.

National Research Council. 1970. Land use and wildlife resources. National Academy of Sciences, Washington, D.C. 262 pp.

Neuenschwander, L.F. 1980. Broadcast burning of sagebrush in the winter. J. Range Manage. 33:233-236.

Patton, D.R., and J.R. Jones. 1977. Managing aspen for wildlife in the Southwest. U.S. For. Serv. Gen. Tech. Rep. RM-37. Rocky Mountain Forest and Range Experiment Station, Fort Collins, Colo. 7 pp.

Pearson, H.A., and J.W. Thomas. 1980. Adequacy of inventory data for management interpretations. Committee on Developing Strategies for Rangeland Management, National Research Council, Range Inventory Workshop, Tucson, Ariz. 23 pp.

Peek, J.M., chairman, and S.R. Hieb, ed. 1976. Proceedings of the elk-logging roads symposium. Forest Wildlife and Range Experiment Station, University of Idaho, Moscow. 142 pp.

Peek, J.M., R.J. Pedersen, and J.W. Thomas. 1982. The future of elk and elk hunting in J.W. Thomas and D.E. Toweill, eds., Elk of North America: ecology and management. Stackpole Books, Harrisburg, Pa. 736 pp.

Pianka, E.R. 1967. On lizard species diversity: North American flatland deserts. Ecology 48:333-351.

Reeker, G.A. 1969. Antelope use on rehabilitated sagebrush range in southeastern Oregon. Proc. West. Assoc. Fish Game Comm. 49:272-277.

Reynolds, T.D., and C.H. Trost. 1980. The response of native vertebrate populations to crested wheatgrass planting and grazing by sheep. J. Range Manage. 33:122-25.

Richards, M. 1980. Economic measure of non-consumptive wildlife values: implications for policy analysis. Ph.D. dissertation. University of Arizona, Tucson.

Rosenzweig, M.L., and J. Winakur. 1969. Population ecology of desert rodent communities: habitat and environmental complexity. Ecology 50:558-572.

Schemnitz, S.D. 1961. Ecology of the scaled quail in the Oklahoma Panhandle. Wildl. Monogr. 8. The Wildlife Society, Washington, D.C. 47 pp.

Schweitzer, D.L., C.T. Cushwa, and T.W. Hoekstra. 1980. Wildlife and fish. Pages 162-242 in An assessment of the forest and range land situation in the United States. FS-345. USDA, Forest Service, Washington, D.C. 631 pp.

Scifres, C.J. 1979. Integration of prescribed burning with other brush control methods: the system concept of brush management. Pages 44-50 in L. D. White, ed., Prescribed range burning in the Rio Grande Plains of Texas: proceedings of a symposium. Texas Agricultural Extension Service, College Station.

Scifres, C.J. 1980. Brush management principles and practices for Texas and the Southwest. Texas A&M University Press, College Station. 360 pp.

Scifres, C.J., G.P. Durham, and J.L. Mutz. 1977. Range forage production and consumption following aerial spraying of mixed brush. Weed Sci. 25:217-218.

Scotter, G.W. 1980. Management of wild ungulate habitat in the western United States and Canada: a review. J. Range Manage. 33:16-27.

Severson, K.E., and C.E. Boldt. 1977. Problems associated with management of native woody plants in the western Dakotas. Pages 51-57 in Kendall L. Johnson, ed., Wyoming shrublands: proceedings of the sixth Wyoming shrub ecology workshop, Buffalo, Wyoming. Society for Range Management. The Wildlife Society. University Stations, Laramie, Wyo.

Sharp, L.A., and K.D. Sanders. 1978. Rangeland resources of Idaho: a basis for development and improvement. Univ. Idaho Forum Wildl. Range Exp. Stn. Contrib. 131. 74 pp.

Short, H.L., W. Evans, and E.L. Boeker. 1977. The use of natural and modified pinyon pine-juniper woodlands by deer and elk. J. Wildl. Manage. 41(3):543-559.

Sisson, L. 1976. The sharp-tailed grouse in Nebraska. Nebraska Game and Parks Commission, Lincoln. 88 pp.

Smith, A.D. 1961. Competition for forage by game and livestock. Vt. Farm Home Sci. 22:8-9. 23 pp.

Smith, H.N., and C.A. Rechenthin. 1964. Grassland restoration: the Texas brush problem. Soil Conservation Service, Temple, Tex. 17 pp. plus maps.

Snyder, W.D. 1978. The bobwhite in eastern Colorado. Colo. Dep. Nat. Resour. Tech. Publ. 32. Denver. 88 pp.

Soil Science Society of America. 1981. Soil and water resources: research priorities for the nation. Executive summary. Soil Science Society of America, Madison, Wis. 45 pp.

Southiere, E.C., and E.G. Bolen. 1972. Role of fire in mourning dove nesting ecology. Proc. Tall Timbers Fire Ecol. Conf. 12:277-288.

Sprunt, A. 1975. Habitat management implications of migration. Pages 81-86 in Proceedings of symposium on management of forest and range habitats for nongame birds. U.S. For. Serv. Gen. Tech. Rep. WO-1. Washington, D.C. 343 pp.

Stoddart, L.A., and A.D. Smith. 1955. Range management. McGraw-Hill, New York. 433 pp.

Stormer, F.A. 1981. Characteristics of scaled quail loafing coverts in northwest Texas. U.S. For. Res. Note RM-395. Rocky Mountain Forest and Range Experiment Station, Fort Collins, Colo. 6 pp.

Taylor, M.A., and F.S. Guthery. 1980. Status, ecology, and management of the lesser prairie chicken. U.S. For. Serv. Gen. Tech. Rep. RM-77. Rocky Mountain Forest and Range Experiment Station, Fort Collins, Colo. 15 pp.

Teer, J.G. 1975. Commercial uses of game animals on rangelands of Texas. J. Anim. Sci. 40:1000-1008.

Thomas, J.W., ed. 1979a. Wildlife habitats in managed forests--the Blue Mountains of Oregon and Washington. U.S. For. Serv. Agric. Handbk. 553. 512 pp.

Thomas, J.W., ed. 1979b. Introduction. Pages 10-21 in Wildlife habitats in managed forests--the Blue Mountains of Oregon and Washington. U.S. For. Serv. Agric. Handbk. 553. 512 pp.

Thomas, J.W., and D.E. Toweill, eds. 1982. Elk of North America: ecology and management. Stackpole Books, Harrisburg, Pa. 736 pp.

Thomas, J.W., C. Maser, and J.E. Rodick. 1979a. Wildlife habitat in managed rangelands--the Great Basin of Southeastern Oregon; riparian zones. Gen. Tech. Rep. PNW-80. Pacific Northwest Forest and Range Experiment Station, Portland, Oreg. 18 pp.

Thomas, J.W., R.J. Miller, C. Maser, R.G. Anderson, and B.E. Carter. 1979b. Plant communities and successional stages. Pages 22-29 in Wildlife habitat in managed forests--the Blue Mountains of Oregon and Washington. U.S. For. Serv. Agric. Handbk. 553. 512 pp.

Urness, P.J. 1981. Food habits and nutrition. Pt. 1, chap. 9, Desert and chaparral habitats. Pages 347-365 in O.C. Wallmo, ed., Mule and black-tailed deer of North America. Wildlife Management Institute, Washington, D.C.

U.S. Department of Agriculture, Forest Service. 1979. Land management plan. Hepner planning unit--final environmental impact statement. USDA, Forest Service, Umatilla National Forest, Pendleton, Oreg. 486 pp.

U.S. Department of Agriculture, Forest Service. 1980. An assessment of the forest and rangeland situation in the United States. FS-345. Government Printing Office, Washington, D.C. 631 pp.

U.S. Department of Commerce, Bureau of the Census. 1981a. 1980 Census of population and housing. Preliminary reports. Preliminary population and housing unit counts. Arizona (PHC80-P-4), Idaho (PHC80-P-14). Government Printing Office, Washington, D.C.

U.S. Department of Commerce, Bureau of the Census. 1981b. 1980 census of population and housing. Advance reports. Final population and housing unit counts. California (PHC80-V-6), Colorado (PHC80-V-7), Kansas (PHC80-VO-8), Montana (PHC80-VO-8), Nebraska (PHC80-V-29), Nevada (PHC80-V-30), New Mexico (PHC80-V-29), North Dakota (PHC80-V-36), Oklahoma (PHC80-V-38), Oregon (PHC80-V-29), South Dakota (PHC80-VO-43), Texas (PHC80-V-34), Utah (PHC80-V-46), Washington (PHC80-V-49), and Wyoming (PHC80-V-52). Government Printing Office, Washington, D.C.

U.S. Department of the Interior, Bureau of Land Management. 1975. Range condition report. Prepared for the Senate Committee on Appropriations by the U.S. Department of the Interior, Bureau of Land Management. Government Printing Office, Washington, D.C.

U.S. Department of the Interior, Bureau of Land Management. 1981. South coast--Curry, timber management environmental impact statement. BLM, Oregon State Office, Portland.

U.S. Senate. 1936. The western range. Senate Doc. 199. 74th Cong., 2nd Sess. Government Printing Office, Washington, D.C. 620 pp.

U.S. Water Resources Council. 1981. U.S. Water Resources Council handbook. Fiscal year 1981. Publ. No. 1980-0-334-533/6993. Government Printing Office, Washington, D.C. 58 pp.

Vogl, R.J. 1967. Controlled burning for wildlife in Wisconsin. Proc. Tall Timbers Fire Ecol. Conf. 6:47-96.

Waddell, B.H. 1977. Lesser prairie chicken investigations--current status evaluation. Kans. For. Fish Game Comm. Prog. Rep. Proj. W-42-R-4. Lawrence. 19 pp.

Waddell, B.H., and B. Hanzlick. 1978. The vanishing sand sage prairie. Kans. Fish Game 35:17-23.

Wagner, F.H. 1976. Livestock grazing and the livestock industry. In H.P. Brokaw, ed., Wildlife and America. Council on Environmental Quality. Washington, D.C.

Wallmo, O.C., ed., 1981. Mule and black-tailed deer of North America. Wildlife Management Institute, Washington, D.C. 605 pp.

Wallmo, O.C., and W.L. Regelin. 1981. Food habits and nutrition. Pt. I, chap. 10, Rocky Mountain and Intermountain habitats. Pages 387-398 in L.D. White, ed., Prescribed range burning in the Edwards Plateau of Texas: proceedings of a symposium. Texas Agricultural Extension Service, College Station.

Westemeier, R.L. 1972. Prescribed burning in grassland management for prairie chickens in Illinois. Proc. Tall Timbers Fire Ecol. Conf. 12:317-338.

Whitson, R.E. 1980. Costs of using prescribed fire. Pages 69-74 in L.D. White, ed., Prescribed range burning in the Edwards Plateau of Texas: proceedings of a symposium. Texas Agricultural Extension Service, College Station.

Wright, H.A. 1978. Use of fire to manage grasslands of the Great Plains: Central and Southern Great Plains. Proc. Int. Rangeland Congr. 1:694-696.

Wright, H.A. 1980. The role and use of fire in the semidesert grass-shrub type. U.S. For. Serv. Gen. Tech. Rep. INT-85. Intermountain Forest and Range Experiment Station, Ogden, Utah. 24 pp.

Wright, H.A., and A.W. Bailey. 1980. Fire ecology and prescribed burning in the Great Plains--a research review. U.S. For. Serv. Gen. Tech. Rep. INT-77. Intermountain Forest and Range Experiment Station, Ogden, Utah. 60 pp.

Yoakum, J. 1958. Seasonal food habits of the Oregon pronghorn. Interstate Antelope Conf. Trans. 10:58-72.

Yoakum, J. 1975. Antelope and livestock on rangeland. J. Anim. Sci. 40:985-992.

Yoakum, J. 1980. Habitat management guides for the American pronghorn antelope. U.S. Dep. Int. Bur. Land Manage. Tech. Note. Denver, Colo. 77 pp.

9
Impacts of Agricultural Trends on Lake and Stream Habitats

DESCRIPTION OF SURFACE WATER HABITATS

This chapter deals with the inland waters, which cover 2 percent of the land of the contiguous United States. These are the bodies of fresh waters that are commonly called lakes, ponds, streams, rivers, and reservoirs, the last being the impounded portions of flowing waters. Excluded from this chapter and covered elsewhere are wetlands and estuaries. No attempt is made here to distinguish by size the bodies of water. Lakes are simply larger bodies of water than ponds. Both have sufficient areas of open water to distinguish them from marshes or other wetlands. Streams are relatively small rivers. Lakes and ponds are standing, or lentic, waters, while streams and rivers are flowing, or lotic, waters. Reservoirs have some characteristics of both lentic and lotic environments.

In size the lentic waters range from numerous farm ponds of less than 1 ha to Lakes Superior and Michigan, each having over 50,000 km^2 within the boundaries of the United States. Streams and rivers range from small spring-fed brooks to the Mississippi River, which has a drainage basin of approximately 3 million km^2 (Reid 1961).

Surface waters are characterized by materials from their watershed, materials that are both natural and man-made. Thus the quality of each stream and lake is directly related to the geology and soil type of the watershed, to climate and precipitation, to the type and amount of terrestrial vegetation, and to the degree and type of human activity within the drainage basin. Because these variables result in many types of interactions, each lake or stream is a unique system affected by the characteristics of its basin. This degree of variability is such that any one practice that severely affects an aquatic system in one area may have little impact on the system in another area. Specific predictions of the impacts of agricultural practices on aquatic systems are difficult to make. Thus such predictions are often limited to generalizations.

In addition to variability in water quality, there are differences in water quantity and basic physical differences among lakes and streams. Deep lakes with large volumes of water behave differently from shallow lakes, and these differently from ponds. Large rivers have characteristics that differ from streams, and streams differ from one another based on their gradient and thus the velocity of the water. Streams and rivers are open systems where few materials accumulate because of the unidirectional flow of water. Reservoirs are less open systems that serve as effective sediment traps. Ponds and lakes are closed systems where materials accumulate and, to some extent, are recycled. Many lakes in the northern latitudes of the United States mix twice a year, in the spring and fall, while lakes in the southern latitudes may mix once or twice in one year or not at all, depending on climatic conditions. Mixing refers to the surface layers of a lake turning warm in the spring or cool in the fall, with the result that the lake becomes homothermous. At those times there is little resistance to mixing by wind. Mixing usually facilitates the cycling of materials in a lake.

While there is great variability among bodies of water, there also are similarities that make general predictions possible. The volume of water in a lake, or the discharge of water by a stream, occurs within a time frame that governs the degree of influence of any activity. A small lake or stream (and likewise short-lived, small organisms) is more sensitive to a particular impact than a large lake or stream. Therefore the accumulation of a given nutrient would be manifested more rapidly as eutrophication or overenrichment in a small lake than in Lake Superior. Although a small aquatic system is more rapidly affected by nutrient input than a large aquatic system, it is much more difficult to change a large volume system where material has been allowed to collect. For this reason, great care must be taken to prevent disruption of large aquatic systems.

The hydrologic cycle that maintains the quality and volume of lakes and streams is a second concept that must be considered. The quality and quantity of precipitation and runoff influence the quality and quantity of water in lakes and streams. Less obvious, but equally or more important, is the relationship between surface water and ground water. In many cases the level of water in lakes is the same as the adjoining underground water table, and any lowering of the water table results in a corresponding lowering of the lake level. The level of the water table also regulates the base flow of streams, except for those in mountain areas. The base flow is the discharge during dry periods in summer and winter after surface runoff has ended and bank storage has been depleted. The base flow is the minimum flow, and it influences the extent and types of animal communities living in the stream.

DISTRIBUTION OF SURFACE WATERS

Just as there are variations in the character of bodies of fresh water, there are also great variations in its distribution. Over 90 percent of our fresh water is in underground aquifers, but, as just noted, ground water cannot be viewed as totally distinct from surface water, since the two are often connected. Of the surface waters in the contiguous United States, nearly 51 percent of the water area is located in the U.S. portion of the Great Lakes (Table 9-1). This would be an even larger percentage on a volume basis. Indeed, on a worldwide basis, about 20 percent of the surface fresh water is in the Great Lakes, making those bodies of water a conspicuous and important resource.

Information on the areas of lakes and miles of streams is readily available by state. The information on surface area is summarized in Table 9-1, which excludes lakes and ponds of less than 16 ha as well as small streams. Excluding the Great Lakes region, the South Atlantic region has the largest area of surface waters. Including the Great Lakes, the East North Central region has the largest area, with Michigan leading all other states.

The glaciated areas of the Northeast and North Central regions are dotted with lakes whose basins were originally created by glacier movements. Many lakes occur in the Rocky Mountain and Appalachian Mountain areas, in the Piedmont area of the South Atlantic region, and in Florida. Large areas of water exist in southern reservoirs and in reservoirs of the Missouri River basin and other major river basins of the Great Plains. The

TABLE 9-1a Summary of Surface-Water Distribution by Regions of the Contiguous United States

Region	Water Area (km^2)	Region	Water Area (km^2)
New England	9,472	East South Central	7,723
Maine	5,944	Kentucky	1,930
New Hampshire	717	Tennessee	2,372
Vermont	886	Alabama	2,334
Massachusetts	1,116	Mississippi	1,088
Rhode Island	427		
Connecticut	381	West South Central	28,731
		Arkansas	3,002
Middle Atlantic	6,286	Louisiana	9,306
New York	4,520	Oklahoma	2,945
New Jersey	816	Texas	13,478
Pennsylvania	951		
		Mountain	20,306
East North Central	10,831	Montana	4,017
Ohio	640	Idaho	2,279
Indiana	502	Wyoming	1,841
Illinois	1,689	Colorado	1,246
Michigan	3,623	New Mexico	658
Wisconsin	4,377	Arizona	1,274
		Utah	7,304
West North Central	24,667	Nevada	1,686
Minnesota	12,378		
Iowa	904	Pacific	12,305
Missouri	1,790	Washington	4,201
North Dakota	3,605	Oregon	2,064
South Dakota	2,828	California	6,040
Nebraska	1,927		
Kansas	1,235	TOTAL	150,899
South Atlantic	30,578		
Delaware	194		
Maryland	1,777		
District of Columbia	16		
Virginia	2,686		
West Virginia	287		
North Carolina	9,811		
South Carolina	2,150		
Georgia	2,080		
Florida	11,577		

SOURCE: Adapted from U.S. Bureau of the Census 1970.

TABLE 9-1b Distribution of United States Portion of the Great Lakes

	Great Lake	Surface Area (km^2)
Illinois	Lake Michigan	3,952
Indiana	Lake Michigan	591
Michigan	Lake Erie	559
	Lake Huron	23,245
	Lake Michigan	33,766
	Lake Superior	42,038
		99,608
Minnesota	Lake Superior	5,729
New York	Lake Erie	1,538
	Lake Ontario	7,855
		9,393
Ohio	Lake Erie	8,954
Pennsylvania	Lake Erie	1,904
Wisconsin	Lake Michigan	19,132
	Lake Superior	6,928
		26,060
TOTAL U.S. area of Great Lakes		156,191

SOURCE: Adapted from U.S. Bureau of the Census 1940.

middle of the United States is drained by a combination of the Mississippi, Missouri, Ohio, Tennessee, and Arkansas rivers. The North Central drainage through the Great Lakes empties into the Atlantic Ocean by way of the St. Lawrence River. The Northwest is drained in large part by the Snake and Columbia rivers. The Colorado and Rio Grande rivers carry water from the central Rockies throughout the Southwest. Many other shorter or smaller rivers drain the Southeast and also the regions mentioned above, but it serves no purpose to mention them all here. The U.S. Geological Survey publishes various statistics on the rivers, including their lengths and the amount of their discharges.

DISTRIBUTION OF MAJOR AQUATIC SPECIES

The distribution of fish and other aquatic animals is well documented. In this report we concentrate on the distribution and water requirements of those species of major economic, cultural, or scientific importance. The salmonids, with considerable economic importance, dominate the tier of states in the Northeast, Great Lakes, and Northwest regions. Trout waters also extend southward in the mountain regions. Coolwater fish species, such as walleye, northern pike, and yellow perch, are important in latitudes adjoining the salmonid areas in the central United States. Warmwater species, such as largemouth and smallmouth bass and catfish, are economically important in the middle and southern states.

Many other species of animals play important roles as forage or for other ecological reasons. The invertebrates are key parts of fish habitats because they form a major portion of the animal food web. Some of these groups, like the mayflies or many of the zooplankton, require water with specific qualities if they are to reproduce and thus serve as food for fish populations. Vertebrates other than fish also have important economic roles. Beaver, muskrat, and mink are examples of aquatic mammals that are trapped for their fur. Alligators, turtles, and frogs lead the list of economically important aquatic reptiles and amphibians. While these other aquatic vertebrates may be as important as fish, fish and many of the invertebrate life forms are usually more sensitive to water quality. They are particularly sensitive to the level of dissolved oxygen in the water and to toxic substances, which are taken up by fish through their gill membranes. Because of this sensitivity, fish and aquatic invertebrates are emphasized in this chapter.

Recent studies have placed dollar values on some previously undervalued activities, such as the recreational pleasures of sport fishing (Talhelm et al. 1979). In many areas, sport fishing has a much greater economic impact than commercial fishing. As an example, Great Lakes sport fishermen in Michigan annually spend in excess of $157 million for their activity, while the ex-vessel value of the commercial catch is estimated to be $4 million annually. Other sport fisheries, such as salmon and trout in the Northwest and Northeast, walleye and perch in Lake Erie, and bass across the southern states, are also "big business."

Commercial fisheries and aquaculture are likewise important economic uses that must be considered when discussing aquatic habitats. Salmonids are cultured in the Northwest, and to a lesser extent in the upper Great Lakes area. Catfish culture is a major enterprise in the southern United States. Aquaculture will probably increase as a method of food production.

HABITAT NEEDS OF AQUATIC ANIMALS

It is important to review the habitat needs of aquatic animals, especially the fish, before discussing agricultural trends and how they affect aquatic habitats. Most needs are similar in type but vary in extent or degree. Primary productivity depends on the fertility of the water and on the amount of sunlight it receives. Nutrients are required in balanced amounts to produce healthy populations of fish. Too many nutrients can upset the conversion of material into desirable biomass and result in unwanted problems, such as excess masses of blue-green algae. Thus the amount and types of nutrients that enter lakes or streams must be controlled if fish populations are to thrive.

Most aquatic animals have temperature preferences and tolerances. Trout need relatively cool water, 11° to 19°C. If water temperatures exceed the upper range by too much or for too long, a trout population will eventually be displaced by warmwater species. The quantity of cool water in some areas depends upon maintenance of a high water table, which results in a good flow of spring water. Spring water has a temperature generally near the mean annual temperature of the area. In northern latitudes this would be within the preferred water temperature range of trout. Springs cool surface waters in summer and warm them in winter, and therefore are critical in maintaining intermediate temperatures.

Dissolved oxygen is needed in water to keep fish populations healthy. At least 5 mg/liter seems to be necessary for an adequate environment. Coldwater species such as trout may require even higher concentrations at some stages in their lives (Federal Water Pollution Control Administration 1968). The production of plant life in lakes and streams is a function of nutrient levels and sunlight, and plant biomass in turn influences the amount of dissolved oxygen in the water. Photosynthesis during the day produces oxygen, while respiration during the night consumes oxygen. A large plant biomass can thus result in concentrations of dissolved oxygen that are high during the day and low at night. This is especially true in standing or slow-moving water, where there is little physical aeration like that which occurs in fast-flowing streams.

Human activities often affect aquatic systems in several ways at the same time, resulting in rapid and dramatic alterations in habitat quality. For example, the addition of nutrients to a stream can increase plant biomass. If at the same time the stream flow is reduced, either directly by water withdrawals from the stream or indirectly by lowering the water table that supplies the stream, the result can be catastrophic for many fish and aquatic invertebrates. The high plant biomass will cause wide fluctuations in the amount of dissolved oxygen, and the low flow will cause increased water temperatures in summer. The saturation levels for dissolved oxygen also decrease with increasing temperature, so that fish with a high requirement for dissolved oxygen will be replaced by fish that can better tolerate extremes in the dissolved oxygen level.

The habitat of aquatic animals can be degraded if water quality is reduced by erosion or the runoff of toxic chemicals. Silts and sediments can degrade habitats by filling deep areas of streams, thus eliminating favorable rearing areas, and also by eliminating spawning areas by filling up spaces in streambed gravel. High levels of suspended sediments can cause abrasive damage to delicate gill structures and make a section of a stream or river unfit for fish.

Toxic compounds entering aquatic systems through runoff can lower habitat quality and significantly alter the structure of the aquatic community. The effects of toxic compounds on an aquatic system vary widely, depending upon the varying tolerances of species or their life history stages, the degree of bioaccumulation, the residence time of the material in the system, and its degradation time.

Water quantity in itself is as important as water quality. Most lakes have basins that slope gently from the water's edge, with the slope increasing or "dropping off" further offshore. This shallow inshore area is the littoral zone, and it is usually the most productive area of a lake because sunlight penetrates to the shallow bottom, allowing attached macrophytes to grow. It also is the preferred spawning area for most fish. If the water level of a lake is reduced by withdrawals either directly from the lake or indirectly from an adjoining aquifer, valuable portions of the littoral zone are lost. The initial lowering of the water level is the most critical because of the relatively large percentage of exposure and thus loss of the gently sloping bottom. Wave action will eventually create a new littoral zone, but it takes many years and the result will be a smaller lake. The surface-to-volume ratio of the smaller lake then increases, contributing further to the eutrophication process.

It is a principle of stream fish ecology that at any point along a stream or river the greater the base flow discharge, the greater the abundance of fish. Enhancing base flow improves fisheries; reducing base flow damages them. Constancy of stream flow is probably the factor of primary importance in maintaining structural habitats, that is, the stream morphometry and availability of cover that encourage fish productivity in flowing waters. Constancy of flow depends largely on the amount of base flow. Natural stream flow regimes include moderate high-water events during the springtime, and these periods of increased flow are important in shaping stream channels and for providing habitats necessary at certain life history stages of various fishes. When base flow then decreases, the meandering channel carved by the high-water flow is less filled with water and provides less useable living space for fish. Instream cover, such as logs, boulders, undercut banks, streamside tree roots, and sheer depth, is rendered progressively less available, and spawning habitats diminish in quantity and quality. Silt accumulates more rapidly, filling pools and smothering benthic food organisms, and water temperatures may become less favorable (White 1981).

Reduced flow also decreases the ability of the water to maintain its natural channel characteristics. The flow of a stream tends to form sinusoidal patterns or meanders in its channel. This is a result of the physical force of the water cutting into the stream bank on the outer or high-velocity sides of curves and depositing entrained materials on the inner or low-velocity sides of the curves. The outer curves or bends thus have deep holes, often with undercut banks. These curves or bends and holes are interspersed with shallower riffle areas. The result is a diversity of habitats, with deep holes for larger fish to hide in and riffle areas for insect life and fish spawning. The dredging and straightening of stream channels remove these pools, destroying the diverse habitats. As stated by Karr and Dudley (1981), these physical alterations reduce the biological integrity of the system. Thus, like reduced water quality, the reduction of water quantity is generally bad for lakes and streams.

In the western United States, biologists have begun to study and define the instream flow needs of fish and other stream-dwelling organisms. Demands on streams in the West are heavy, and water allocations for irrigation, industrial and mining purposes, and municipal needs have been specified. The instream flow needs for fisheries, however, have not been legally recognized as a beneficial use by many states.

AGRICULTURAL TRENDS RELATED TO SURFACE WATERS

This section deals with emerging trends in agricultural practices (see Chapter 4). However, some practices that have been ongoing for years and that continue to affect lakes and streams also will be discussed.

Water Management and Use

Irrigation is a common agricultural practice, and in the 17 western states irrigation accounts for about 90 percent of the fresh water used (see Chapter 4). Nationally, agriculture accounts for about 83 percent of the fresh water consumed (U.S. Water Resources Council 1978). Supplying water to crops at critical times has allowed agriculturists to farm areas that would otherwise be too dry, and to greatly increase the production of food. Agriculture will continue to use the water allocated for irrigation in the West, and irrigation is predicted to increase in the eastern United States as well. Some researchers feel that if world food problems continue, the volume of water used in the western United States also will increase. As demands for water increase, irrigation methods that conserve water will become more prevalent, including sprinkler and drip-trickle irrigation. Other types of large-scale irrigation, such as center pivot systems, require large volumes of water and high water pressure.

Increases in water use, whether the withdrawals are directly from lakes or streams or indirectly from ground-water sources, usually will have negative effects on surface-water ecosystems. The impact of dewatering will be greatest on smaller streams and lakes. Small, spring-fed trout streams, trout-feeder streams, and marginal trout streams are extremely vulnerable to reduced flow. The so-called trout-feeder streams are important spawning and nursery streams that "feed" young fish and food organisms into larger streams and are necessary to maintain viable trout populations. Marginal trout streams usually have trout populations maintained by stocking programs and provide politically important fisheries, often near population centers. It is probable that many of the larger streams in the eastern United States have discharges in excess of instream flow needs. Research is needed to identify the streams that would be affected and by how much. Cooperation would then be needed to limit irrigation withdrawals to streams that would be harmed the least.

While the greatest impact of irrigation on surface-water ecosystems arises from water withdrawals, return flow also is potentially harmful. While returning water helps to restore instream flow, it is usually much warmer and often carries nutrients, biocides, and sometimes silt. Filtration through the soil and tile drainage would be helpful in removing chemical compounds that adsorb to soils. In most cases, tile drainage in the eastern United States is used to facilitate the use of wet soils and not to facilitate the return flow of water used for irrigation. In the West, however, tile drains are used to return irrigation water to streams and to prevent the build-up of minerals in the soil.

Water management in agriculture includes removing excess water from the land as well as adding water to the land. In the spring and the fall, when heavy rains sometimes occur, the success of farming may depend on moving water off the land. Tile drainage and channel modification of drains and streams are the two major means of doing so. Channel modification is an ongoing practice and is now controlled by many state and federal regulations. The U.S. Soil Conservation Service has information on channel modifications in progress or planned (Table 9-2). Of the almost 34,000 km listed in Table 9-2, over 17,000 km are constructed or under contract, and planning for the remaining kilometers is being carried out. But unless these modifications are made with the intention of retaining fish habitats, the result will be a negative impact on fisheries. The establishment of new channels and the realignment of existing channels often result in straight channels offering little in the way of habitats for fish or other aquatic animals. The removal of snags during the cleaning of channels often removes cover and productive areas used by fish. Recommendations have been made for channel modification practices that minimize the destruction of aquatic habitats (Nunnally 1978). It should be noted that of the almost 34,000 km listed in

TABLE 9-2 National Summary of Channel Work

Type of Work	Channel (km)
Establishment of new channel including stabilization	4,237
Enlargement or realignment of existing channel or stream	23,609
Cleaning out natural or man-made channel	2,962
Clearing and removal of loose debris	2,767
Stabilization	368
TOTAL	33,943

SOURCE: Data are from Soil Conservation Service, informal communication, March 12, 1980.

Table 9-2, fewer than 11,000 km are unmodified, well-defined, natural channels. Mississippi has over 2,800 km of natural streams scheduled to be modified, followed by Texas with almost 1,300 km and Georgia with nearly 1,200 km, these three states accounting for nearly half of the total in this category. The remainder are man-made ditches, previously modified channels, or poorly defined channels. Unless modification is done properly, however, over 10,000 more kilometers of stream channel will be affected. Straightened channels will, after many years (60 to 70 or more), revert to their natural meandering pattern if left alone. But if modified channels are continuously maintained there will be no reversion, and the continuing process of channel modification will remove many kilometers of channel from the natural stream category.

Tillage and Soil Conservation

Soil erosion has been and continues to be a major water-related problem (see Chapters 4 and 5). There are no short-term incentives for farmers to control soil erosion, even though it may have a negative impact on long-term soil productivity. Increasing energy costs now seem to be an indirect incentive to reduce erosion, however, and have stimulated the use of conservation tillage, reduced tillage, or no-till methods (Giere et al. 1980). The use of these methods has been increasing and is predicted to continue to increase. At the present time, about 20 percent of cropped acreage is cultivated by reduced tillage and 2.6 percent by the no-till method. These percentages are expected to increase to at least 40 percent and 10 percent, respectively, by 2010. Conservation tillage exposes less soil and thus should decrease erosion. Soils cultivated by such practices are not traveled over as often by heavy agricultural equipment and are not plowed deeply as often. Although these two factors have opposite effects on soil compaction, it is anticipated that their use will mean better water infiltration and less surface runoff. This could lead to greater replenishment of ground water and better stream stability. A higher water table would increase the amount of cool water supplied from springs to streams. Because the soil would be covered by more plant residues, runoff water would carry less soil. All of these results would be beneficial.

In 1975 the average loss of soil from cropland was 19 metric tons per hectare, but in some areas the average was as high as 57 metric tons per hectare, and there are reports of isolated situations where losses reached 225 metric tons per hectare. The mouth of the Mississippi River is reported to transmit an annual load of about 270 million metric tons of sediment. Clearly, surface-water habitats would benefit greatly from the implementation of conservation tillage practices.

While conservation tillage will reduce erosion, continued fall plowing and double cropping will increase it (see Chapter 5). The practice of fall plowing may decrease because of soil conservation efforts, but double cropping will probably increase in an effort to increase production. Other ways of increasing production will also be attempted. Agriculturists will continue to bring marginal lands into crop production, expanding field size by reducing grass-filled water drainage areas and plowing closer to stream banks or lake shores. But grassed waterways and green belts filter and trap silt, thereby reducing the amount of silt entering surface waters. These marginal lands often have steeper slopes that ordinarily would not be tilled, and they are more easily eroded when the soil is exposed.

Efforts to increase crop production also will include the conversion of woodland and pastureland to tilled land. Conversion of forest land to row crops may increase erosion by a factor of 100 to 1000, while conversion of grassland to row crops may increase erosion by a factor of 20 to 100 (U.S. Water Resources Council 1978).

Thus there are reasons for predicting both increases and decreases in soil erosion. Rising energy costs will favor reduced tillage and less soil erosion, but pressures to increase crop production will result in more soil erosion. The latter will probably predominate unless soil conservation efforts increase. Greater attention to soil conservation for the sake of long-term agricultural productivity as well as for fishery resources is a worthy and essential goal.

Use of the Riparian Zone

Riparian zones are areas associated with surface water that reveal, through their vegetation, the effects of that water. A riparian zone, in short, is the interface between an aquatic environment and a drier terrestrial zone that filters or traps pollutants moving from the land to the water. Riparian areas are usually attractive sites for crops or grazing. In the western United States especially, riparian zones usually stand out as the most productive timber and forage sites available. Cattle seek forage on such areas more frequently than they do in adjacent drier areas. Agriculturists have not made many predictions about their use of riparian zones, but present use often affects adjacent surface waters in ways that are bad for fish habitats. As discussed previously, these include reduction of the width of the riparian zone to increase tilled acreage, and livestock grazing of riparian zones.

Some streamside zones are not riparian. Examples of nonriparian sites are areas where sagebrush reaches the water's edge or where the streamside zone is composed of bedrock, steep-sided canyons, or boulders and rubble. Nonriparian zones also can be affected by livestock grazing, but to a lesser degree than riparian zones. As pressures increase to use land for agriculture, it seems reasonable to believe that there will be a temptation to increase the use of the riparian zones, and that such use will cause problems for adjacent surface-water fish habitats.

Use of Chemicals

Modern agriculture depends on fertilizers and pesticides to maintain high levels of production (see Chapter 5). These high levels of production have been costly in terms of energy use, however. The prediction is that the use of chemicals will be more judicious and efficient, but also more widespread. The overall use of chemicals is expected to increase at a rate of 2.5 percent annually between 1977 and 1990, compared to an increase of 4.5 percent between 1970 and 1977 and an annual increase of 8 percent in the 1960s. The reduction in the rate of increase of chemical fertilizers is due to better timing and placement, better forms of fertilizers, and reductions in fertilizer losses. Integrated pest management (IPM) has greatly improved pest control by utilizing biological controls and other innovative methods that reduce dependence on pesticides. While these methods have reduced the rate of chemical use, other agricultural activities will continue to stimulate increased chemical use. Double cropping, intercropping, and the use of marginal lands will all require more fertilizers, and conservation tillage will result in large increases in the use of herbicides and pesticides to control weeds and pests previously controlled to some degree by tillage. Fortunately, more restrictive regulations have led to the development of biocides that are shorter-lived. If these biocides degrade rapidly into nontoxic products, chemical-induced problems will be minimized.

Aquaculture

A final agricultural trend that can affect surface-water habitats is an increase in aquaculture. In freshwater areas a significant increase in production is predicted for such fish as channel catfish, buffalo fish, and tilapia. This increase will occur in the southern tier of states, with a concentration in the mid-South. Although the rate of increase may be large, the base is small, and total annual production will reach only 1 million metric tons by 2000. Aquaculture takes place in raceways, in open water ponds, or in cages suspended in lakes or other surface waters. The problems associated with aquaculture arise from the nutrients released into the water from unused food and from the metabolic wastes of the fish. If the nutrients are in organic form they will support bacterial populations, causing a reduction in dissolved oxygen in the water.

IMPACT OF TRENDS

The foregoing discussion focused on continuing and predicted agriculture practices that may affect surface-water habitats (see Chapter 4). The following discussion focuses on the impacts as we know them or anticipate them, based on past experience. These are the impacts that affect water quantity, water quality, and the physical aspects (morphometry) of lakes and streams.

Impacts on Water Quantity

The agricultural trends that will influence water quantity are conservation tillage and irrigation (see Chapters 4 and 5). Reduced tillage and no-till methods are assumed to increase water infiltration into the soil and reduce runoff, although it has been argued that these tillage methods may increase soil compaction, thus decreasing water infiltration. Anything that lowers the water table and thus the base flow of streams reduces stream habitats.

Irrigation is predicted to use less water because of more efficient methods that may save as much as 30 percent of the water consumed under some conditions. These water savings will occur primarily in the West. The water saved, however, will then be used to expand irrigation. Reductions in ground-water recharge due to crop irrigation, and wetland drainage caused by a diminution of base flow discharge, must be minimized, since less water in streams and rivers will mean fewer fish. This point deserves to be emphasized. Wisconsin is one of the few states that has policies that effectively regulate the withdrawal of water from streams (Ellis et al. 1970). Legislation is needed elsewhere to regulate withdrawals from streams as well as from ground water. The problem is intensified during drought periods when all water needs become critical at the same time.

Porous soils tend to result in the ground-water conditions that produce the "coldwater" streams that support trout. These soils also tend to be suitable for irrigation farming. In sandy central and northeastern Wisconsin, for example, irrigation farming has developed greatly in the past 20 years. Pumping ground water for irrigation has severely reduced base flow, to the extent that some streams have lost their value for trout fishing (White 1975, Hunt 1979). Irrigation farming is also increasing on sandy soils in some of the major trout stream areas of Michigan as well as in warmwater stream areas of southwest Michigan and northern Indiana. These increases in water withdrawal for supplemental irrigation present a serious threat to fish habitats in the eastern United States. Where increased irrigation needs are projected, fisheries biologists should work closely with agriculturists to minimize the damage to streams.

Impacts on Water Quality

Many agricultural practices influence water quality. Nutrients are contributed by runoff or drainage from fertilized areas, by the return flow of water used for irrigation, by water runoff from feedlots, and by erosion. Silt also reduces water quality. Eutrophication is a natural aging process whereby a lake gradually becomes shallower and smaller as it is filled with organic materials resulting from plant growth caused by nutrient accumulation. Any activity that increases the amount of nutrients hastens the eutrophication process. The accelerated version usually is manifested by excessive growths of macrophytes (rooted aquatic weeds) and blue-green algae. Despite considerable study, more research is needed to learn how to direct nutrients into desirable vegetative species that will result in greater production of useful fish.

The news media spoke of the "death" of Lake Erie during the past decade. Lake Erie did not die, but the lake did suffer severe overenrichment. In the process, great volumes of its lower waters became devoid of oxygen, losing the mayfly populations that were so important as fish food. A remarkable effort to control nutrients from point sources, such as wastewater treatment facilities, helped to slow the eutrophication process in Lake Erie, allowing restoration of the economically valuable walleye and yellow perch fisheries. Waste treatment efforts have also been widespread and effective in bodies of surface water other than Lake Erie. These efforts must be continued.

The National Eutrophication Survey (U.S. Environmental Protection Agency 1975) estimated that 8 percent of the lakes and reservoirs in the Northeast and North Central

United States are in an advanced state of eutrophication. A much larger percentage are in a moderate state of overenrichment and suffer from weed-choked conditions that interfere with any form of water recreation, including fishing. Studies of nonpoint sources (storm runoff from municipal streets and residential lawns) in 143 drainage areas revealed that urban runoff to surface waters contributed 28 km of phosphorus and 680 km of nitrogen per square kilometer of drainage area. Agriculture was responsible for an even greater influx of phosphorus, the main element contributing to overenrichment in the majority of our surface waters.

The amount of runoff from agricultural land into lakes and streams can be reduced, and more efficient forms of fertilizer will help reduce the concentration of nutrients. Consistent use of grass cover in water runways, and green belts along streams and lake shores, will also help. Maintenance of marsh areas in watersheds will help to trap nutrients from waters draining through on the way to lakes or streams. Any practice that reduces the time that soils are exposed without plant cover to air or water erosion will help. Fall plowing is an example of a practice where soil is exposed for a lengthy period of time. Soil particles eroded by water or wind contribute to the sediment in lakes and streams. In addition to the problems of the sediment itself, the soil particles also carry adsorbed biocides and nutrients, especially phosphorus.

Estimates of phosphorus loading in Lake Michigan (Anonymous 1978) include 30 percent from diffuse sources and 26 percent from the atmosphere. It was estimated in the same report that 71 percent of the diffuse source phosphorus comes from agriculture. Delumyea and Petel (1977) reported that a majority (73 to 90 percent) of the atmospheric phosphorus input to southern Lake Huron was due to agricultural activity. If the atmospheric load in Lake Michigan has a similar origin, agriculture's contribution to the total phosphorus load in the lake can be estimated at 71 percent of the 30 percent from diffuse sources plus 73 percent of the 26 percent from the atmosphere, or about 40 percent of the total phosphorus load in the lake. The practice of fall plowing contributes phosphorus to the diffuse load during runoff and contributes phosphorus to the atmospheric load during dry, windy periods. It should be noted that agriculture's portion of the atmospheric phosphorus load in Lake Michigan in all probability includes airborne soil particles from as far away as Iowa, Nebraska, and the Dakotas.

Obviously, reduced tillage or no-till methods will reduce soil exposure and thus the transfer of soil particles with their adsorbed nutrients and biocides. Such a change would benefit aquatic systems and fishery resources. However, the increase in herbicides and pesticides projected with conservation tillage may pose other problems if not carefully managed. Giere et al. (1980) predict less movement of phosphorus under no-till methods, but greater loss of nitrogen to the atmosphere. Research into conservation tillage is needed to determine its long-term effects on soil compaction and chemical movements.

Increased costs will force more efficient use of pesticides and herbicides, but, as with nutrients, an overall increase as a result of conservation tillage and conversion of marginal lands is expected. Any practice that allows increased runoff and erosional loss of soil will be accompanied by the movement of biocides into the aquatic environment. Past experience with DDT, dieldrin, PBB, and PCBs is sufficient to illustrate how easily these chemicals move within our environment. The aquatic environment is ideal for the bioaccumulation of chemicals. Not only do aquatic animals ingest these chemicals with their food, but the gill-breathing animals also absorb many chemicals directly from the water, thus causing more rapid accumulation. Once a biocide is concentrated in fish, the stage is set for movement into any fish-eating animal, such as eagles, ospreys, and human beings. The decline in fish-eating birds of prey was traced to eggshell thinning caused by long-lived pesticides (Ratcliffe 1967, Hickey and Anderson 1968), and reproductive failure in some salmonids has been related to pesticides (Burdick et al. 1964, Johnson and Pecor 1969). In the Great Lakes, a ban was placed on the sale of commercial species of fish, and people fishing for sport species were given warnings about the potential hazards. These bans and warnings are still in effect, but the decline in most pesticides after their use was discontinued has been more rapid than predicted, and in most fish the concentrations are now within safe limits for human consumption. While the decline was more rapid than expected, it still took about 5 years for the concentrations to reach safe levels as defined by the federal Food and Drug Administration (FDA). Even though most Great Lakes fish are below action levels (the level at which restrictions on human use are imposed), some catches are still made in which the fish are above the action levels for dieldrin, PCBs, and mercury.

The economic value of the fisheries is in the millions of dollars annually, so economic losses in fisheries partially offset the gains in other areas of food production resulting from pesticide use. Furthermore, the economic loss resulting from permanent loss of a major commercial or sport species would be compounded for many years. But even more important would be the overall degradation of the aquatic environment and the loss of its biological integrity for all aquatic animals. Finally, and most important, is the ultimate hazard to human beings. Even though agriculturists predict an increase in the total use of pesticides and herbicides, there is cause for some optimism. Integrated pest management is being more widely practiced, and regulations have restricted the development of new biocides to more short-lived forms. Maintenance of these regulations is necessary for the future protection of the aquatic habitat.

Impacts on Lake and Stream Morphometry

Damage caused by siltation in aquatic habitats is well known (Ritchie 1972). Conservation tillage should help reduce soil erosion, but this benefit will be reduced by increased use of marginal lands that are often hilly or otherwise highly erodable. Consolidation of farm ownership and loss of fencerows, the discarding of crop rotational practices, and an increase in fall plowing will cause the siltation problem to become worse. The loss of fencerows and wind breaks from consolidation of farms has already led to an increase in wind erosion that, according to some reports, is reminiscent of the dustbowl conditions of the 1930s. Much of this wind-eroded soil finds its way into lakes and streams. Stream siltation fills in pools, depriving pool-dwelling fish of space and concealment. Silt covers streambed riffles and is deposited in other gravel areas, smothering spawning grounds of certain fish and decreasing benthic invertebrate populations that provide the major share of food for stream fish (King and Ball 1964). In lakes, silt contributes to the formation of deltas and otherwise to the filling-in process. Siltation is also the major factor contributing to the loss of useful aquatic life in reservoirs, where the basins are filled by the reduction of velocity of the stream and the subsequent deposition of silt.

Streamside vegetation is directly affected by grazing because riparian zones are usually grazed more heavily than upland areas. When cattle are reintroduced into a rested area, riparian vegetation can be expected to decline 35 percent in a short period. Studies have shown that the willow canopy in a riparian area excluded from grazing provided up to 75 percent more shade on the stream than areas subjected to year-round grazing. Streamside vegetation was 77 percent more abundant in an ungrazed section than in a grazed section. In addition to destroying riparian vegetation, livestock grazing contributes to the actual elimination of riparian areas by channel widening and aggradation. Streams thus modified are wider and shallower, the channels contain more fine sediment, the stream banks are more unstable and erodable, there are fewer undercut banks, and summer water temperatures are higher.

Livestock grazing and the reduction of stream flow are the greatest threats to the integrity of trout stream habitats in the western United States. They also contribute seriously to degradation of aquatic habitats in the eastern United States.

A study in Nebraska (Van Velson 1978) in an area fenced to exclude livestock revealed that the stream improved within 3 years from a nonproducer to a good producer of trout. The stream width decreased, the stream banks stabilized, and summer water temperatures were lowered. An Oregon study (Clair and Storch 1977) found that within an enclosed area along the Deschutes River over a 10-year period of nongrazing the fish population shifted from predominately dace to rainbow trout. In Montana, brown trout biomass per unit area in a stream within a nongrazed section was 340 percent higher than in an adjacent section that was heavily grazed (Gunderson 1968). In Oregon, trout biomass was reported 240 percent higher in ungrazed than in grazed sections, and in Utah the increase was 360 percent.

Channel modification of streams may include dredging and straightening of channels and snagging the clearance of logs or other natural debris from channels. The unfavorable effects on stream habitats of "channelization" and snagging have been well documented (Funk 1973, White 1973, Marzolf 1978). Straight dredging eliminates the pool-riffle or pool-bar conformation found in meandering channels, creating a highly unnatural and unproductive situation (Leopold and Langbein 1966). Removal of logs and other snag debris, if done without regard for fish habitat protection, eliminates the very features upon which most important stream fish depend for shelter. The uniform watercourses created by channelization and snagging projects usually result in drastic declines in fish abundance, with little recovery for many decades and perhaps even centuries (Irizarry 1969). The fish that repopulate shallow straightened channels tend to be far smaller, and the resultant biomass of the total population is typically only 10 to 20 percent of prealteration conditions.

Some states have statutes regulating stream channel alteration to some extent, and federal agencies involved in channel modification have adopted policies that allow for some degree of prevention and mitigation of damage to fish habitats. The degree to which protection of fish habitats is incorporated into projects varies considerably, however.

CONCLUSION

Two common-sense concepts should be considered in the context of this report. One concept is that an accumulation of relatively small impacts can severely weaken the ecological integrity of natural systems (Karr and Dudley 1981). We must be aware of these interacting and cumulative effects.

The other concept is that large natural systems are very difficult to restore after they have been degraded. This concept also extends to large, long-lived organisms. Many of the highly valued fish in the Great Lakes are large, long-lived species, such as the lake trout. Such species may take several years or longer to reach sexual maturity and thus reproduce over a long period of time. Once such populations are endangered, they need many years to recover. Thus, in response to stress we can expect shifts from fish communities dominated by large, long-lived piscivores to communities of smaller, short-lived planktivores (Regier and Loftus 1972). Such concepts can be useful in guiding long-range planning. The latter concept relates particularly to the Great Lakes. These large bodies of fresh water are a unique resource, and their water quality must be maintained.

Aquaculture has a great potential for protein production and should be developed. This development, however, must be accomplished with due regard for its impacts on the quality of associated surface waters.

There are a number of unifying interests that bring agriculturists and fisheries and wildlife ecologists together. Broad land use management is one such interest. Urban sprawl and other such uses continue to encroach upon prime agricultural land. The loss of such land forces agriculturists to use marginal lands where it takes more acreage, more fertilizer, more time and effort, and higher expenditures to achieve the same levels of crop production. A concerted effort to retain high-quality farmland for agriculture would have many benefits. Likewise, in the long term, both agriculturists and fisheries and wildlife interests are dependent on our soil and water resources. We need to protect the quality of these resources and use them in a manner allowing for their perpetuity.

Conservation tillage methods appear to have strong benefits that outweigh their disadvantages and therefore should be promoted. But research is still needed to answer questions about conservation tillage. Will these methods increase soil compaction over the long term? Will these methods actually increase water infiltration and reduce runoff? Will there be less runoff of phosphorus and more loss of nitrogen to the atmosphere?

Soil conservation should be brought into vogue again. Maintenance of grassed waterways and green belts along streams and around lakes would help, as would reduction of fall plowing. Marginal lands with highly erodable gradients should not be cultivated, and riparian zones must be protected from overgrazing. Windbreaks and fencerows should be encouraged. Soil conservation methods are well known and have been used for many years. Economists should investigate the cost-benefit ratio of soil conservation over the long term for society as a whole and not just for agriculture (White et al. 1980).

The virtues of sprinkler and drip-trickle irrigation should be emphasized. Significant benefits can be gained by encouraging irrigation methods that conserve water. Water shortages in the western United States will probably force this trend in that area, but these water-conserving methods should also be promoted in the eastern United States. Much research has been undertaken in the West to define instream flow needs for salmonids; similar research is needed for fish in the eastern United States.

Efforts to improve the efficiency of fertilizer use should be encouraged. We should promote efforts to optimize the timing of fertilizer applications to maximize plant uptake and thereby minimize loss due to runoff or wind erosion. The development and use of fertilizers that are more efficient also appear to be possible and should be encouraged.

Regulation of pesticide and herbicide development and use must be maintained so that the trend continues toward short-lived forms with harmless degradation products. Integrated pest management makes good sense and should be promoted.

Channel modification of natural streams should be examined very closely to ensure that the benefits clearly outweigh all costs. Determining which modifications will cause least damage to fish habitats must be part of the analysis. If the cost of the modification relative to fish is too high, the modification should not be made. Recent progress in channel modification regulations and policies has been positive and should be strengthened.

RESEARCH NEEDS

- Studies are needed with conservation tillage to determine changes of soil compaction, water infiltration, and runoff of water and entrained or dissolved chemicals. Previous studies show better infiltration, less runoff, reduced loss of phosphorus, and increased loss of nitrogen to the atmosphere. Long-term studies are needed to confirm the very optimistic and beneficial results shown by previous studies.
- Increased irrigation is predicted for the eastern United States. This means increased pressures on streams especially. The instream flow needs for eastern streams must be determined so guidance can be given to agriculturists as to where water can be taken with the least habitat damage.
- Research must be continued on new herbicides and pesticides to determine toxicity to nontarget species. Tests should use sublethal criteria such as metabolism, growth, behavior, and reproduction in these evaluations.
- Research must continue on understanding the dynamics and interactions of nutrients in aquatic systems so we will eventually be able to manage the flow of nutrients into desired production.

LITERATURE CITED

Anonymous. 1978. Environmental management strategy for the Great Lakes system. Pollution from Land Use Activities Reference Group final report to the International Joint Commission. Windsor, Ontario. 115 pp.

Burdick, G.E., E.J. Harris, J.H. Dean, T.M. Walker, J. Shea, and D. Colby. 1964. The accumulation of DDT in lake trout and the effect on reproduction. Trans. Am. Fish. Soc. 93:127-136.

Clair, E., and R. Storch. 1977. Stream site management and livestock grazing: an objective look at the situation. In John Menke, ed., Symposium on livestock interactions with wildlife, fish, and their environments, Sparks, Nev. USDA, Forest Service Pacific Southwest Forest and Range Experiment Station, Berkeley, Calif.

Delumyea, R.G., and R.L. Petel. 1977. Atmospheric inputs of phosphorus to southern Lake Huron, April-October 1975. EPA-600/3-77-038. U.S. Environmental Protection Agency. 54 pp.

Ellis, H.H., J.H. Beuscher, C.D. Howard, and J.P. DeBraal. 1970. Water-use law and administration in Wisconsin. Department of Law, University of Wisconsin-Extension, Madison. 694 pp.

Federal Water Pollution Control Administration. 1968. Water quality criteria: report of the National Technical Advisory Committee to the Secretary of the Interior. 234 pp.

Funk, J. 1973. Stream channel suitability for warmwater fish. Proc. 28th Annu. Meet. Soil Conserv. Soc. Amer.

Giere, J.P., K. Midohnson, and D.H. Perkins. 1980. A closer look at no-till farming. Environment 22:15-41.

Gunderson, D.R. 1968. Flood plain use related to stream morphology and fish populations. J. Wildl. Manage. 32(3):507-514.

Hickey, J.J., and D.W. Anderson. 1968. Chlorinated hydrocarbons and egg-shell changes in raptorial and fish-eating birds. Science 162:271-273.

Hunt, R.L. 1979. Removal of woody streambank vegetation to improve trout habitat. Wis. Dep. Nat. Resour. Tech. Bull. 155. 36 pp.

Irizarry, R.A. 1969. The effects of stream alteration in Idaho. Idaho Fish and Game Department, Boise.

Johnson, H.E., and C. Pecor. 1969. Coho salmon mortality and DDT in Lake Michigan. North Am. Wildl. Nat. Res. Conf. Trans. 34:159-166.

Karr, J.R., and D.R. Dudley. 1981. Ecological perspective on water quality goals. Environ. Manage. 5(1):55-68.

King, D.L., and R.C. Ball. 1964. The influence of highway construction on a stream. Mich. State Univ. Agric. Exp. Stn. Res. Rep. 19. East Lansing, Mich. 4 pp.

Leopold, L.B., and W.B. Langbein. 1966. River meanders. Sci. Am. 214:60-70.

Marzolf, G.R. 1978. The potential effects of clearing and snagging on stream ecosystems. U.S. Fish Wildl. Serv. Biol. Serv. Program Publ. FWS/OBS-78/14. 31 pp.

Nunnally, N.R. 1978. Improving channel efficiency without sacrificing fish and wildlife habitat: the case for stream restoration. In R.R. Johnson and J.F. McCormick, eds., Strategies for protection and management of floodplain wetlands and other riparian ecosystems. U.S. For. Serv. Gen. Tech. Rep. WO-12.

Ratcliffe, D.A. 1967. Decrease in eggshell weight in certain birds of prey. Nature 215:208-210.

Regier, H.A., and K.H. Loftus. 1972. Effects of fisheries exploitation on salmonid communities of oligotrophic lakes. J. Fish. Res. Board Can. 29(6):959-968.

Reid, G.K. 1961. Ecology of inland waters and estuaries. Reinhold, New York.

Ritchie, J.C. 1972. Sediment, fish, and fish habitat. J. Soil Water Conserv. 27:124-125.

Talhelm, D.R., R. Bishop, K. Cox, N. Smith, D. Steinnes, and A. Tuomi. 1979. Current estimates of Great Lakes fisheries values: 1979 status report. Great Lakes Fishery Commission, Ann Arbor, Mich.

U.S. Bureau of the Census. 1940. Areas of the United States.

U.S. Bureau of the Census. 1970. Area measurement reports. Ser. GE-20, No. 1.

U.S. Environmental Protection Agency. 1975. A compendium of lake and reservoir data collected by the National Eutrophication Survey in the Northeast and North-central United States. Working Pap. No. 474. 212 pp. (NTIS No. PB 248-894)

U.S. Water Resources Council. 1978. The nation's water resources--1975-2000. Vol. 2, Water quantity, quality, and related land considerations. Pt. II: Water management problem profiles, pp. 1-72. Second national water assessment. U.S. Water Resources Council, Washington, D.C.

Van Velson, C. 1978. The effects of livestock on Otter Creek, Nebraska. *In* A forum on livestock grazing and riparian flash stream ecosystems. Trout Unlimited, Denver, Colo.

White, F.C., J.E. Hairston, W.N. Musser, J.F. Perkins, A. Ersoz, and J.F. Reed. 1980. Nonpoint source pollution and economic tradeoffs associated with rural land use changes in Georgia. Univ. Ga. Coll. Agric. Exp. Stn. Res. Bull. 260. Athens, Ga.

White, R.J. 1973. Stream channel suitability for coldwater fish. Proc. 28th Annu. Meet. Soil Conserv. Soc. Amer., pp. 61-79.

White, R.J. 1975. Trout population responses to streamflow fluctuation and habitat management in Roche-a-Cri Creek, Wisconsin. Verh. Int. Verein. Limnol. 19:2469-2477.

White, R.J. 1981. Stream flow requirements for fisheries. *In* L.G. Wolfson, ed., Competition for water in Michigan: proceedings of a conference held April 4, 1981, at Kalamazoo. Michigan State University Institute of Water Research, East Lansing, Mich.

10
Impacts of Agricultural Trends on Interior Wetland Habitats

WETLAND DIVERSITY AND DISTRIBUTION

Wetlands are shallow basins that hold water and contain a nutrient-rich substrate that allows growth of water-loving and water-tolerant plants. Depending on the kind of soil, water quality and availability, and temperature patterns, the dominant plants in wetland areas may be mosses, grasses, sedges, bulrushes, cattails, shrubs, or trees (or any combination of these) that have become adapted to the water regime. The nature of this habitat affects the animal species that settle in the wetland community. Although the soils in such basins have evolved underwater with reduced aeration, soil classification systems recognize such soils. A wetland therefore may be identified even when hydric plants are absent.

Wetlands have been classified through a variety of systems, the most common of which involve descriptive terms of vegetation type, mean water depth, and water permanence. The most commonly used system (and the current legal description) is from Martin et al. (1953) as elaborated in Shaw and Fredine (1956). Among the major types are seasonally flooded basins or flats (Type 1), inland fresh meadows (Type 2), inland shallow fresh marshes (Type 3), inland deep fresh marshes (Type 4), and inland open fresh water (Type 5). Nationally, there are 20 types in all, including shrub swamp, wooded swamp, bogs, salt marshes, and mangrove swamps. Stewart and Kantrud (1971) significantly improved the classification of wetlands in the glaciated prairie region by emphasizing water and vegetation patterns and processes. Water permanence is an inherent factor in the classification of wetlands and includes ephemeral (Class I), temporary (Class II), seasonal (Class III), semipermanent (Class

IV), and permanent (Class V). In addition, vegetation can be identified by such things as drawdown or germination phase, emergent phase, and open water phase, since vegetation in many wetlands proceeds through various phases, dependent on water depths and water constancy. Various plant communities may occur in different phases, water depths, and long-term successional stages in a single wetland.

A federal interagency task force recently completed a new classification system for wetlands and deep-water wildlife habitats (Cowardin et al. 1979). This system is designed to serve broader resource interests than the systems currently in use and will form the classification basis for the current national survey of wetlands. This system might describe a midwestern deep fresh marsh as follows: system = palustrine; class = emergent wetland; subclass = persistent; dominance type = cattail-bulrush. A southern wooded swamp might be a palustrine, persistent, forested wetland. All of these descriptors can be converted to numerical terms for computer processing. Because the system is hierarchical, various levels of detail can be determined.

Major wetland regions in the United States are a product of geomorphology, climate, and local floras, but each region may have a variety of wetland types present, according to localized conditions.

Prairie Pothole Region These diverse shallow wetlands, ponds, and lakes were glacially formed and originally occurred in northwest Iowa, western Minnesota, northern and eastern North Dakota, eastern South Dakota, and the Prairie Provinces of Canada (southern Manitoba, Saskatchewan, and Alberta). Vegetation descriptions can be found in Stewart and Kantrud (1972). Vegetation in the surrounding drier regions is predominantly prairie grasses and forbs, but aspen is common in the transition zones between prairies and boreal forests. Small grain and row crop agriculture is the primary land use and, along with grazing, strongly influences upland vegetation as well as wetlands.

Northern Forests and Forest-Prairie Ecotone These are wetlands, often glacially formed, that are surrounded by and often invaded by trees. Edges are often boglike, even in open areas, and include sedges and mosses as well as alder and willow shrubs or trees. These range from the interlake region in the Great Lakes states eastward to Maine and north to the tundra ecotone. Descriptions of these wetlands are found in Cowardin and Johnson (1973) and Golet and Larson (1974). Successional patterns in the northeastern United States are outlined in Golet and Parkhurst (1981).

Western Great Basin and Intermountain These are shallow wetlands formed in pluvial lake basins that persisted after the Pleistocene period. They occur in cold desert and steppe country, and are often saline (or alkaline) due to high rates of evaporation. Classic examples are the Bear River Marshes (Utah), the Malheur Lake Marshes (Oregon), Stillwater Marsh in the Carson Sink (Nevada), the Tule-Klamath Basin (California and Oregon), and the marsh systems of the central valleys of California. The general vegetative and limnological characteristics of this type of wetland, as well as its use by wildlife, are outlined in Duebbert (1969).

Southern Great Plains In this region there are several extensive regions of shallow wetlands, ponds, and lakes that serve as wildlife habitats in summer and winter. These include over 121,000 ha (300,000 acres) of marshes and lakes in the Sand Hill region of northwestern Nebraska (Sanderson and Bellrose 1969) and about 100,000 ha (250,000 acres) in the Playa Lakes in the High Plains region of northwestern Texas (Bolen et al. 1979). Many artificial ponds and reservoirs have been constructed to add open water habitats attractive to migratory and some wintering waterfowl (Hobaugh and Teer 1981), but they do not replace natural wetlands as breeding or wintering habitats.

River Oxbow Swamps and Delta Marshes These may occur anywhere in North America but are most prominent in the south central region. They are characteristic of slow-moving rivers with broad, ancient basins, and those with large silt loads. Older wetlands are forested by water-tolerant trees, such as cypress and pin oak (Fredrickson 1979a), but younger delta areas are dominated by emergent marsh. One of the best examples is the Mississippi River Delta, which formed a massive marsh in Louisiana that now is being lost due to water level control structures that have deprived the area of nutrient-rich and revitalizing silt, with a resultant invasion of salt water (Gagliano 1981).

Southern Wooded Swamps Large basins that hold water much of the year because of geologic formation, river influence, or vegetative characteristics, these occur as far north as the Mingo Swamp of southeast Missouri, Reelfoot Lake in northwestern Tennessee, and the Great Dismal Swamp of Virginia and North Carolina, and range southward to the Okefenokee Swamp of southeastern Georgia and Lake Okeechobee and the Everglades in Florida. Many are river-oriented and river-influenced. Several were drained early in the history of the United States but later were restored.

Inland Coastal Marsh Often large marshes formed behind beach ridges of large lakes, these are characteristic of the glacially influenced Great Lakes and the large lakes of southern Manitoba. Some are influenced by the water levels of the lake, including wind tides, whereas others are separated from the lake, are older, and are in eutrophic or boglike stages. Large marshes of this type are still common along the Great Lakes but are much reduced in size. In Michigan, 71 percent of the marshes of this type have been lost (Jaworski and Raphael 1979).

WETLAND DYNAMICS

Wetlands retain enough vegetation characteristics to be put into classes or types, but they vary in water permanence and vegetation and are characterized by fluctuating water levels. In the western Great Basin, Intermountain, and Prairie Pothole regions, water fluctuation is caused by early spring snowmelt or heavy rainfall and late-season drying. In river flood plains, spring floods are regular in some drainages and periodic in others. Throughout the Prairie Pothole region, late summer drying and year-to-year runoff are major influences on wetland conditions. Many emergent plants do not tolerate permanent inundation and are characteristic of temporarily flooded areas. These include sedge, arrowhead, and moisture-tolerant grasses, such as manna grass. Others, such as cattail, tolerate standing water but do not seed well in such sites. Only a few true hygrophytes, such as certain bulrushes, submergents, and floating-leafed plants, germinate and grow well in deeper water.

Stability in wetlands seems to produce anaerobic conditions that tie up nutrients in substrates and concentrate toxic chemicals (Cook and Powers 1958, Harter 1966). Periodic drying, on the other hand, oxygenates, detoxifies, decomposes, and reactivates the flow of nutrients. Concurrently, natural seedbeds result in germination of diverse emergent and submergent plants as well as terrestrial plants, depending on soil moisture levels. Hence stabilization of water levels produces lakelike conditions that reduce the production of typical wetland flora and fauna.

Animal populations may be temporarily eliminated by such periodic water fluctuations, but species that have evolved in such dynamic settings survive by virtue of drought-tolerant eggs (invertebrates), bird-carried eggs (amphibians and fish), immigration (mammals and invertebrates), migration (birds), and other mechanisms. However, regional climatic changes can affect wetlands and their wildlife populations. Moreover, some species--the more aquatic ones, like fish--are slower to return after wetlands have dried than are semiaquatic forms.

Man-induced changes in vegetation and invertebrates have been studied by Kadlec (1962) and Harris and Marshall (1963). Examples of responses to short-term water cycles in prairie wetlands have been documented by Weller and Spatcher (1965) and Smith (1971). Natural long-term successional changes in vegetation have been observed in northeastern forests by Golet and Parkhurst (1981).

WETLAND WILDLIFE VALUES

Numerous species of invertebrates, fish, amphibians, reptiles, birds, and mammals occur in wetlands (Shaw and Fredine 1956, Sanderson and Bellrose 1969, Chabreck 1979, Landin 1979, Weller 1979a,b). Rather than attempt to list all these species, this discussion will focus on selected vertebrates of economic or aesthetic prominence as a means of assessing wildlife values and losses due to wetland alteration.

Several important furbearers are always associated with water: muskrats, (introduced) nutria, mink, beavers, otters, and raccoons. Muskrats, mink, and nutria achieve their greatest density and productivity in marshes. The lodge-building muskrat is a good species for denoting the depth and condition of marshes, and its populations reflect major habitat patterns. Several studies have shown that the water cycle is a major factor in year-to-year population variation (Weller and Spatcher 1965, Weller and Fredrickson 1974, Neal 1977).

Harvest data on furbearers taken during the 1975-1976 season reflect both the abundance and the economic importance of these species (Table 10-1). Nutria are harvested in Louisiana, Maryland, the Carolinas, Texas, Oregon, and Washington. Mink and muskrats are taken in almost all states, but the majority are taken in the wetland-rich states of the upper Midwest, the Dakotas, and Louisiana. The total harvest value of these three species in the United States exceeded $33 million in 1975-1976 (Deems and Pursley 1978).

About 44 species of waterfowl occur in the wetlands of North America (Bellrose 1980), of which 4 species of geese and 10 to 13 species of ducks are harvested in sizable numbers annually (U.S. Fish and Wildlife Service 1975, Chabreck 1979, U.S. Department of Agriculture 1980b). The total harvest of ducks varied from 4.5 to 16 million ducks annually between 1955 and 1977 with an increasing trend for 1963 to 1975 (Figure 10-1). This variation was generally correlated with population fluctuations that, in turn, were dependent on water conditions in wetlands, which influence the reproductive success of breeding ducks. Several regional studies have detailed this cause-effect relationship (Yeager and Swope

TABLE 10-1 Harvest, Average Pelt Price, and Total Value of Some Wetland Mammals Harvested in 1975-1976

	Mink	Muskrat	Nutria
Harvest	235,069	6,415,861	1,570,083
Mean pelt price	$10.00	$3.50	$5.25
Total value	$2,350,690	$22,455,514	$8,242,936

SOURCE: Adapted from Deems and Pursley 1978.

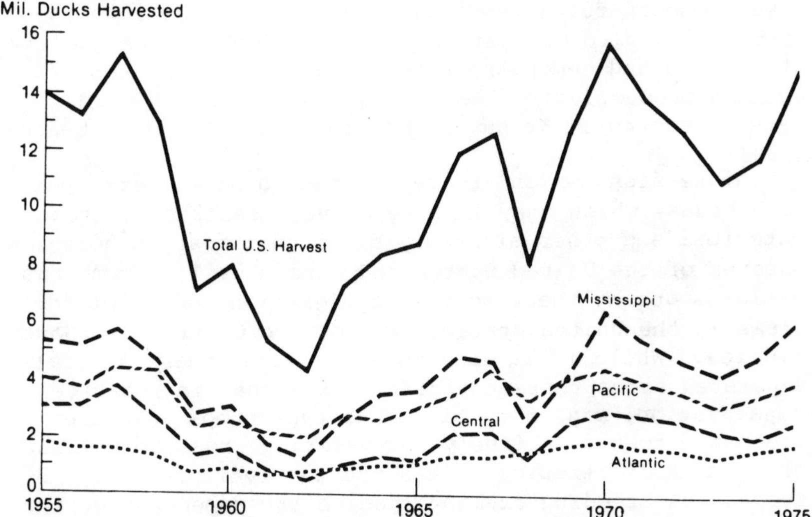

FIGURE 10-1 Total duck harvests in the United States and harvest by flyways. SOURCE: USDA 1980b.

1956, Smith 1971, Weller 1979b). The numbers of geese vary less dramatically because of their use of more stable and northerly Canadian wetlands, and the harvest averaged about 1.6 million birds per year during the period 1955-1977. Geese also are more terrestrial and often graze on wet meadows and shallow marsh during the breeding season as well as in winter. Large wetlands are important for rest and protection during southward migration.

In addition to waterfowl, many species of birds are dependent on wetlands, ponds, and lakes, and are termed "waterbirds." These include loons, grebes, coots, gallinules, rails, white pelicans, and other species. Certain terns and gulls also are associated with marshes, and may nest and feed there during the summer, but gulls also feed in the uplands. The waders and shorebirds include those species associated with water but more inclined to wade the shallow shorelines or mudflats, such as herons, cranes, sandpipers, and plovers. Other birds nest and feed in the marsh-edge vegetation.

Long-term studies done in northwestern Iowa provide data on common species in emergent marshes and relate estimates of minimal nest density to variations in habitat conditions (Weller and Fredrickson 1974). These studies, like those on furbearers and waterfowl, assess responses of breeding bird populations to variations in the quality of marshes and demonstrate the "boom-or-bust" nature of wetland productivity. Additional data on marsh birds were presented by Krapu and Duebbert (1974) and Duebbert (1981).

Unlike fish, which are restricted to water, or amphibians, which stay in a relatively restricted area, waterfowl and other migratory birds that nest in northern marshes of the United States and Canada utilize numerous wetlands during their southward migration and on wintering areas in the United States, Mexico, and Central and South America. While it is easy to assume that these spatially separated areas represent different issues in resource conservation, migratory birds use rest stops when they go south and then move freely on wintering areas to utilize any available resource. Thus the survival, return, and successful breeding of many species are dependent on the availability of wetlands in widely separated areas (see, for example, Heitmeyer and Fredrickson 1981). Recent legal rulings impose responsibility for maintaining these resources in the United States to the federal government under the Migratory Birds Treaty.

WETLAND LOSSES DUE TO DRAINAGE

Insufficient or incomplete baseline data on wetlands in North America prevent an accurate appraisal of wetland losses. However, several observations and assessments document a drastic and continuing decline in wetland area, numbers, and quality.

Information derived from Swamp Reclamation Acts, and various estimates of wet soils by the Soil Conservation Service, led to an estimate that there was an original wetland area of more than 51 million ha (127 million acres) in the contiguous United States (Shaw and Fredine 1956). This included an unknown amount of coastal marsh. In a partial wetlands survey by the USDA in 1922, nearly 3 million ha (7.4 million acres) of tidal marsh were included. The 1955 estimate of Shaw and Fredine (1956) included almost 3.8 million ha (9.3 million acres) of coastal marsh (1.6 million ha of fresh and 2.2 million ha of saline). However, to simplify calculations, no attempt was made to separate coastal from inland marsh.

Shaw and Fredine (1956) estimated that by 1955 there were 33 million ha (82 million acres) of wetlands, or a loss of over 18 million ha (35.4 percent). A Soil Conservation Service estimate in 1977 (USDA 1980a) showed 28.5 million ha (70.5 million acres) (Figure 10-2), or 44 percent of the original estimate. This estimated loss of almost 4.7 million ha (11.5 million acres) in 20 years equals over 233,000 ha (575,000 acres) per year.

Losses of wetlands have varied by region and time. As civilization moved westward and urbanization and agriculture expanded, the eastern states were the first to lose wetlands through drainage followed by such soil-rich areas as Indiana, Illinois, and Iowa. The major Prairie Pothole region extended from the Wisconsin glacial lobe of north central Iowa through western Minnesota, eastern South and North Dakota, northeastern Montana, and into Canada. Drainage in Iowa has been fairly well documented (Figure 10-3) and has caused an estimated loss of 94 percent (Bishop 1981).

In 1955 it was estimated that 57 percent of the wetlands of the entire Prairie Pothole region (Schrader 1955) had been lost. Considering only Types 3, 4, and 5, Haddock and DeBates (1969) estimated that over 40,000 ha (100,000 acres) had been lost in the three major Prairie Pothole states of Minnesota, South Dakota, and North Dakota during the years 1966-1968. Because some areas have significant numbers of Types 1 and 2 (which

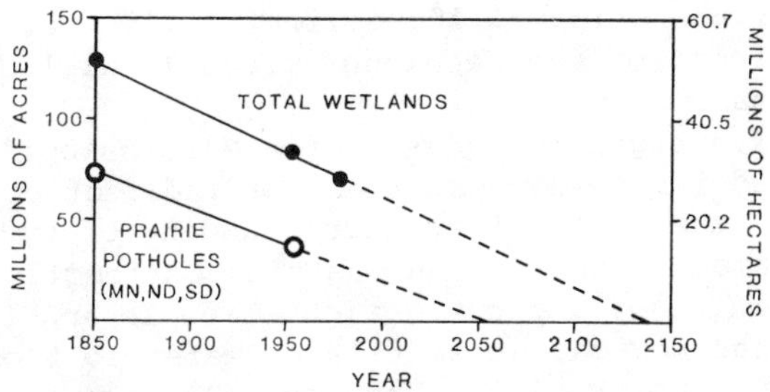

FIGURE 10-2 Estimated area of remaining wetlands in the United States and in the Prairie Pothole states, 1850-1977. SOURCE: Adapted from Shaw and Fredine 1956 and USDA 1980a.

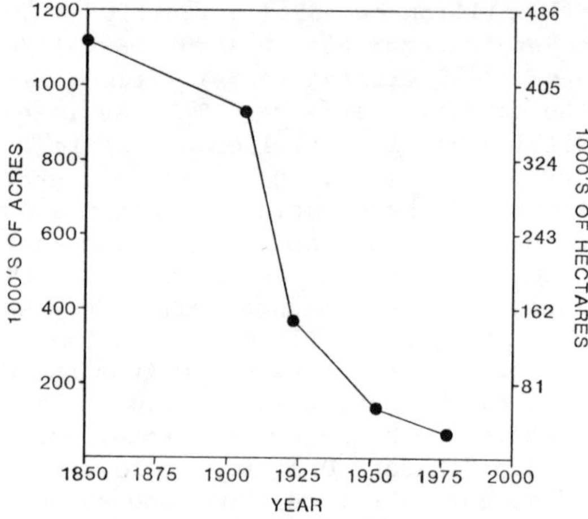

FIGURE 10-3 Area of Iowa's remaining wetlands. SOURCE: Based on data in Shaw and Fredine 1956 and Bishop 1981.

constituted about 40 percent of the 1955 survey), it is obvious that this estimate was a minimal one.

The most dramatic loss of a wetland type has been in river bottom swamp and overflow wetlands that have been converted to cropland. Data from the Missouri "boot heel" summarized by Korte and Fredrickson (1977) showed a loss of 96 percent since the original estimate was made (Figure 10-4). Losses of such bottomland forests throughout the Mississippi River valley total nearly 80 percent of the original 10 million ha (25 million acres), and 25 percent of the remainder probably will be drained by 1995 (MacDonald et al. 1979).

Loss of emergent marshes of the Mississippi River Delta in Louisiana demonstrates the indirect consequences of action taken without an understanding of hydrologic relationships. This action was the construction of levees, drainage, and navigation channels and forest removal that now causes silt-laden water to flow directly into the Gulf of Mexico. Because silt from the Mississippi River builds substrate and recharges the nutrients for a diverse emergent plant community, its loss (combined with invasion by salt water) has resulted in the loss of 10,000 ha (25,000 acres) of marsh per year. The loss has amounted to 324,000 ha (800,000 acres) since 1890 (4,000 ha per year), with the rate per year increasing geometrically (Gagliano 1981).

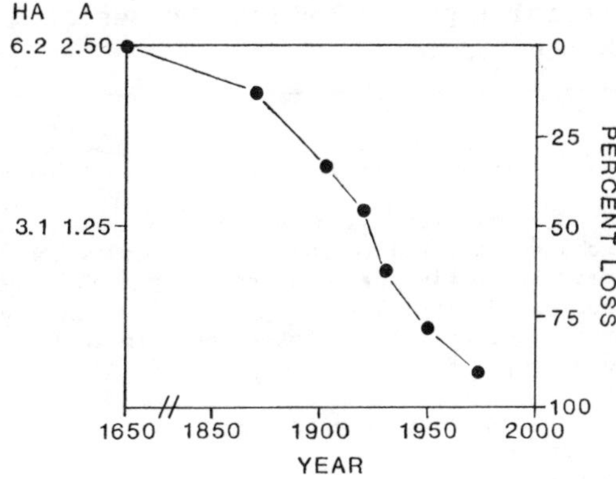

FIGURE 10-4 Area remaining and percent loss of Missouri's swampland forests. SOURCE: Based on data in Korte and Fredrickson 1977.

Mean annual rates of wetland loss can be calculated from the limited data shown in Figures 10-2, 10-3, and 10-4. Nationally, the loss has been about 0.4 percent per year since 1850. Losses in Iowa were greatest between 1906 and 1922 (about 3 percent per year) and have decreased to 0.2 percent per year since 1955, presumably because so few wetlands are left to drain, and many of them are protected by state or federal agencies. Loss of Missouri's lowland forest has been more rapid, with average loss rates of 1 percent per year before 1900 and 1.2 percent between 1900 and 1920, dropping to 0.5 percent by 1950, when 78 percent had been lost.

TYPES OF WETLAND ALTERATIONS IN RELATION TO WILDLIFE

The usual man-induced perturbations on a midcontinent wetland are listed in Table 10-2. Such perturbations sometimes are specific to the plant community of part of a wetland (e.g., wet meadow, shallow marsh, deep marsh), but usually the entire wetland is affected. Vast regions of wetland clusters thus are sometimes lost or modified.

Marginal wet-meadow vegetation suffers most from intensive land use because it is lost when drainage allows encroachment of agricultural and construction activities. Partial drainage of wetlands, which occurs

TABLE 10-2 General Types of Wetland Losses in Midcontinent North America

---

Total loss
- A. Drainage followed by farming, construction, or other use of the site.
- B. Tiling of adjacent areas with encroaching agricultural or other land use resulting in loss of wet meadow zone.
- C. Filling from the perimeter creating abrupt shorelines as well as decreased size.
- D. Siltation by poor uphill soil management in agricultural or urbanized areas.

Modified productivity due to pollutants
- A. Fertilizer runoff
- B. Livestock wastes
- C. Sewage disposal
- D. Pesticides

Water-level modification
- A. Flooding
- B. Water stabilization
- C. Use for irrigation, industry, or human water supply

Introduction of exotic plants or animals
- A. Carp and sunfish
- B. Trout stocking for aquaculture
- C. Aquatic plants

Cluster modification with loss of diversity of wetland types by complete or partial drainage
- A. Drainage of small units into streams, reducing size of both large and small units.
- B. Drainage of smaller units into larger wetlands, flooding larger wetlands.

Flooding of wetland clusters
- A. Flood control impoundments
- B. Irrigation impoundments
- C. Hydroelectric power production

---

during tiling operations, may result in a successional shift toward wet-meadow vegetation at a lower contour level while reducing deep-marsh vegetation (Table 10-3). In such cases, wet-meadow wildlife might increase. However, partial drainage of wet meadows combined with draining of adjacent uplands and/or intensive use of the marsh edge seriously reduces wet-meadow bird populations. Thus it is not surprising that marsh hawks, short-eared owls, and sandhill cranes are now uncommon in the much-drained and modified Prairie Pothole region. Marsh birds may be replaced by upland species that favor weedy cover

TABLE 10-3 Some Relative Population Changes and Habitat Shifts by Wildlife Following Natural or Man-Made Wetland Perturbations

Wildlife Arranged by Vegetative Community--from Dry (top) to Wet (below)[a]	Drained Tiled/or Construction	Drained Drought	Partially Drained	Partially Flooded	Flooded
Upland edge					
R.N. pheasant	-	+	+	-	-
M. dove	-	+	+	-	-
Deer*	-	+	+	-	-
Meadowlark	-	+	+	-	-
Bobolink	-	+	+	-	-
Marsh edge (mud flat)					
Shorebirds*	-	-	+	-	-
Herons*	-	-	+ or 0	00 or -	-
Marsh edge (shrub)					
R.W. blackbird	-	-	0	0 or -	-
Wet meadow					
Swamp sparrow	-	-	0	-	-
Sedge wren	-	-	0	-	-
Marsh hawk	-	-	- or 0	-	-
SE owl	-	-	- or 0	-	-
King rail	-	-	- or 0	-	-
Mink	-	-	- or 0	0 or +	-
Shallow marsh					
R.W. blackbird	-	-	0	0 or -	-
Am. bittern	-	-	0 or +	0 or -	-
Sora	-	-	0 or +	-	-
Dabbling ducks	-	-	0 or -	0 or +	-
Gallinules	-	-	-	0 or +	-
Deep marsh					
LBM wren	-	-	-	- or 0	-
Va. rail	-	-	0 or -	0 or +	-
Y.H. blackbird	-	-	-	- or +	-
Coot	-	-	-	0	-
Diving ducks	-	-	-	0 or +	-
Grebes	-	-	-	0	-
L. bittern	-	-	-	0 or -	-
Muskrat/nutria	-	-	-	0 or -	-

NOTE: Based mainly on midcontinent, semipermanent prairie marshes.

[a]Based on breeding populations except as indicated by asterisk.

(pheasants, meadowlarks, doves, and song sparrows), but these are small in numbers unless other habitats are available.

One of the most difficult losses to evaluate is that of small, seasonally flooded wetlands (Types 1 and 2) that are easily drained and that often are not regarded as of high value for wildlife because they dry out by midsummer. Some studies (Evans and Black 1956) have noted high use by breeding waterfowl, while other researchers feel these wetlands are of lesser importance. Because these wetlands reduce farming efficiency and are easily drained by tile or ditch, these areas have been reduced severely. Most federal and state regulations offer little or no protection for these shallow wetlands.

A related loss is the drainage of these smaller wetlands into larger ones, which often seasonally or permanently floods the larger unit, making it more lakelike. Some good examples of this in urban forest-succession wetlands have been noted in the Northeast (Golet and Parkhurst 1981). Attractive deep-marsh vegetation is thereby reduced or eliminated, and this loss directly affects nesting birds (Table 10-3). Such permanently changed water levels may have only temporary impacts in reducing the areas of emergent vegetation, since plant succession may advance upslope. This depends, however, on basin contours, since abrupt shores are not conducive to the growth of emergent plants. Even then, the character of the wetland is changed by the addition of more open water in the center. Where wetlands become open lakes (Type 5), alternate uses by birds (such as postbreeding or migrational rest stops) may occur if adequate food is available in the vicinity. But the stability of the water level may also modify stands of submergent plants, thus influencing the kinds of waterbirds found there. Moreover, such conversion seriously limits habitat diversity in a region.

Wetland losses resulting from impoundment of streams for irrigation or for use in hydroelectric power plants are increasingly common. The construction of the Garrison diversion irrigation project in North Dakota will eliminate 89,000 ha (220,000 acres) of agricultural land and wetlands. Such actions once were most common in populated areas, but proposals for such projects in Canada and Alaska threaten vast areas of wetlands once regarded as safe because of their isolation and severe weather.

Although many of the impacts of such perturbations on wildlife and precise assessment of the wildlife population losses are difficult to measure, the potential consequences seem staggering.

MEASUREMENT OF WILDLIFE LOSSES ON WETLANDS

Ideally, the impacts of wetland losses on wildlife should be measured by continuous censusing of wildlife populations over time concurrent with drainage patterns in different types and sizes of wetlands. But this involves expensive, long-term studies with uncertain outcomes. Moreover, such work has customarily been viewed as mere documentation of the demise of wildlife rather than involvement in aggressive and innovative programs to preserve wildlife habitats. Thus only qualitative assessments can be made. Judgments such as those in Table 10-3 are based on general observations of the natural successional changes in wetland communities and year-to-year changes produced by climatic conditions. Better data are available on these changes with respect to vegetation than to wildlife, however.

A decline in the diversity and abundance of birds, and an increase in small mammals, was recorded as a result of drainage and channelization of Missouri's bottomland forest (Fredrickson 1979b). Evans and Black (1956), Smith (1971), and Yeager and Swope (1956) noted declines in waterfowl populations as a product of drought and drainage in prairie potholes. Dramatic changes in bird and muskrat populations were noted for Type 4 marshes in Iowa by Weller and Spatcher (1965) and Weller and Fredrickson (1974). Waterfowl responses to changing water levels in a pothole cluster have been noted by Weller (1979b).

Total drainage of a wetland for some alternate use will obviously result in a major impact on all wildlife, but the losses often are partially due to incomplete drainage. Moreover, there has been no assessment of the impacts on wildlife of flooding, a common result of the drainage of several smaller wetlands into a larger one. By using natural variations in wildlife response to fluctuations in the quality of a Type 4 wetland, Weller (1981b) estimated the losses of wildlife due to flooding or partial drainage. Although the losses were not as great as for drainage, flooding was calculated to eliminate 65 to 70 percent of the muskrats and nesting birds.

Such techniques are useful only if data on other wetland types and vegetation communities are available. There is considerable variation among wetlands, and it is important to record not only different levels of productivity but also the range of normal variation found in these dynamic, climate-sensitive habitats.

WETLAND PROTECTION AND ACQUISITION

The continuing loss of wetlands has induced a variety of efforts to slow the loss and retain sufficient area to maintain typical faunal and floral diversity and the production of wildlife for hunting. Waterfowl hunters have been especially involved in forceful conservation programs resulting in the acquisition, protection, and management of wetlands for both breeding and wintering waterfowl.

The earliest acquisitions were refuges to protect specific birds and were initiated by the National Audubon Society. Subsequently, the Biological Survey of the U.S. Department of Agriculture initiated an acquisition (and sometimes restoration) program in 1908, resulting in a large number of National Wildlife Refuges managed by the U.S. Fish and Wildlife Service. This system of refuges now includes some 2.5 million ha (6 million acres). The present goal is to acquire about 810,000 ha (2 million acres) more by 1986 through lease or purchase in Minnesota, South Dakota, and North Dakota (Ladd 1978). There has been considerable local resistance to such programs, however. In 1977 the governor of North Dakota declared that no further acquisitions of land by the federal government would be permitted in the state. This was legally tested by the U.S. Fish and Wildlife Service, and in 1981 the courts held that the federal government has a mandate to provide habitats for water birds under international migratory bird treaties with Canada, Mexico, Japan, and Russia, and that states cannot obstruct such acquisitions.

The U.S. Department of Agriculture once aided farmers in draining wetlands. Now, the department manages the Federal Water Bank program and expends some $10 million annually for the protection of wetlands and adjacent uplands that help protect watersheds, prevent floods, and serve wildlife needs. As of 1978, over 160,000 ha (400,000 acres) had been protected for a 10-year period (Ladd 1978).

States also have acquired blocks of land for wildlife habitats that now total 2 million ha (5.1 million acres) (Ladd 1978), mostly acquired through the Pittman-Robertson Act, which taxes firearms and ammunition to provide funds for the acquisition and management of wildlife habitat. Minnesota also has a state water bank program and gives farmers property tax credits if they abstain from draining wetlands. A recent analysis suggests that such economic incentives are effective and that the compensation is fair (U.S. Corps of Engineers 1981).

Private organizations and individuals also have been involved. Ducks Unlimited (Canada) initiated protective easements on wetlands in the Prairie Provinces of Saskatchewan, Manitoba, and Alberta after a severe drought had reduced duck populations in the 1930s. Both Canadian and U.S. hunters contribute sizable amounts annually to this ongoing program. Smaller and often pristine areas have been acquired by the Audubon Society, the Nature Conservancy, and local nature study centers.

Many biologists believe that outright purchase can only provide an example, and that maintenance of a harvestable waterfowl population will depend upon a changed philosophy of land use that considers the long-term advantages of wetlands to all society. As a result, various efforts are under way to protect significant and often larger wetlands at the state as well as the national level. Some 15 states now have some type of wetland protection law. In addition, Section 404 of the 1972 Federal Water Pollution Control Act provides federal protection of wetlands from dredge and fill activities. The U.S. Corps of Engineers is charged with taking protective actions under this act, and the U.S. Environmental Protection Agency (EPA) oversees the permit process. However, both agencies currently limit their actions to wetlands near rivers and do not believe they are authorized to regulate perturbations elsewhere. Hence drainage continues in many states where wetlands are most abundant.

WETLAND RESTORATION AND CREATION

A number of major wetlands that were drained later were found to be less than satisfactory for agriculture and other purposes and have since been restored. These include the Great Dismal Swamp in Virginia, Horicon Marsh in Wisconsin, the Souris Marshes in North Dakota, and Klamath Lake in Oregon and California. Many restorations have been successful where remnant flora and fauna persisted, but the response has also been good even where agricultural activities have been practiced for many years. Many marsh plants have seeds that remain viable for 15 years or more and thus are adapted to the dynamic water cycles characteristic of marshes. Other seeds are spread easily by wind (e.g., cattail), so that plant establishment can be rapid when conditions are ideal. Currently, there is considerable interest in marsh restoration and creation, partly as a mitigation measure and partly to encourage placement of new marshes in desirable locations, such as nature study centers.

ESTIMATING FUTURE WETLAND LOSSES

In spite of increased efforts to conserve wetlands through state and federal legislation, tens of thousands of hectares are drained annually for agriculture, construction, and other intensive land uses. Moreover, skyrocketing land values, political influences that hamper land acquisition, the trend toward clean farming, the need for more intensive production on available land, increased opportunities to sell products abroad, and lack of appreciation of wetland values will further stimulate drainage where it is not prohibited by law.

One can calculate a mean loss of 233,000 ha (575,000 acres) per year between 1955 and 1977, based on data plotted in Figure 10-2. The current rate of loss has been estimated at more than 120,000 ha (300,000 acres) per year nationally (USDA 1980a). Certain areas undoubtedly will suffer great losses, both because wetlands are still available and because economic incentives exist for land use changes. Two crucial areas for the production and wintering of waterfowl, respectively, are the Prairie Pothole region and the Mississippi River Delta forests and emergent marshes. Losses of bottomland forests to agriculture by 2000 were projected at 2.3 million ha (5.6 million acres) in the Second National Water Assessment (U.S. Water Resources Council 1980). Calculations by MacDonald et al. (1979) suggest that 86 percent of the original Mississippi bottomland will be destroyed by 1995. Calculated delta marsh losses in Louisiana were 10,000 ha (25,000 acres) per year for 1980 (Gagliano 1981), and projections suggest that such losses may reach over 15,000 ha (38,000 acres) per year by 2000. At this rate, several entire parishes would be lost within the next 50 to 200 years, creating great economic loss to the public and loss of habitats for furbearers, waterfowl, and other wildlife.

Losses in the Prairie Potholes can be assessed by projection of the weak data points in Figure 10-5, which indicate that the current area is about 10.5 million ha (26 million acres), or 35 percent of the estimated 29.8 million ha (73.6 million acres) in the area originally. All of the remaining area will be lost by 2055 if the present rate of drainage continues. Unfortunately, the 1977 survey does not give state or regional estimates for Prairie Potholes in a manner comparable to the 1955 survey.

Studies of Prairie Pothole loss have been sporadic and regional. A study by Evans and Black (1956) showed how minor losses of wetlands drained into larger units decreased duck habitat on one small area. A study of losses in three states (Minnesota, South Dakota, and North Dakota) showed a loss of about 24,500 ha (60,440 acres) of mostly Types 1-3 wetlands because of subsidized drainage programs of the Soil Conservation Service (SCS) between 1954 and 1958 (U.S. Fish and Wildlife Service 1961). Moreover, deeper wetlands also were drained because drought had reduced these to less permanent waters. In 1964-1968, over 50,000 ha (125,000 acres) of wetlands were drained in these three states (Horwitz 1978). More recently, the channelization of small watersheds under SCS-sponsored programs clearly increased the ease and extent of drainage both in Minnesota (Choate 1972) and in South Dakota (Erickson 1975).

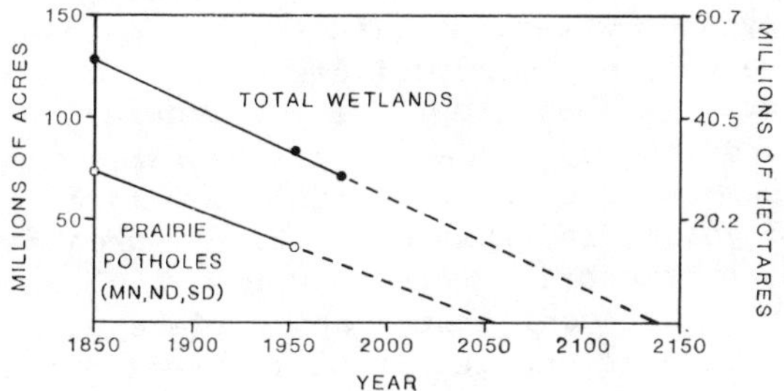

FIGURE 10-5 Projected losses of total U.S. wetlands and Prairie Potholes at present drainage rates. SOURCE: Weller 1981a.

What factors will influence the rate at which wetlands are drained in the future? The easiest wetlands to drain are small ones in shallow basins, so that larger, deeper wetlands tend to be preserved. But wetland drainage techniques also have improved, and filling is common in certain areas. It is apparent that existing laws are slowing but not stopping the drainage of wetlands and that more effective laws are needed.

WETLAND MANAGEMENT

Management may be defined as human activity directed toward manipulation of habitat for the good of wildlife and man. The production of wildlife has been maximized on a reduced number of hectares and areas by a variety of management practices. Management practices to enhance threatened or endangered plant species, as well as common plants useful for biomass production or water purification, also are possible.

Techniques useful in wetland habitat management have been reviewed by Sanderson and Bellrose (1969), Linde (1969), and Weller (1978, 1981a). We can classify these techniques as either "natural" or "artificial" processes. The natural processes common to wetlands are water level fluctuations, grazing, and fire. Of these, water level manipulation has been most effectively used by wildlife managers and produces one of the least expensive, longest lived, and most aesthetically pleasing (i.e., natural) results.

Because the flora and fauna of wetlands have evolved with changing water levels, the stabilization of water levels seems to be detrimental to most species of marsh wildlife. Therefore, when emergent vegetation has been eliminated by high water, herbivores, or disease, water levels can be reduced to reactivate nutrients and reduce toxic elements. A lush growth of new vegetation results, which, when reflooded, attracts invertebrates, amphibians, birds, and semiaquatic mammals. The resulting "boom" may last several years, and this production increases the long-term mean production level. However, there has been confusion over what constitutes appropriate water level fluctuations because changes in water level during the nesting of birds or muskrats can cause loss of nests and eggs or death of young. Hence water levels should be relatively stable during breeding periods, but not all year or year to year. In some years a loss of breeding populations will result from management, but subsequent revitalization of the marsh will attract larger numbers of wildlife and increased production.

Only managed wetlands have water control structures, and management often is difficult on areas lacking control structures. Water diversion by instream impoundments or irrigation channels is used in some western marshes. In most cases, management is restricted to regulation of herbivores. Grazing by muskrats, nutria, moose, and domestic livestock is difficult to control, and the impact can be dramatic.

Fire has been used to temporarily eliminate excessively dense vegetation, such as cattails, to create open spaces attractive to water birds, and to return nutrients to circulation.

Dugouts, level-ditching, and blasting are techniques that affect small areas and that can be used to create artificial nesting sites, improve cover-water interspersion, or fulfill other specific habitat needs. Herbicides have also been used to create temporary openings, but this practice seems feasible only where water hyacinths or other exotic plants have created continuing choking of wetlands.

Wetland losses have been so extensive that only a modest part of these can be replaced. Since losses continue to occur, sound management programs will be required to increase wildlife production on remaining wetland areas managed primarily for wildlife. Moreover, other uses of land surrounding wetlands will further modify remaining wetlands and require tighter controls over manageable factors.

PROJECTED IMPACTS OF CURRENT AGRICULTURAL TRENDS

Agricultural trends vary by region, and the impacts of wetland destruction or degradation on wildlife are therefore not uniform nationally (see Chapter 4). Although this section attempts to cite the concerns of biologists regarding various areas, it emphasizes those areas where the prospects of further wetland losses are greatest, namely, the Prairie Pothole region and the lowland hardwood forests.

Beneficial Effects Any action that reduces further drainage, or the conversion of prime or submarginal lands to row crops, will significantly aid wildlife in wetlands. In drier regions, where agricultural productivity is low and erratic, a trend away from the conversion of grasslands to cropland would mean less drainage. Maintenance of grass cover on uplands through the proper regulation of livestock grazing would reduce erosion into wetland basins. Improved watershed management also would improve water quality and reduce eutrophication and siltation of wetlands. If high energy costs lead to reduced cultivation, there will be more upland cover, and integrated pest management would result in reduced water pollutants.

Detrimental Effects Continued tiling, channelization (Fredrickson 1979b), and drainage of small watersheds (Choate 1972) and of wetlands that normally store water will dry out uplands and enlarge remaining wetlands. This will result in lakelike rather than marshlike conditions in some wetlands, which will negatively affect wildlife. Urban development on former farmlands will compound this problem. Concurrently, flooding will lower wildlife production on enlarged wetlands.

Increases in the size of feedlots in watersheds, the use of high-sulfur coals that produce acid rain, and increased fertilizer and herbicide use in no-till agriculture could negatively affect water quality in wetlands.

Increased farm size, increased equipment size, irrigation, and other intensive farming practices all produce "clean farming" and encourage further drainage or the use of uplands adjacent to wetlands. Irrigation is viewed with particular concern by several observers in western areas because of its role in lowering water tables and eliminating surface wetlands. This impact varies by location, water availability, and intensity of irrigation.

Uncertain Impacts Aquaculture may prove beneficial by providing further economic incentives to maintain wetlands. The timing of aquaculture harvests, however, could have negative effects on breeding birds or furbearer populations. Moreover, aquaculture creates competition among all species that feed on the invertebrates of marshes and negatively affects wildlife and native fish by the sheer numbers of introduced fish (Swanson and Nelson 1970). Additionally, there is a tendency to modify natural Type 5 wetlands in some areas to provide freeze-proof depth in winter, good summer oxygenation, and drawdown of water for harvest. The general pattern of fish growth and removal is such that the wetlands could be lost to most wetland birds except for predaceous mergansers and herons, which could become a problem in fish production.

Biomass production in uplands would influence wetlands by stimulating increased farming intensity and possibly siltation. Growing of wetland plants such as cattail or reed for biomass could add useful interspersion and openings to densely vegetated areas. However, water reduction to dry such upland areas for harvest must be in late fall or early winter, rather than during bird and mammal breeding seasons.

Forest cutting practices are pertinent to wetland wildlife only if tree-cutting produces siltation or flooding in the wetlands.

PROTECTION OF WETLANDS

Intensive wildlife management, however good it may be, cannot fully compensate for wetland losses of 50 to 95 percent. Wildlife harvests will be reduced proportionately, and management strategies must be devised to prevent the loss of threatened species. Some mitigation of losses may be possible, and some artificial wetlands can be created, but these contributions to wildlife survival will be relatively minor.

Some wetlands may be of greater long-term economic value for the harvesting of furbearers and the leasing of land for waterfowl harvesting than for agricultural crops, but this use will require different business approaches than have been developed in the modern farm management system.

Although data on wetland drainage are difficult to gather, and the long-term effects of drainage can only be estimated, the evidence is overwhelming that the values of wetlands to hydrologic and other life-support systems are indispensable. Several recent reviews (Good et al. 1978, Greeson et al. 1979) provide extensive summaries of the values of wetlands. Field studies by Novitzki (1979) in Wisconsin and Brun et al. (1981) in North Dakota, and modeling studies by Moore and Larson (1979) provide excellent evidence that wetlands influence stream flow and reduce floods. Wetlands influence underground water tables (Sloan 1972), though often only in small amounts.

They also improve water quality, reduce wind and water erosion, store organic material, purify the air, and add visual diversity. Localized, short-term benefits should not take precedence over long-term values important to the entire continent, and even the world. Thus, both for wildlife and for other values, wetland losses must not continue. Wetland values must be carefully documented, and the public informed of these values.

Implementation of the following recommendations is essential to preserve North American wetlands (recommendations are not in priority order):

1. Legal responsibility for enforcement of federal wetland protection laws must be clarified.

2. All types of wetlands should be protected from siltation and other perturbations that reduce wildlife habitats, water-holding capacity, or water quality. Those wetlands for which flooding is not a natural phenomenon should be protected from flooding. Currently, dredge and fill operations can be regulated mainly on wetlands associated with streams.

3. Wetlands of all types should be protected to preserve natural flora and fauna, to prevent endangering any species, and because each wetland type serves a different wildlife community. Currently, most wetland protection laws do not cover Class II (temporary) or Class III (seasonal) wetlands.

4. Federal and state policies that encourage or subsidize the drainage or alteration of wetlands should be abolished.

5. Suitable land management systems should be devised and demonstrated to encourage certain wetland use and preservation by private owners. The provision of economic incentives has been the major means of preserving wetlands, but better assessments of the value of furbearer harvests and of leasing land for hunting may increase voluntary protection.

6. Knowledge about wetlands and wetland preservation programs should be directed to farmers and other land managers so that preservation efforts are based on understanding and cooperation.

7. Evaluation of wetlands should be done on a long-term basis, incorporating data on the annual contributions of wetlands to water quality and storage, flood control, and recreation as well as to wildlife.

RESEARCH AND INFORMATION NEEDS

Several kinds of information are needed to understand fully the current impacts of agriculture on wildlife habitats and populations. Obtaining such information often requires expensive, long-term research on wildlife habitat ecology. The following are a few examples of the types of studies needed.

- Determine wildlife density by habitat type. Populations of nongame birds, of wetland mammals, and of common species of ducks still are insufficiently related to vegetation type and quality. There are examples from a few habitats, but information recorded under various habitat quality conditions is needed to serve as baselines for models to predict loss.
- Perform experimental studies on vegetation and wildlife. Most data are based on observational studies that cannot be replicated. Uncontrollable variables influence the quality of the data and refinement of assessment techniques. Several study designs are possible, but water control structures are essential to create areas of sufficient size to attract wildlife.
- Perform observational studies of wetland size and wildlife. Data on the relationship between wildlife numbers or species diversity and wetland size are essential to assess the impacts of drainage where wetlands of different sizes are eliminated. Small wetlands tend to be drained first and are of different types than larger wetlands and serve different bird or mammal species and therefore suffer differential losses of species. Descriptions of the communities and of the impacts of drainage on them are inadequate.
- Develop wildlife assessment techniques. Various qualitative techniques are being developed. The Habitat Evaluation Procedures (HEP) of the Fish and Wildlife Service are species-oriented, whereas the Corps of Engineers' Habitat Evaluation System (HES) is community-oriented. Both have advantages and disadvantages, but both are necessary because of the need for speed of assessment and the lack of a data base on the vegetation and wildlife characteristics of various types of habitats. Greater emphasis is needed on quantitative bases on which to make qualitative judgments. New techniques have been developed by Burnham et al. (1980) and others, who are perfecting rapid census techniques that provide density estimates as well as data on species diversity and habitat selection.

• Assess wetland losses. Variation in the techniques of classifying and quantifying the distribution and area of wetlands makes assessment of loss rates difficult. Each new system must be adjusted so that equivalent habitats are recorded. Currently, uncertainty exists as to the equivalency of certain wet soil types and certain ephemeral wetlands.

• Determine socioeconomic influences on drainage. Federal programs that provided financial assistance for draining wetlands increased the loss of wetlands in many areas until a presidential decree mandated a change in such policies. National and state systems to preserve wetlands include outright purchase, or easements, by the Fish and Wildlife Service and such things as tax incentives not to drain wetlands for agriculture. However, resistance to these programs suggests that social influences and nuisance factors of wetlands may be of overriding importance (Leitch and Danielson 1979). Not only is better understanding of farmer decision-making necessary, but new methods of information dispersal are essential to inform landowners of the values of wetlands and the economic and tax benefits of maintaining them in their natural state.

• Determine values of Types 1-3 wetlands. Most wetland regulations at the state and national level do not protect these temporary wetlands, which dry out in most years and do not occur in some years. Their value to wildlife is known but not quantified, and their role in water retention, flood control, and water recharge is uncertain. Drainage of these types of wetlands is great, and their loss will continue unless research documents their value more convincingly.

• Study mitigation needs and processes. Agricultural and other activities often result in lowered quality, if not total loss, of wetlands. Replacement of lost habitat tends to be judged on surface area of water even though the substrate shape, richness, and the vegetative community it supports differ greatly. As a result, there is no mitigation based on wildlife production units or other more realistic values. Such approaches need to be explored, tested, and activated.

• Assess the effects of pesticides and fertilizer. Experimental studies should be conducted to measure the inflow of herbicides and fertilizers into marshes and to assess the possible consequences on flora and fauna richness and productivity.

LITERATURE CITED

Bellrose, F.C. 1980. Ducks, geese, and swans of North America. 3rd ed. Wildlife Management Institute, Washington, D.C. 540 pp.

Bishop, R.A. 1981. Iowa's wetlands. Proc. Ia. Acad. Sci. 88:11-16.

Bolen, E.G., C.D. Simpson, and F.A. Stormer. 1979. Playa Lakes: threatened wetlands of the southern Great Plains. Pages 23-30 in Riparian and wetland habitats of the Great Plains. U.S. For. Serv. Publ. 91. Fort Collins, Colo. 88 pp.

Brun, L.J., J.L. Richardson, J.W. Enz, and J.K. Larsen. 1981. Stream flow changes in the southern Red River Valley of North Dakota. N.D. Farm Res. 38(5):11-14.

Burnham, K.P., D.R. Anderson, and J.L. Laake. 1980. Estimation of density from line transects sampling biological populations. Wildl. Soc. Wildl. Monogr. 72. 202 pp.

Chabreck, R.H. 1979. Wildlife harvests in wetlands of the United States. Pages 618-631 in P.E. Greeson, J.R. Clark, and J.E. Clark, eds., Wetland functions and values: the state of our understanding. American Water Resources Association, Minneapolis, Minn. 674 pp.

Choate, J.S. 1972. Effects of stream channeling on wetlands in a Minnesota watershed. J. Wildl. Manage. 36:940-944.

Cook, A., and C.F. Powers. 1958. Early biochemical changes in soils and waters of artificially created marshes in New York. N.Y. Fish Game J. 5:9-65.

Cowardin, L.M., and D.H. Johnson. 1973. A preliminary classification of wetland plant communities in north central Minnesota. U.S. Fish Wildl. Serv. Spec. Sci. Rep. Wildl. No. 168. 33 pp.

Cowardin, L.M., V. Carter, F.C. Golet, and E.T. LaRoe. 1979. Classification of wetland and deepwater habitats of the United States. U.S. Fish and Wildlife Service, Office of Biological Services. 103 pp.

Deems, E.F., Jr., and D. Pursley. 1978. North American furbearers, their management, research, and harvest status in 1976. International Association of Fish and Wildlife Agencies, College Park, Md. 171 pp.

Duebbert, H.F. 1969. The ecology of Malheur Lake and management implications. U.S. Fish Wildl. Serv. Refuge Leafl. No. 412. 24 pp.

Duebbert, H.F. 1981. Breeding birds on waterfowl production areas in northeastern North Dakota. Prairie Nat. 13:19-22.

Erickson, R.E. 1975. Effects of P.L. 566 stream channelization on wetlands on the Prairie Pothole region. M.S. thesis, South Dakota State University, Brookings. 91 pp.

Evans, C.D., and K.E. Black. 1956. Duck production studies of the Prairie Potholes of South Dakota. U.S. Fish Wildl. Serv. Spec. Sci. Rep. Wildl. No. 32. 59 pp.

Fredrickson, L.H. 1979a. Lowland hardwood wetlands: current status and habitat values for wildlife. Pages 296-306 in P.E. Greeson, J.R. Clark, and J.E. Clark, eds., Wetland functions and values: the state of our understanding. American Water Resources Association, Minneapolis, Minn. 674 pp.

Fredrickson, L.H. 1979b. Floral and faunal changes in lowland hardwood forests in Missouri resulting from channelization, drainage, and improvement. Final contract report to Office of Biological Services, Fish and Wildlife Service, Washington, D.C. 131 pp.

Gagliano, S.M. 1981. Special report on marsh deterioration and land loss in the Deltaic Plain of coastal Louisiana. Coastal Environments, Baton Rouge, La. 14 pp.

Golet, F.C., and J.S. Larson. 1974. Classification of freshwater wetlands in the glaciated northeast. U.S. Fish Wildl. Serv. Resour. Publ. 116. 56 pp.

Golet, F.C., and J.A. Parkhurst. 1981. Freshwater wetland dynamics in South Kingston, Rhode Island, 1939-1972. Environ. Manage. 5(3):245-251.

Good, R.E., D.F. Whigham, and R.L. Simpson, eds. 1978. Freshwater wetlands: ecological processes and management potential. Academic Press, New York. 378 pp.

Greeson, P.E., J.R. Clark, and J.E. Clark, eds. 1979. Wetland functions and values: the state of our understanding. American Water Resources Association, Minneapolis, Minn. 674 pp.

Haddock, J.L., and L.W. DeBates. 1969. Reports on drainage trends in the Prairie Pothole region of Minnesota, North Dakota, and South Dakota. Mimeographed. U.S. Fish and Wildlife Service, Minneapolis, Minn. 8 pp.

Harris, S.W., and W.H. Marshall. 1963. Ecology of water-level manipulations of a northern marsh. Ecology 44:331-342.

Harter, R.D. 1966. The effects of water levels on soil chemistry and plant growth of the Magee Marsh Wildlife Area. Ohio Dep. Nat. Resour. Game Manage. Publ. No. 2. 36 pp.

Heitmeyer, M.E., and L.H. Fredrickson. 1981. Do wetland conditions in the Mississippi Delta hardwoods influence mallard recruitment? Trans. North Am. Wildl. Nat. Resour. Conf. Vol. 46.

Hobaugh, W.C., and J.G. Teer. 1981. Waterfowl use characteristics of flood-prevention lakes in North Central Texas. J. Wildl. Manage. 45:16-26.

Horwitz, E.L. 1978. Our nation's wetlands. Council on Environmental Quality, Washington, D.C. 70 pp.

Jaworski, E., and C.N. Raphael. 1979. Mitigation of fish and wildlife habitat losses in Great Lakes coastal wetlands. Pages 152-156 in G.A. Swanson, ed., The mitigation symposium. U.S. For. Serv. Gen. Tech. Rep. RM-65. Rocky Mountain Forest and Range Experiment Station, Fort Collins, Colo. 684 pp.

Kadlec, J.A. 1962. Effects of a drawdown on a waterfowl impoundment. Ecology 43:267-281.

Korte, P., and L.H. Fredrickson. 1977. Loss of Missouri's lowland hardwood ecosystem. Trans. North Am. Wildl. Nat. Resour. Conf. 42:31-41.

Krapu, G.L., and H.F. Duebbert. 1974. A biological survey of Kraft Slough. Prairie Nat. 6:33-55.

Ladd, W.N., Jr. 1978. Continental habitat status and long-range trends. Ducks Unlimited Int. Waterfowl Symp. 3:14-19.

Landin, M.C. 1979. The importance of wetlands in the North Central and Northeast United States to non-game birds. Pages 179-188 in R.M. DeGraff and K.E. Evans, eds., Proceedings of workshop on management of north central and northeastern forests for non-game birds. U.S. Dep. Agric. Gen. Tech. Rep. NC-51. North Central Forest Experiment Station, St. Paul, Minn. 268 pp.

Leitch, J.A., and L.E. Danielson. 1979. Social, economic, and institutional incentives to drain or preserve prairie wetlands. Dep. Agric. Appl. Econ. Econ. Rep. ER79-6. University of Minnesota, St. Paul.

Linde, A.F. 1969. Techniques for wetlands management. Wis. Dep. Nat. Resour. Rep. No. 45. 156 pp.

MacDonald, P.O., W.E. Frayer, and J.R. Clauser. 1979. Documentation, chronology, and future projections of bottomland hardwood habitat loss in the lower Mississippi alluvial plain, Vol. I, Basic report. HRB Singer, Inc., State College, Pa. 133 pp.

Martin, A.C., N. Hotchkiss, F.M. Uhler, and W.S. Bourn. 1953. Classification of wetlands of the U.S. U.S. Fish Wildl. Serv. Spec. Sci. Rep. Wildl. 20. 14 pp.

Moore, I.D., and C.L. Larson. 1979. Effects of drainage projects on surface runoff from small depressional watersheds in the North Central Region. Univ. Minn. Water Resour. Res. Cent. Bull. 99. 225 pp.

Neal, T.J. 1977. A closed trapping season and subsequent muskrat harvest. Wildl. Soc. Bull. 5:194-196.

Novitzki, R.P. 1979. Hydrologic characteristics of Wisconsin's wetlands and their influence on floods, stream flow, and sediment. Pages 377-388 in P.E. Greeson, J.R. Clark, and J.E. Clark, eds., Wetland functions and values: the state of our understanding. American Water Resources Association, Minneapolis, Minn. 674 pp.

Sanderson, G.C., and F.C. Bellrose. 1969. Wildlife habitat management of wetlands. Ann. Acad. Bras. Cienc. 41(Supp.):153-204.

Schrader, T.A. 1955. Waterfowl and the potholes of the North Central states. Pages 596-604 in Yearbook of agriculture, 1955. U.S. Department of Agriculture, Washington, D.C. 751 pp.

Shaw, S.P., and C.G. Fredine. 1956. Wetlands of the United States. U.S. Fish Wildl. Serv. Circ. 39. 67 pp.

Sloan, C.E. 1972. Ground-water hydrology of prairie potholes in North Dakota. U.S. Geol. Surv. Prof. Pap. 585-C. 28 pp.

Smith, A.G. 1971. Ecological factors affecting waterfowl production in the Alberta Parklands. U.S. Fish Wildl. Serv. Resour. Publ. No. 98. 49 pp.

Stewart, R.E., and H.A. Kantrud. 1971. Classification of natural ponds and lakes in the glaciated prairie region. U.S. Fish Wildl. Serv. Resour. Publ. No. 92. 57 pp.

Stewart, R.E., and H.A. Kantrud. 1972. Vegetation of Prairie Potholes, North Dakota, in relation to quality of water and other environmental factors. U.S. Geol. Surv. Prof. Pap. 585-D. 36 pp.

Swanson, G.A., and H.K. Nelson. 1970. Potential influences of fish rearing programs on waterfowl breeding habitat. In E. Schneberger, ed., A symposium on the management of midwestern winterkill lakes. North Cent. Div. Am. Fish Soc. Midwest Fish Wildl. Conf. 32. Winnipeg, Manitoba.

U.S. Corps of Engineers. 1981. The economics of wetland drainage on agricultural Minnesota. St. Paul District, Corps of Engineers, St. Paul, Minn. 51 pp. plus appendix.

U.S. Department of Agriculture. 1980a. Soil and Water Resources Conservation Act, appraisal 1980. Government Printing Office, Washington, D.C.

U.S. Department of Agriculture. 1980b. An assessment of the forest and range land situation in the United States. U.S. For. Serv. FS-345. Washington, D.C. 631 pp.

U.S. Fish and Wildlife Service. 1961. Waterfowl production habitat losses related to agricultural drainage. North Dakota, South Dakota, and Minnesota--1954-1958. Branch of River Basin Studies, Minneapolis, Minn. 39 pp. plus appendix, 23 pp.

U.S. Fish and Wildlife Service. 1975. Final environmental statement for the issuance of annual regulations permitting the sport hunting of migratory birds. Washington, D.C. 710 pp. plus appendix, 13 pp.

U.S. Water Resources Council. 1980. Second national water assessment, Washington, D.C.

Weller, M.W. 1978. Management of freshwater marshes for wildlife. Pages 267-284 in R.E. Good, D.F. Whigham, and R.L. Simpson, eds., Freshwater wetlands, ecological processes and management potential. Academic Press, New York. 378 pp.

Weller, M.W. 1979a. Wetland habitats. Pages 210-234 in P.E. Greeson, J.R. Clark, and J.E. Clark, eds., Wetland functions and values: the state of our understanding. American Water Resources Association, Minneapolis, Minn. 674 pp.

Weller, M.W. 1979b. Birds of some Iowa wetlands in relation to concepts of faunal preservation. Proc. Ia. Acad. Sci. 86:81-88.

Weller, M.W. 1981a. Freshwater marshes: ecology and wildlife management. University of Minnesota Press, Minneapolis. 146 pp.

Weller, M.W. 1981b. Estimating wildlife and wetland losses due to drainage and other perturbations. Pages 337-346 in B. Richardson, ed., Selected Proceedings of the Midwest Conference on Wetland Values and Management. Minnesota Water Planning Board, St. Paul. 660 pp.

Weller, M.W., and L.H. Fredrickson. 1974. Avian ecology of a managed glacial marsh. Living Bird 12:269-291.

Weller, M.W., and C.E. Spatcher. 1965. Role of habitat in the distribution and abundance of marsh birds. Ia. Agric. Home Ec. Exp. Stn. Spec. Rep. No. 43. 31 pp.

Yeager, L.E., and C.M. Swope. 1956. Waterfowl production during wet and dry years in north central Colorado. J. Wildl. Manage. 20:442-446.

11
Impacts of Agricultural Trends on Coastal Wetland and Estuary Habitats

The coastal wetlands are the marine shores of the United States, excluding Alaska and Hawaii. They consist of approximately 8,000 linear kilometers of the coastal shoreline and approximately 86,000 km of tidal shoreline as shown in Table 11-1. The coastal zone is an area where urban, industrial, and recreational activities are increasing.

The estuaries of the United States range from the deep, stable bays of the Northwest, such as Puget Sound, at one extreme, to waters around the tropical reefs of the Florida Keys, at the other. In between these extremes are systems of every kind and gradation where nearly every combination of natural fish and wildlife productivity occurs.

Within these ecological systems, the characteristics of which are largely determined by natural factors, such as geological history, tidal amplitude, weather, water currents, and geographical location, human impacts have become a major cause of alteration of water and water-related resources. Within each coastal region of the United States, one of the major concerns is pollution. In some areas, such as southwest Florida and California, the major sources of concern are domestic wastes, while in other regions, such as New England, the Pacific Northwest, and Alaska, industrial pollution is the major concern.

Other major concerns are conservation of wetlands in New England and the mid-Atlantic and south Atlantic regions; erosion in the south Atlantic region and the eastern Gulf of Mexico; water diversion in the lower Mississippi region; and freshwater supply in the Gulf of Mexico.

TABLE 11-1 Size and Shape Comparisons Among Biophysical Regions

	North Atlantic	Middle Atlantic	Chesa-peake Bay	South Atlantic	Caribbean
Ocean coastline (mi)	1,358	1,286	11.3	817	1,542
Tidal shoreline (mi)	4,419	7,992	5,469	9,793	3,437
Estuarine water area (mi^2)	3,401	5,130	4,554	3,973	717
Marsh area (mi^2)	97.6	603.1	595	2,267	616.4
Coastal counties area (mi^2)	11,177	19,237	13,859	24,839	9,869
Descriptive ratios					
Tidal shoreline/ocean coastline	3.3	6.2	408.0	12.0	2.2
Estuarine water area/ocean coastline	2.6	4.0	400.0	4.9	0.46
Estuarine water area/tidal shoreline	0.77	0.64	0.83	0.41	0.21
Marsh area/ocean coastline	0.07	0.47	53.0	2.8	0.40
Marsh area/tidal shoreline	0.02	0.08	0.11	0.23	0.18

	Gulf of Mexico	Pacific South-west	Pacific North-west	Alaska	Pacific Islands	Total
Ocean coastline (mi)	2,270	1,194	669	14,899	1,194	25,230
Tidal shoreline (mi)	15,476	3,060	4,793	33,904	1,328	89,571
Estuarine water area (mi^2)	10,944	799	1,946	14,353	15	45,832
Marsh area (mi^2)	8,427	191	44.5	[a]	15	12,841
Coastal counties area (mi^2)	48,151	31,168	42,768	334,413	6,703	552,184
Descriptive ratios						
Tidal shoreline/ocean coastline	6.8	2.6	7.2	2.3	1.1	3.6
Estuarine water area/ocean coastline	4.8	0.67	2.9	0.96	0.01	1.8
Estuarine water area/tidal coastline	0.71	0.26	0.41	0.42	0.01	0.5
Marsh area/ocean coastline	3.7	0.16	0.07	--	0.01	0.5
Marsh area/tidal shoreline	0.54	0.06	0.01	--	0.01	0.1

[a]No data.

SOURCE: Brokaw 1978.

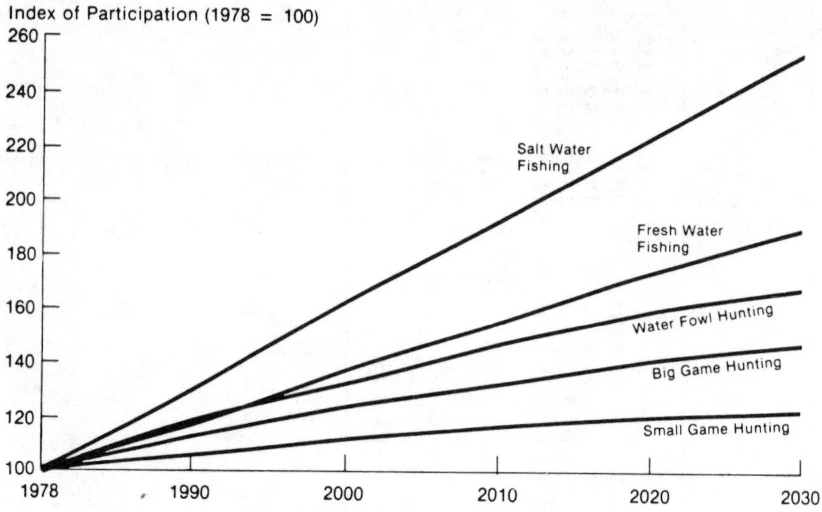

FIGURE 11-1 Projections of participation in major hunting and fishing activities under medium-level population assumptions, 1978-2030. SOURCE: USDA, Forest Service 1980.

Concern for estuarine and nearshore marine areas is appropriate. In 1972 the value of commercial fish harvests was $750 million (U.S. Department of Commerce 1972); in 1970 expenditures for saltwater recreational fishing were estimated at nearly $1.25 billion, and at $244 million for waterfowl hunting (U.S. Department of the Interior 1972); and during the 1975-1976 season the total market value of fur harvests exceeded $150 million (Deems and Pursley 1978). Other uses of estuarine and nearshore marine areas, such as recreational boating, bird watching, and swimming are also dependent upon the quality of the water and water-related resources. Figure 11-1 shows the projected impact of sport fishing in salt waters through the year 2030. Most coastal ecologists agree that coastal fisheries are at their maximum sustaining yield. However, most estuarine areas of the United States have been modified more or less severely by human activities. Thus it is imperative to manage the coastal environment to avoid further degradation.

Conflicts between recreational and commercial users of estuaries highlight the problems of allocating both the shoreline and the adjacent waters for different purposes. These conflicts will increase in frequency and intensity, particularly if projected increases in recreational demands and consumption of fisheries products are realized as the population continues to grow and the population density of coastal regions intensifies. The population of the United States, excluding Alaska and Hawaii, rose from 12 persons per square kilometer in 1790 to 150 in 1970, and the population within 80 km of the coast rose from 60 to 108 million people between 1940 and 1970.

GEOGRAPHICAL AND ECOLOGICAL DESCRIPTIONS OF ESTUARIES

The shorelines of the United States are generally divided into the Pacific, Gulf, and Atlantic regions. The reader is directed to U.S. Department of the Interior (1970a) for detailed maps of the estuarine zones of the United States. The Pacific region, with its narrow shelf, cold coastal waters, emerging shoreline, and few estuaries, is quite different from the Gulf and Atlantic regions, which have a broad shelf, many estuaries, and a subsiding shoreline and are warmed by the Gulf Stream. Shoreline types and areas are shown in Table 11-2. The term "estuaries," as used in this chapter, includes bays, lagoons, fjords, other semienclosed saltwater-influenced bodies of water, and river delta areas.

The Pacific Coast is a tectonically rising area. This produces a coastline with alternating sandy beaches and cliffs that extend into deep water near shore. Water circulation along this kind of coast tends to reduce the effects of events on land, either natural or man-induced. Therefore there may not be significant major agricultural impacts on the coastal waters of the Pacific Coast. The bays of the West Coast were tectonically formed with deep basins into which empty streams from mountainous areas, fertile valleys, forests, rangeland, and cropland. The northern area has abundant rainfall, while the southern area is arid. While there are numerous small, semienclosed natural bays, the large estuaries are Puget Sound, San Francisco Bay, and the Gulf of California, where the Colorado River enters Mexican waters. Smaller estuaries are found along the northern coast of Washington, where weathering of the shore has produced low coastal flats. These rise to more rocky coasts at Cape Mendicino. In the southern portion of the Pacific Coast, San Diego and Tomales bays have fringing marshes, but Newport Bay and other areas adjacent to Los Angeles have been almost completely replaced by urban development.

TABLE 11-2 Shoreline Types for the United States

		Shoreline[a]		Coastline[a]		Estuarine Surface Area[b]		Gravel or Rocky Beach[d]	
		(mi)	(km)	(mi)	(km)	(acres)	(km²)	(mi)	(km)
New England	Maine	2,500	4,011.5	228	366.9	39,400	159.4		
	New Hampshire	40	64.4	13	20.9	12,400	50.2		
	Massachusetts	1,200	1,930.8	192	308.9	207,000	837.7		
	Rhode Island	340	547.1	40	64.4	94,700	383.2		
	Connecticut	270	434.4			31,600	127.9		
	Total	4,350	6,999.2			385,100	1,558.4		
Middle Atlantic	New York	638	1,026.5	127	204.3	376,600	1,524.1		
	New Jersey	469	754.6	130	209.2	778,400	3,150.2		
	Delaware	226	363.5	38	45.1	395,500	1,600.6		
	Maryland	1,939	3,119.9	31	49.8	1,406,100	5,690.5		
	Virginia	993	1,597.7	112	180.2	1,670,000	6,768.5		
	Total	4,265	6,862.3	438	688.6	4,626,600	18,733.4		
South Atlantic-Gulf	North Carolina	3,661	5,890.5	301	484.3	2,206,600	8,930.1		
	South Carolina	3,063	4,928.4	187	300.9	427,900	1,731.7		
	Georgia	204	328.9	100	160.9	170,800	691.2		
	Florida	8,426	13,557.4	1,350	2,172.2	1,051,200	4,254.0		
	Mississippi	359	577.6	44	70.8	251,200	1,016.6		
	Alabama	607	976.6	53	85.3	530,000	2,144.8		
	Total	16,320	26,239.4	2,035	3,274.4	4,637,700	18,768.4		

		Sandy Beach		Unclassified Beaches		Marsh or Mangrove		Unconsolidated Cliffs		Rocky Shore[d]	
		(mi)	(km)	(mi)	(km)	(mi)	(km)	(mi)	(km)	(mi)	(km)
New England	Maine	50	80.5	10	16.1					2,440	3,926.0
	New Hampshire			25	40.2						
	Massachusetts	305	490.7	635	1,021.7						
	Rhode Island	45	72.4	140	225.3						
	Connecticut			145	233.3						
	Total			955	1,536.6						
Middle Atlantic	New York			331	532.6						
	New Jersey	215	345.9			205	329.8				
	Delaware	76	122.3			100	160.7				
	Maryland	46	74.0								
	Virginia	294	473.0			530	852.8				
	Total										
South Atlantic-Gulf	North Carolina	1,269	2,041.8			1,503	2,418.3				
	South Carolina	196	315.4								
	Georgia	102	163.6								
	Florida										
	Mississippi	1,375	2,212.4[c]			2,423	3,898.6[c]				
	Alabama										
	Total										

TABLE 11-2 (continued)

		Shoreline[a]		Coastline[a]		Estuarine Surface Area[b]		Gravel or Rocky Beach[d]	
		(mi)	(km)	(mi)	(km)	(acres)	(km^2)	(mi)	(km)
Lower Mississippi	Louisiana	7,721	12,423.1	397	638.8	3,545,100	14,346.3		
Texas-Gulf	Texas	1,792	2,883.3	373	600.3	1,344,000	5,438.9		
California-South Pacific	California	3,427	5,514.0	840	1,351.6	552,100	2,234.2	17.5	28.5
Columbia-North Pacific	Washington	3,026	4,868.8	157	252.6	193,800	784.3		
	Oregon	1,410	2,268.7	296	476.3	57,600	233.1		
	Total	4,436	7,136.5	453	728.9	251,400	1,017.4		
Alaska	Alaska	33,904	54,551.5	6,640	10,683.8	11,022,800	44,607.1		
Great Lakes	Wisconsin	9,571	15,399.7			10,600	42.9		
	Michigan					151,700	613.9		
	Ohio					37,200	150.5		
	New York					48,900	197.9		
	Total	9,571	15,399.7						
Hawaii	Hawaiian Is.	1,052	1,692.7	750	1,206.7				
Caribbean	Virgin Is.	175	281.6	117	188.2				
	Puerto Rico	700	1,126.3	311	500.4				
	Total	875	1,407.9	428	688.6				

		Sandy Beach		Unclassified Beaches		Marsh or Mangrove		Unconsolidated Cliffs		Rocky Shore[d]	
		(mi)	(km)	(mi)	(km)	(mi)	(km)	(mi)	(km)	(mi)	(km)
Lower Mississippi	Louisiana	835	1,343.5			1,108	1,782.8				
Texas-Gulf	Texas	674	1,084.5			359	577.6	421	677.4		
California-South Pacific	California	622	1,065.6			202	325.8	757.0	1,218.0		
Columbia-North Pacific	Washington										
	Oregon										
	Total										
Alaska	Alaska										
Great Lakes	Wisconsin	2,107	416.4								
	Michigan										
	Ohio										
	New York										
	Total										
Hawaii	Hawaiian Is.										
Caribbean	Virgin Is.										
	Puerto Rico										
	Total	259	3,390.6								

[a] Data are from U.S. Department of Commerce 1975.
[b] Data are from U.S. Department of the Interior 1970b.
[c] Includes Gulf Coasts of Florida, Mississippi, and Alabama.
[d] Source material not sufficiently explicit to classify. Most beaches in these categories are probably shelly, pebbly, or gravel or mixtures.

The estuaries of the Gulf of Mexico are extensive and contribute much of the fish catch of the United States. These estuaries are somewhat similar to those on the Atlantic Coast, in that they were formed on a shallow coastal shelf during the rise of the sea after the last ice age. The estuarine environments of the Gulf range from the hypersaline Laguna Madre of south Texas to the Mississippi River Delta to the carbonate mangrove swamps of the Florida Everglades. The estuaries of the Gulf receive a large inflow of fresh water, since approximately 50 percent of the rainfall in the United States falls within the Gulf's watershed. Since much of this rain originates from the evaporation of Gulf waters, the Gulf's estuaries and shoreline are highly sensitive to agricultural trends. The marshes in the estuaries are highly productive of seagrasses and phytoplankton, vary constantly with variations in rainfall and coastal energy patterns, and have been greatly affected by activities like development of the intercoastal canal and the ports of Galveston, Corpus Christi, Sabine, and Mobile and those on the Mississippi River. The Gulf coastal waters are highly turbid because the rivers carry heavy loads of silt.

The estuaries of the Atlantic region are divided into flooded river valleys and water in glaciated areas of the northern Atlantic Coast. Within this region is Chesapeake Bay, a drowned river valley highly affected by ocean tides and river inflow. Marshes are extensive throughout the bay area and are highly productive of wildlife. The Hudson River estuary is heavily affected by human activities in New York and its port.

All the coastal regions are highly productive for many kinds of aquatic life, ranging from anadromous fish, like salmon, to various species of crabs, shrimp, and oysters, and numerous marine fish species. The total marine catch of the United States for 1979 was about 3.5 million metric tons, or about 5 percent of the world catch (U.N. Food and Agricultural Organization 1979). The Gulf of Mexico contributed roughly half of the country's commercial fish and shellfish catch. The sport fish catch may equal or exceed the commercial catch, depending on the area and species of fish.

The estuaries are normally transitional freshwater-saltwater systems influenced by weather patterns on both land and sea. They are generally highly productive and sometimes eutrophic, depending on variations in the nutrient input from rivers and local runoff. The nutrients are generally diluted by offshore currents, tidal action, and rainfall.

Until recent times there was little scientific understanding of estuaries as distinct environments, although the estuaries of the great river systems have always been a primary source of human food. The interchange of fresh and saline waters within estuaries makes them suitable environments for the spawning and growth of various fish and crustaceans, and their shoals are the site of extensive beds of mussels, clams, and oysters. While it may be true that estuaries are transitory environments because they are subject to all the changes that occur where land and sea meet, these transitory conditions do not occur with such suddenness as to destroy the estuarine environment itself. However, it is possible for human activity to result in the destruction of estuaries. This has happened in the past and could occur with greater frequency in the future. Much of this destruction by alteration is insidious (Odum 1970).

LEGISLATIVE ACTION RELATED TO ESTUARINE HABITATS

Throughout most of its recorded history the competitive economic system of the United States has led most of its citizens to choose to ignore the environmental consequences of that system. But when it was realized that Lake Erie, the Hudson River estuary, and other large bodies of water were slowly becoming unfit as aquatic habitats for most species, the nation enacted legislation to reverse the destructive trends. The National Environmental Policy Act of 1969, the Federal Water Pollution Control Act of 1972, the Marine Protection, Research and Sanctuaries Act of 1972, the Safe Drinking Water Act of 1974, and the Coastal Zone Management Act of 1972 all included recommendations for regulating most of the human activities that affect coastal waters.

These various acts and federal regulations issued pursuant to the acts were intended to regulate all discharges of wastes, water, dredge materials, and so on, into the waters and wetlands of the United States. The acts resulted in a vast and comprehensive evaluation of the nation's waters and their capacity to absorb wastes.

Through implementation of the various acts, U.S. waters have been greatly improved during the past decade. With the help of these laws and regulations, many polluted environments have restored themselves rapidly, although it is difficult to determine the extent of the restoration because there are no complete historical records of natural ecosystems. However, almost no control exists over effluents from nonpoint sources. These are due to water use and changes in the normal water flow of drainage areas, streams, and lakes, as well as soil erosion, nutrient runoff, agricultural chemical runoff, and street runoff, whose impact may be greater than effluents from point sources.

HOW AGRICULTURE AFFECTS ESTUARIES

The impacts of agriculture on estuarine systems are primarily due (1) to river load and runoff from adjacent uplands, and (2) the direct use of coastal wetlands for agriculture. Figure 11-2 shows the water budget for the United States, indicating the flow of fresh water to the coasts.

The greatest impacts of agricultural trends on estuaries are caused by river burdens. These can be separated into major and minor impacts. In general, multiple agricultural activities occur in the drainage areas of the major U.S. rivers. Approximately 50 percent

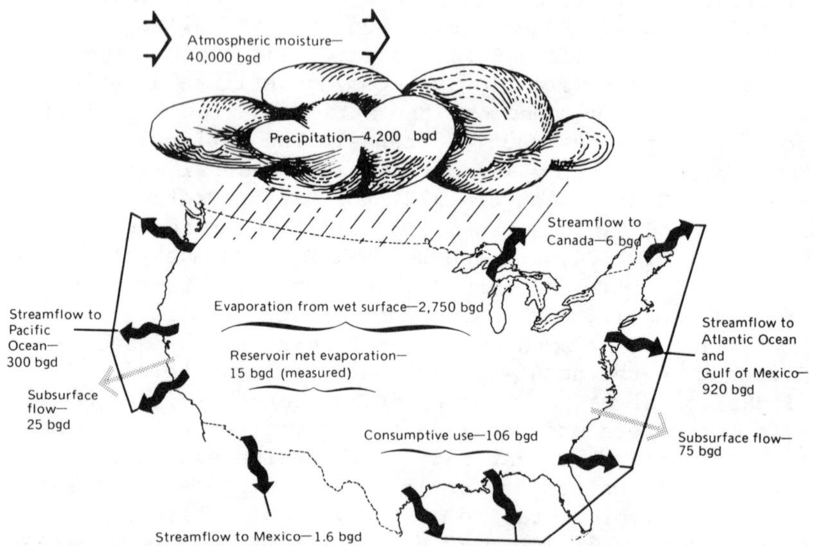

FIGURE 11-2 Water budget for the conterminous United States. SOURCE: U.S. Water Resources Council 1978.

of the United States is included in the drainage basin of the Mississippi River, and roughly 75 percent of the river return flow moves through its extensive river system. The downstream impacts on estuaries will be influenced by all known agricultural practices and potential changes. Much of the anticipated increase in agricultural area will be in the drainage basins of the major and minor river systems east of the Mississippi. Erosion, nutrient, and chemical levels, as well as water quantity, will all be influenced. The degree of upland change will influence the impact of agriculture on estuaries.

The ecological balance of the Chesapeake Bay, for example, is regulated by four major rivers and 50 tributaries. The bay is intensively used for both commercial and sport fishing and for other recreational purposes. Its marshes are havens for a multitude of birds, and oysters from the bay are world-renowned.

San Francisco Bay is influenced by the Sacramento and San Joaquin rivers, which originate in the mountains and fertile valleys of California. Diversions of these two rivers may cause changes in the habitats of the bay by an increase in salinity and a decrease in nutrients. The flow from small rivers in the southern California area passes directly through ocean outfalls to the Pacific Ocean, bypassing estuarine systems.

The deep waters of Puget Sound and the Strait of Juan de Fuca are affected by numerous rivers, including the Skagit, which supplies 60 percent of the fresh water that enters the sound.

Almost all the other estuaries of the United States are affected by the many smaller river systems in coastal areas. Each of these may reflect the agricultural impacts of a more specific type of activity.

The quality of freshwater input to estuarine systems in the United States is regulated by local and upriver wastewater criteria established by the U.S. Environmental Protection Agency (EPA). In general, these criteria have resulted in an improvement of the environmental balance of estuarine systems since 1970. There is a concurrent move toward control of agricultural and urban runoff from nonpoint sources that may further improve estuarine systems. The productivity and aesthetic value of estuarine systems are determined by nutrient availability and the amount of toxic materials entering the systems. If the toxic materials are removed but the nutrients are not, the result may be an increase in wildlife and plant productivity. If nutrients are reduced in eutrophic systems, the result will be an increase in estuarine productivity. Nutrient-limited systems may be affected negatively.

Agricultural activities and changes in the amounts of suspended materials, nutrients, pesticides, and chemicals in coastal waters are related. The fertility of estuaries is related to water runoff from land and the rates of flushing due to tides and currents. Major storms have flushing effects, removing accumulations of sediment, reducing salinity, and often opening passages between estuaries and coastal waters. The management of estuaries must therefore consider a wide range of variables, some man-made and some natural.

GENERAL EFFECTS OF AGRICULTURAL TRENDS

The only approach that can be used is to devise scenarios delineating ranges of causes and effects. It is impossible to provide information on the impacts of all agricultural trends on the wide range of coastal habitats, because the net effect of any trend cannot be estimated by means of a quantitative methodology.

There are some general agricultural trends whose effects are applicable to all coastal habitats (see Chapter 4). There is a general consensus that, because of energy constraints, one of the general changes in agricultural practices will be a reduction of irrigation in the arid western regions of the United States and a trend toward more livestock grazing. This reduction in cropland, coupled with the impact of the estimated 50 percent increase in world population by the year 2000, will lead to an increase in the conversion of forests and rangeland to cropland east of the Mississippi River. Estimates of the land that will be converted range from 16 to 40 million ha. In general, this transformation will take place in areas where water is available and probably in riverine wetlands. The impact on aquatic systems will be an increase in chemicals and nutrients, and changes in amount of runoff.

This will result in a general reduction of agricultural effects on arid western environments and increase the agricultural effects on estuarine systems in the East.

Water Availability and Irrigation

Because of energy constraints, there will be a general trend in western irrigation to shift to the more efficient drip method. This will have the general effect of reducing erosion and the movement of nutrients and chemicals into the watershed.

In the East, on the other hand, there will be an increase in water use, and unless more emphasis is placed on erosion control there will be a general increase in sediment in bodies of water. More nutrients and chemicals will also be used, but these materials may be more efficiently utilized as their costs continue to rise. Whether or not more efficient use of fertilizers and chemicals will lead to reduced amounts of both in natural bodies of water, given greater agricultural production, is hard to predict. No mechanisms are available to determine the total impact of such changes on an entire watershed, such as the Mississippi River or Chesapeake Bay system.

Forest Practices

In general, there will be an emphasis on increasing the harvesting of trees (see Chapter 7). This will require greater use of nutrients, chemicals, and silviculture methods to develop tree species that grow more rapidly. The net effect on the environment will depend on the areas of the country involved, the types of nutrients and chemicals used, and the efficiency of their application.

Nutrients and Chemicals

The amounts of plant nutrients and chemicals used in agriculture will increase because of a need for greater production. The net quantitative effect cannot be anticipated because the current trend is toward developing more specialized chemicals for specific uses, and because greater emphasis will be placed on biodegradability and toxicity control. While the local effects of such chemicals on wildlife may be greater, the increase in biodegradability will reduce downstream effects. Thus the net result of this trend may be a lower overall impact on wildlife in estuaries.

SPECIFIC EFFECTS OF AGRICULTURAL TRENDS

Water Use and Changes in Flow to Coastal Waters

Water use is related to irrigation trends, while changes in runoff depend on soil preparation and management. Figure 11-3a shows the irrigation water budget for the United States and the Caribbean during a normal year, while Figure 11-3b shows the irrigation water budget for the 17 western states during a normal year.

The data indicate that trends in water use and their effects on estuaries may not be as significant in the East because of relatively high rainfall and relatively little irrigation. Some trends indicate that current agricultural lands will not change much, while other trends suggest that the irrigation of arid land in the West will be reduced as more farmland in the East is brought into production.

On the Pacific Coast, because of rapid urban development in southern areas and substantially greater rainfall in the north, water distribution practices may damage wildlife habitats. Urban areas in southern California initially relied on the limited amount of water available locally and on water from the Colorado River. Eventually, however, these resources proved inadequate, and now water is diverted from northern to southern California by means of the California Aqueduct at a rate of 7.5 billion liters per day. This water comes from the San Joaquin-Sacramento river system and would otherwise enter San Francisco Bay, thereby maintaining a habitat typical of the estuarine interface between tidal salt water and fresh river water. The San Joaquin-Sacramento river system provides water to irrigate the fertile Sacramento Valley area, but because of evaporation and the salinity of the river, the soil in the valley is becoming more saline. The San Luis drainage system returns excess ground water of high salinity to San Francisco Bay. Scientists believe that the present diversion of river water to the south and the salty return flow from the drainage system are making the San Francisco estuary more saline, thus changing the environmental balance of the bay.

A ruling of the U.S. Supreme Court providing the state of Arizona with more water from the Colorado River may add to the problems of the San Francisco Bay system. This ruling will reduce the amount of water available for irrigation and urban use in southern California, and steps are being taken to increase the capacity of the

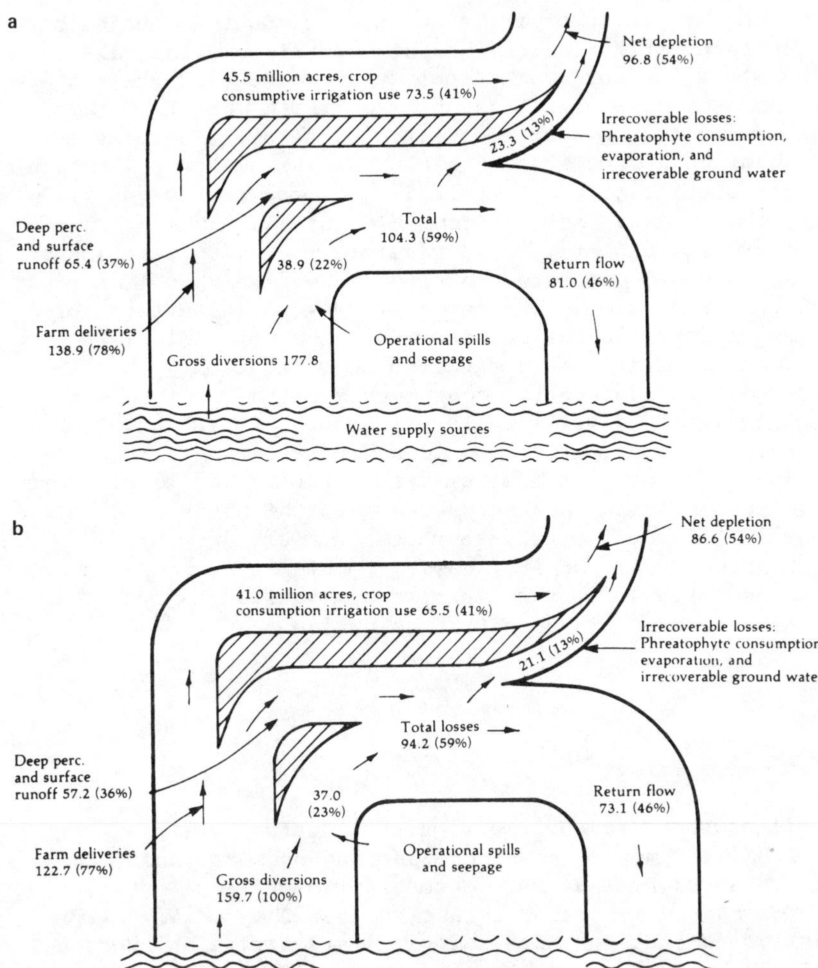

FIGURE 11-3 Irrigation water budget, in millions of acre-feet, at 1975 level of development for (a) the United States and Caribbean, and (b) the 17 western states (Second National Water Assessment). SOURCE: Adapted from U.S. Department of the Interior et al. 1979.

California Aqueduct to make up the difference. The net effect of all this would be to decrease the freshwater inflow and increase the salinity return flow to the bay area, and there is controversy as to how much this will change the estuary.

Some states, such as Texas, have conducted studies on the fresh water requirements of estuaries. Since all of the state's river systems but one originate in the state, methods of controlling the flow of fresh water in Texas estuaries can be designed without interstate agreements.

Dams on rivers also affect estuarine systems, although it is difficult to assess their regional or national impact. Dams retard nutrient flow by causing settling in reservoirs, and they may accelerate the biodegradation of chemicals because water in reservoirs remains standing longer than normal running river water. The effects of dams on agricultural trends, and hence on wildlife habitats, merit future research consideration.

There is substantial controversy on the role of dams in regulating river flow to estuaries. During high rainfall, water may be stored behind a dam and later released to provide a more even rate of river flow. Some scientists think that estuaries need the burst of river water that would otherwise reach them at times of intensive rain. Others, however, think that the more stable estuarine environment resulting from a more constant river flow benefits estuaries.

Water Quality Changes

Suspended Solids

Soil erosion from U.S. agricultural lands averages over 3.7 billion metric tons per year and on some lands may reach as high as 34 metric tons per hectare per year, which has an impact on estuaries (see Chapter 4). It is estimated that the Mississippi River carries an average of 273 million metric tons of suspended solids per year. There is a general trend toward the use of such soil conservation methods as contouring, reduced tillage, and drip irrigation that may reduce the annual loss. Figure 11-4 indicates the areas where erosion or sedimentation are major problems.

If the general trends toward erosion control are realized, it is estimated that the reduction in the amount of soil lost through erosion would offset the amount of erosion caused by an increase in the amount of land used for agriculture, at least in national terms. Regional assessments of the amount of erosion, however, may still show that it exceeds the amount of soil saved through erosion control methods. It should also be noted

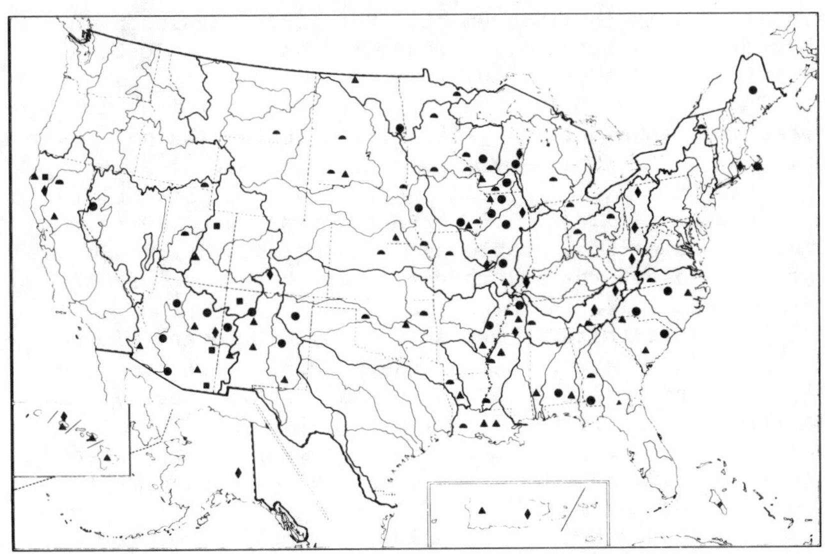

Explanation

Area problem

- Area in which erosion or sedimentation is a significant problem
- Unshaded area may not be problem-free, but the problem was not considered major

Nature of erosion or sedimentation problems

- ● Cropland or rangeland erosion or sedimentation
- ♦ Urbanization, mining, or industrial and highway construction
- ■ Natural erosion of stream channels
- ◓ Shoreline, streambank, or gully erosion
- ▲ Sedimentation of farm ponds, lakes, water supply, and flood-control channels

Boundaries

- ▬ Water resources region
- — Subregion

FIGURE 11-4 Erosion and sedimentation problems.
SOURCE: U.S. Water Resources Council 1978.

that a reduction in the amount of soil sediment reaching estuaries may in some areas reduce nutrient loading and therefore diminish estuary productivity.

Nutrient Runoff

The high cost of fertilizers will require the use of more efficient application methods. This will reduce the runoff of nutrients. If such an effect occurs in estuaries that have become eutrophic, reduced runoff should result in improvement. But if it occurs in an estuary where nutrients are limited, there would be a decrease in productivity.

The total amount of nitrogen in runoff from an average area (Vollenweider 1968) is 16.6 to 28.1 kg/ha per year. Of this, 2.3 to 5.8 kg/ha per year, or 13.8 to 20.6 percent, comes from arable land. The total amount of phosphorus is 1.7 to 2.5 kg/ha per year, and 5.9 to 20 percent comes from arable land. Nutrient enrichment produces a substantial reduction in the amount of dissolved oxygen in the water.

About one third to one half of U.S. food and fiber production is attributed to the use of fertilizers (Hobbie and Copeland 1977). Fertilizer is heavily applied to cultivated crops, particularly in the coastal plains of the southeastern and Gulf states, and these areas contain some of the most extensive estuaries in the country (McHugh 1976).

The residents (particularly suburbanites) of large metropolitan areas adjacent to coastal waters also use large quantities of fertilizers (Hobbie and Copeland 1977). Per hectare, the amount of fertilizer used often is much greater than on agricultural land. Usually these materials are recycled through municipal sewage treatment plants, but during heavy rains some, if not all, of these wastes bypass the treatment plants and go directly to estuaries.

The principal effect of fertilizer runoff from agricultural fields into estuarine habitats is eutrophication--i.e., increased amounts of algae, increased biological oxygen demand (BOD), instability in dissolved oxygen levels, and periodic fish kills. These impacts have been thoroughly documented for both freshwater and saline waters (Likens 1972). In coastal Louisiana the impacts are exacerbated by the drainage canal network, which discharges nutrients directly into coastal lakes.

Pesticides and Herbicides and Other Toxic Substances

Runoff is probably the single most significant cause of pesticide and herbicide contamination of surface water flowing into estuaries. A pesticide may be adsorbed on eroding soil particles or suspended in runoff water, or both. Chlorinated hydrocarbons, because they are persistent and have low solubility in water, are usually transported on soil particles. Organic phosphates are usually more soluble than chlorinated hydrocarbons. Herbicides, particularly the inorganic type, are highly soluble in water. The greatest dangers from the runoff of soluble pesticides exist in the period immediately following application, prior to their becoming adsorbed onto soil particles. To some degree these dangers are under control in major agricultural areas because weather conditions are closely observed to determine when pesticides are best applied (Li 1977a,b). However, rain does not always fall when predicted.

Pesticides, especially the more persistent and toxic ones, are more dangerous than plant nutrients to anadromous fish species. In the 10-year period of 1963 to 1972, agricultural pollution of all kinds accounted for 7.8 percent of all fish kills; agricultural pesticides accounted for almost two thirds of the kill caused by agricultural pollution. Manure and silage drainage killed about one third. Fertilizer runoff accounted for only a minute portion of all fish kills (Li 1977a,b). It can be assumed that when anadromous species were present (and that includes a good part of the year), they were predominant in these kills.

Shellfish are particularly vulnerable to toxins because they cannot migrate to escape pesticides, and closing their shells is a limited protective device. Shellfish can survive brief encounters with toxins, but they cannot survive continued exposure above certain levels. Moreover, their bodies can accumulate quantities of some toxic substances far in excess of the average amounts in the natural environment. Analysis of 8095 samples of _Crassostea virgineca_, _C. gigas_, and _Merceneria merceneria_ for 15 organochlorine compounds showed that DDT residues were ubiquitous (Butler 1973). The maximum DDT residue detected was 5.39 ppm. Dieldrin was the second most commonly detected compound, with a maximum residue of 0.23 ppm. Endrin, Mirex, and polychlorinated biphenyls were found only occasionally. A clear downward trend in DDT residues in mollusks began in 1969. At no time were the residues of such magnitude as to cause harm to mollusks, but they were large enough to pose a threat to other elements of the biota through recycling and magnification (Butler 1973).

The effects of pesticide on wildlife in the United States are difficult to determine. Knowledge of urban and agricultural runoff is accumulating through studies of waste loads to estuaries. In many areas, chemicals from urban industry may have more significant effects on the environment than chemicals carried into bodies of water by agricultural runoff. There is a trend in agriculture toward the use of chemicals with greater degradability and toward more specific application. If this trend continues, one could expect the harmful effects of chemicals on estuaries to decrease.

Other effects of agriculture on the quality of water in estuaries may include the accumulation of heavy metals used for trace nutrients, drainage of river bottomlands, changing storage capacity, and runoff of litter from the forest floor.

Ongoing research may indicate the actual effects of chemicals on the food chain. Louisiana is an excellent example area since it has a major portion of the forested wetland habitats in the United States. The Mississippi River alluvial flood plain, including the Atchafalaya Basin, was and still is the largest contiguous wetland area in the United States. This habitat is undergoing rapid change (Turner and Craig 1981). Plummer (1979) lists some 53 pesticides used in Louisiana agriculture. These include three major classes of pesticides, each having distinctive effects on the environment. Organochlorines, for example, are still being used in cotton, rice, and soybean agriculture in Louisiana. Organophosphate compounds are less persistent than organochlorines, degrading within a few months, and they do not accumulate in the tissues of organisms that consume them. They are, however, highly toxic to mammals and invertebrates. Carbonates are similar in structure to organophospates, but vary in toxicity to mammals.

Fungicides being used include a broad range of compounds, both organic and inorganic. Examples are fixed copper, sulfur, Bordeaux, and Benomyl.

A large number of organic herbicides, such as dinitroanaline, dinitrophenol, chlorophenoxy-substituted urea, Triazine, organic arsenicals, and Paraquat, are also in current use.

Corn, cotton, soybeans, rice, sugarcane, and sweet potatoes are the major agricultural products of the Mississippi River alluvial flood plain. To protect over 5.7 million ha, pesticides were used on the three major crops of the Southeast (soybeans, cotton, and rice) at an average rate of 1 kg/ha per year. This figure excludes 0.9 million kg of defoliants, 2.4 million kg of soil fumigants, and unknown quantities of fungicides (Schmitt and Winger 1980).

Methyl parathion and EPN, both organophosphates, accounted for over one half of the total insecticide use in the region. Toxaphene, an organochlorine, accounted for one third.

The effects of these chemicals on the environment are determined by a number of factors, including climate, soil type, hydrology, method of application, amount used, and time of year. An important factor is the inherent longevity of the compound itself. This characteristic is moderated by such external conditions as pH, amount of rainfall, temperature changes, and biodegradation.

Agricultural chemicals are transferred into the wetlands of Louisiana by wind movements (especially chemicals sprayed by aircraft) by being dissolved in water runoff, and by being incorporated in detritus carried by water. Most of the pesticides that reach aquatic ecosystems, though, are those adsorbed on eroded soil (Bailey et al. 1974, Woolhiser 1976).

An EPA study of pesticides and polychlorinated biphenyls in the Atchafalaya Basin of Louisiana (Hern et al. 1979) reported no trace of organophosphorus pesticides in the basin's water or sediments. Nor were the persistent organochlorines, such as benzene-hexachloride, Captan, Dachtal, Endosulfan, Endrin, or Toxaphene, detected. But DDT, banned in 1972, was detected in 78 samples of bottom sediments, and samples taken near agricultural areas showed concentrations as high as 150 parts per billion (ppb).

Pesticides at low or undetectable concentrations in aquatic systems can result in extremely high levels in animals. Aldrin and Dieldrin were not detected by the Atchafalaya Basin study in any water sample and were found in only one sediment sample, but two thirds of the fish sampled contained one or both pesticides. Water samples showed a maximum Toxaphene concentration of 0.01 ppm, while fish tissues contained over 100 ppm of Toxaphene, a 10,000-fold concentration. Thus although Endrin, Dieldrin, and Chlordane were banned from agricultural use in 1975, significant levels continued to be found in the wildlife of the basin.

Applications of as little as 0.02 to 0.06 kg/ha of DDT have caused declines in populations of shrimp, amphipods, crayfish, isopods, annelids, fish, fiddler crabs, and blue crabs in aquatic systems (Woodwell et al. 1967). These declines are often caused by spectacular die-offs, which disrupt food chains and ecosystems. Inspection of several species of fish that suffered mass mortality in the early 1960s in south Louisiana showed lethal concentrations of the pesticide Endrin in their tissues (Blus et al. 1979). Herbicides such as Triazine have been shown to act at the base of the food chain by destroying macrophytes, filamentous algae, and several species of invertebrates (Scorgie and Cooke 1979). The ramifications of producer and herbivore destruction extend to all trophic levels of the ecosystem.

Pesticides may reduce wildlife populations by interfering with their reproductive processes as well. There is evidence implicating DDT and Endrin in the decline of the Louisiana population of brown pelicans in the mid-1970s. Organochlorines may be linked to the thinning of eggshells and reproductive failure (Blus et al. 1979).

An increasingly urgent problem is the rapid increase in pest populations resistant to control by existing pesticides. Lethal compounds applied to pests are agents of selection. The more lethal the agent and the more frequently the population is exposed, the more rapid is the development of resistant strains of pests. Newsom (1972) reports that the development period can be as short as 4 years, and that in some cases (for example, the rice water weevil and the soybean looper), no known insecticide will effectively control the insect. The adoption of IPM and resulting decreased use of pesticides may slow down the selection process and, although not "eliminating" the pest in the short term, extend the effective life of the pesticide.

Coastal Land or Estuarine Use Modification

Conversion of Habitats to Agricultural Use

A comparison of the net rate of wetland conversion for different areas is shown in Table 11-3. From 1849 to 1934 the loss rate was estimated at about 0.10 percent annually, assuming that 3 million of the original 4.6 million ha had already been reclaimed by 1849. For 1964 to 1974, the rate was 1.3 percent per year for Louisiana as a whole. In comparison, the annual conversion rate for coastal swamps and marshes in Louisiana was 0.4 percent per year and 0.5 percent for all U.S. coastal wetlands. It was 2.1 percent per year for the Mississippi River alluvial flood plain, where most of Louisiana's forested wetlands are located (Turner and Craig 1981).

TABLE 11-3 Wetland Loss Rates for in Louisiana Compared with Those for the United States

	Percent Remaining Lost Annually (interval)
Mississippi River Alluvial Floodplain (MRAF)	2.1 (1967-1977)
Louisiana forested wetland	
State total	1.3 (1964-1974)
MRAF only	1.96 (1964-1974)
Coastal wetlands of the United States	0.5 (1954-1974)
Louisiana coastal swamps and marshes	0.4 (1954-1974)

SOURCE: Turner and Craig 1981.

Conversion of River Basins Bottomland hardwoods are dominant tree species that grow on soils that are moisture-saturated or inundated during part of the year. They include oak-gum-cypress and elm-ash-cottonwood as the dominant timber associations. Cottonwood, willow, ash, elm, hackberry, maple, beech, sycamore, and sugarberry are considered minor species. Surveys by the Forest Service provide a basis for determining the present status and recent changes in the extent of bottomland hardwoods in the southeastern United States. From the 1960s to the 1970s, the annual net loss of forested bottomlands in the 12 southeastern states was about 170,000 ha. From the 1950s to the 1970s the loss rates in each state generally approached 1 percent per year. A major decline in forested bottomland acreage occurred in Arkansas, Georgia, Louisiana, Mississippi, Missouri, North Carolina, and Virginia (Turner et al. 1981).

The reason for the changes was that farmers anticipated economic gains from the conversion of these bottomlands to crop production. Land drainage, financed primarily by the federal government, stimulated further land clearing (Turner et al. 1981).

In Louisiana, as well as in the rest of the flood plain, flood control, bank stabilization, and agricultural drainage projects have resulted in the conversion of about 7.3 million of the original 9.3 million ha of forested wetlands to other uses (Gill 1973, Bragg and

Tatschi 1977). Most of this land has been transformed into farmland, primarily for soybean and cotton cultivation (Sternitzke 1976, MacDonald et al. 1979). The net economic return per hectare is reported to be 2 times higher for farmland than for forest (MacDonald et al. 1979). However, crayfish farms in combination with forested wetlands may be economically competitive with farmland (Gary 1974).

Of the original 4.5 million ha of forested wetlands in Louisiana, about 49 percent remain. Most of the habitat losses in Louisiana have been within the Mississippi and Atchafalaya river drainage basins. The majority of these losses have occurred in order to increase agricultural production and are clearly permanent (Turner and Craig 1981).

Louisiana is now losing about 36,000 ha of forested wetlands annually, or 1.3 percent of the remaining area. MacDonald et al. (1979) have shown that this rate of change increases in dry years, when bottomlands can be cleared of trees more easily. The most recent rates of net loss are higher than ever. If continued, one half of the remaining area will be lost by the year 2005. Since the last Forest Service survey in 1974, about 10 percent of the remaining forested wetlands has been converted to some other ecosystem, primarily agriculture. There is every indication that a dramatic policy change is necessary to reverse this long-term trend (Turner and Craig 1981).

The impacts of bottomland clearing have been documented in several recent reports. Among these impacts are the following:

1. Deterioration of water quality because of increased erosion from the cleared flood plain (Livingston 1978) and because the forest no longer exists to serve as a kind of filter, removing nutrients, sediments, and agricultural toxins from flood waters and from runoff across the flood plain (Kemp 1978, Mitsch et al. 1979).

2. Stream flow instability because the riparian forest acts as a reservoir during floods, releasing water slowly as the stream returns to normal levels. Gosselink et al. (1981a) estimate that the forests of the Mississippi River alluvial flood plain historically had the capacity to store a volume of water equivalent to 60 days of discharge of the Mississippi River. Because of channeling and levees, this has been reduced to about 12 days of flow. This change is important to downstream

areas. It means river stages are higher for a given discharge rate during floods and lower during low-water periods (Littlejohn 1977).

3. Reductions in the movement of organic materials, which are potential food for downstream aquatic organisms (Mulholland and Kuenzler 1979).

4. Loss of habitats for birds, mammals, and for spawning fish (Gosselink et al. 1981b).

Conversion of Coastal Wetlands Projects to reclaim marshlands for agricultural purposes in Louisiana reached a peak between 1915 and 1920. The majority of these did not last because of poor drainage, deterioration of levees, seepage, and the shrinkage and oxidation of organic soils. The marshes of the Louisiana coastal zone have numerous rectangular lakes documenting these failures (Gagliano 1973). Conversion of wetlands to agricultural land still occurs, however. In Barataria Basin, Louisiana, approximately 8000 ha of marshland was recently converted to agricultural land (Adams et al. 1976).

Wetlands in Florida have also decreased in extent dramatically in this century, due to conversion to agricultural land. In general, the effect has been decreased fisheries and fewer habitat areas for waterfowl. In the upper St. John's River basin, waterfowl populations have declined so substantially that the Florida Fish and Game Commission no longer bothers to count the remaining birds. Fish populations were measured twice a year during the early 1970s in isolated marshes and in marshes close to large pastures. Fish in unaltered areas amounted to about 220 kg/ha, but there were only 5 to 10 kg of fish per hectare in marshes adjacent to improved pasture (Florida Fish and Game Commission 1972).

In the Chenier Plain of Louisiana, agricultural activities take place in areas that were formerly wetland, ridge, or upland forest. Over 80 percent (7000 ha) of the increase in agricultural area since 1952 has resulted from draining natural and impounded wetlands. Most of the land currently in agriculture was being farmed many years before 1952. These farms were originally established on the prairies of the Chenier Plain, then on cleared upland forests, and finally on drained wetlands. At the same time, agricultural land has been taken over for urban uses. Between 1952 and 1974 there were no changes in this pattern; that is, no agricultural land reverted to natural wetlands or uplands (Gosselink et al. 1979).

The impacts of wetland conversion to other purposes are well documented. Major effects are as follows:

1. Direct loss of wetland habitats for fish and wildlife. Both nutria and muskrats are commercially harvested in Louisiana. Although fur harvests are historically variable, there has been a fairly sharp and persisting decline in harvests of nutria and muskrats since about 1972 in Louisiana, which is the major domestic fur-producing state (Gosselink et al. 1979). The reasons for the decline are difficult to identify with certainty, but one is the disruption of habitat. Virtually all commercial fish species on the Gulf Coast are dependent on marshes as nursery grounds. Turner (1977) has shown a direct relationship between marsh nursery area and shrimp yields worldwide. Fresh marshes appear to be just as important as salt marshes to this relationship.
2. Reductions in the movement of nutrients between wetlands and estuaries. Marshes send large amounts of organic matter to adjacent estuaries. This organic matter is believed to be important in estuarine food chains. Marshes also buffer the flow of nutrients between uplands and estuaries and act as a sink for nitrogen and sulfur (Gosselink et al. 1974).
3. Changes in drainage patterns and flooding because of the network of artificial canals necessary to farm wetlands. The extensive network of agricultural canals has been documented by Gael and Hopkinson (1979), Bedient (1975), Gosselink et al. (1979), and others. Their impacts are discussed below under channelization.

In addition to these impacts, the conversion of wetlands to rice fields in southwest Louisiana and eastern Texas has caused changes in waterfowl habitats. Before the 1970s, snow geese wintering in Louisiana and Texas were found mainly in coastal marshes. As rice cultivation subsequently increased, large numbers of birds that had wintered in eastern Louisiana shifted to rice fields in the western and northern parts of the state (Bellrose 1976). In general, it is thought that the loss of marshlands as wildlife habitats has been partially offset by the development of rice cultivation (Dillon 1957). Reservoirs used to provide water for rice fields provide habitats for wintering waterfowl, such as birds displaced by the clearing of bottomland hardwoods (Linduska 1964). Waste rice left after harvesting is an important food source (Dillon 1957), especially in wet years when the growth of marsh grasses and sedges declines (McGinn 1963). Fulvous whistling ducks nearly always rest in rice fields in Louisiana (Linduska 1964). Many geese now winter exclusively in rice fields, cattle pastures, and other agricultural lands (Lynch and Shingleton 1967). This is a positive development in that the loss of certain habitats has been succeeded by the creation of others that offer a dependable source of food. But it is negative in that it encourages large concentrations of birds, resulting in crop damage and eventually in attempts to control the birds, which come to be considered pests.

Channelization

Channelization has been widely used in coastal Louisiana to aid in the drainage of agricultural fields. Channelization refers to two types of activities. The first is the dredging of new canals, and the second is the deepening and straightening of natural streams. In both cases, deep and hydrologically efficient water courses are formed. In addition, dredged spoil is placed alongside the channel. This spoil material forms a continuous barrier that impedes the movement of water between the waterway and adjacent wetlands. Thus channelization in coastal Louisiana has had two general consequences. The channels have speeded the flow of upland runoff to coastal bodies of water, and the exchange of water between wetlands and water bodies has been reduced. In earlier times, most upland runoff flowed through wetlands before reaching estuaries.

The impacts of channelization are becoming increasingly well understood and include the following:

1. Along with the clearing of forests, channelization has increased the volume of runoff. For example, it is estimated that runoff from the uplands surrounding the upper Barataria Basin will increase by 4.2 times between 1975 and 1995. Nutrient runoff will increase by 28 percent for nitrogen and 16 percent for phosphorus (Hopkinson and Day 1980). A similar finding of increased runoff has been shown for the Lake Pontchartrain Basin by Turner and Bond (1982).

2. Upland runoff through channels leads to an increase in nutrients in estuaries downstream. This has caused widespread eutrophication in estuarine bodies in Louisiana (Craig and Day 1977, Seaton and Day 1979). Gael and Hopkinson (1979) showed that eutrophic conditions in the Barataria Basin were related to channel density.

3. The directing of upland runoff into canals and the reduction of water exchanges because of spoil banks have reduced the possibility that upland runoff will be affected by overland flow. Studies have shown that significant amounts of suspended particulate matter, nitrogen, and phosphorus are removed if upland runoff flows through wetlands (Kemp 1978, Hopkinson and Day 1980). This overland flow can also lead to increased wetland productivity (Conner et al. 1981).

4. The decrease in water exchange caused by spoil banks can also lead to decreased wetland productivity. Conner and Day (1976) have shown that swamp productivity in the southeastern United States is related to water exchange. Conner et al. (1981) reported that the productivity rate in a semi-impounded swamp in the Barataria Basin was 50 percent lower than the rate of productivity in an adjacent swamp. The water exchange was substantial.

5. Channelization can affect the size of furbearer populations. Gray and Arner (1977) found that furbearer populations were significantly lower in channelized sections of the Louxapalila River in Mississippi and Alabama than in an unchannelized section. This was true even in a section channelized 55 years before the study.

6. Spoil banks reduce the movement of nutrients and sediments into wetlands and allow more rapid saltwater intrusion (Craig et al. 1979).

7. Spoil banks make wetlands less able to absorb flood waters. A study by Hopkinson and Day (1980) indicated that an unchannelized swamp can carry a greater flood discharge at lower stages than one with channelization. Because the spoil on stream banks confines water to the channel, water from the stream cannot flow over wetlands.

8. Streams draining wetland watersheds export more organic carbon than those draining upland watersheds. When a wetland drainage stream is channelized, it takes on the characteristics of an upland draining stream (Mulholland and Kuenzler 1979).

Grazing

Cattle grazing is a well-established practice on wetlands. The rapid plant growth and large area make these areas attractive for year-round grazing. The one important criterion for grazing cattle on marshland is the ability of these soft soils to support the weight of the cattle. Chabreck's (1964) study of cattle grazing preferences on different marsh elevations showed that cattle spent half of their time on "high" marsh (firm, well-drained soil with sparse vegetation) and half on "intermediate" and "low" marshes (soft moist soils, open bodies of water). Documented grazing impacts are as follows:

1. Grazing changes the vegetation of the natural area. It sets back plant succession in much the same way as cultivation and burning. When cattle crop the tall rough vegetation, they create openings for the growth of annual grasses.
2. Grazed areas are characterized by short sparse vegetation, usually composed of minor species. The trampling of the soft soils by cattle often has as much effect as actual grazing in bringing about this change. Indeed, the process of revegetation takes longer after compaction caused by trampling and flooding (Chabreck 1964).
3. The removal of plants with high forage value by cattle means that wildlife are left with the nonpalatable types of vegetation.
4. Light or moderate grazing encourages the growth of certain plants that provide valuable food for wildlife (Chabreck 1964, Neely 1967). Opening areas for annual grasses and removing competitive species create seed stock and food materials for waterfowl and furbearers.

Aquaculture

It is doubtful that upland aquaculture will have any effect on estuarine habitats. Aquaculture should result in little loss of water, and return flow will be absorbed through normal downstream processes.

Aquaculture will be delayed until the industry is integrated with regulatory restrictions. At present, land costs are excessive for efficient economic gain and wetlands are protected by strict federal permitting requirements. The viable increase in aquaculture may be somewhat restricted to areas devoted to cooling water or ponding for water treatment purposes. This land is dedicated to water use, and the cost of levy development is already spent. Modifications may be within economic justification.

Aquaculture technology is rapidly gaining momentum. In the Northwest, salmon and trout cultivation is becoming economically advantageous. In the South and Southeast, oyster culture has been economically viable for many years in leased bottom waters traditionally dedicated to this purpose. Crayfish can be cultivated in rice fields with little or no effect on estuarine habitats. Crayfish culture in wetlands where diking is required, however, would be environmentally damaging. Shrimp culture is a viable technique that provides good yields, in warm estuarine areas, providing that dedicated waters are available at reasonable cost.

Oyster culture has been practiced for more than a century (Van Sickle et al. 1976, Hofstetter 1977). The harmful effects of oyster bottom culture as practiced on the Gulf Coast are minimal (Herke 1976), and the positive effects are significant. Oyster cultivation involves supplying culch, which provides a substrate where naturally produced larvae can set and mature. At oyster maturity, the beds are harvested by dredging. Oysters are produced using similar techniques in estuaries of the Northeast and Northwest wherever adequate water environments are available.

Unlike oyster culture, the cultivation of crayfish and catfish constitutes a potential threat to wetlands. Although catfish can become acclimated to brackish water (Allen and Avault 1970), the soil required for pond construction (Davis and Hughes 1977) generally means that catfish are not farmed in coastal areas. Where they are, however, pond effluents drain into coastal waters. These effluents are sources of pollution (Hinshaw 1973) because of wastes from fish feed (Mac et al. 1979), disease-management-related compounds (Schnick and Meyer 1979, Table 1), and eutrophication of pond waters (Hinshaw 1973). For instance, Finucane (1969) reported the toxic effects of Antimycin on marine habitats. Effluents from catfish farms are of such great concern that legislation has been introduced (Williams et al. 1977).

The impact of crayfish farming on wetlands depends on whether the crayfish are grown in naturally vegetated ponds, as in rice culture, or in swamp forest (Gary 1974). The construction of naturally vegetated ponds usually involves the conversion of swamp or freshwater marshes. The devegetated ponds, separated hydrologically from surrounding wetlands, no longer exchange nutrients, store excess storm waters, or provide habitats for native biota.

Wetland forests managed as crayfish farms are subjected to modified flooding that mimics the seasonal flooding of riparian wetlands. These forests change composition toward typical bottomland hardwood sites (Conner et al. 1981), and normal wetland functions are modified (Gosselink et al. 1981a,b). Paille (1980) showed how crayfish production and predation change under these circumstances.

Cultivating crayfish with rice presents few problems to estuarine habitats, other than those inherent in rice culture itself. In fact, the need to modify the use of pesticides on rice to avoid poisoning the crayfish probably leads to a better environment. The problem of pesticide use in rice-crayfish operations is discussed by Hyde et al. (1972), Cheah et al. (1980), and Jolly et al. (1976).

Local Runoff from Agricultural Land

Very little information is available on the direct effects of local agricultural runoff on estuarine habitats. In some arid areas there may be increased salinity due to the leaching of soils during runoff. In dense crop areas, pesticides and herbicides may affect habitats. Silting, filling, and delta formation from channelized runoff may reduce estuarine areas or change their general biological balance. Changes in forest management may reduce litter and thus the movement of organic matter into the estuaries. There are insufficient data to analyze these impacts, however.

RESEARCH NEEDS

- Inorganic and organic loads on estuaries must be monitored. Continued research to determine the effects of agricultural trends on the country's estuaries should be supported. All estuaries are important. Therefore what goes into them should be known and analyzed.
- Aquatic and estuarine resources for aquaculture should be evaluated. As fishing pressures from sport and

commercial interests increase, fish resources will decline. This decline could be offset by a gradual transition to intensive aquaculture. This transition will require a reevaluation of aquatic and estuarine resources and will invoke a change from established tradition. This will be a serious problem that may affect the natural habitat, if not now, in the near future.

• Research on the correct balance between the use of pesticides and herbicides and their harmful effects is needed to permit the use of these materials for agricultural production at levels compatible with the environment of estuaries.

• Any regulation of upland agricultural practices should be based on knowledge of agriculture's effects on water quantity and quality in estuaries downstream.

• Analysis of ecosystems should be undertaken to determine where agricultural trends can be related to water quantity and quality, changes during flow, storage in lakes and dams, and river discharge into estuaries. River systems and the combined agricultural activities in their drainage areas are too complicated to evaluate, however. Therefore data on river discharge to estuaries are necessary to understand and predict effects from upland agricultural trends.

LITERATURE CITED

Adams, R.D., B.B. Barrett, J.H. Blackmon, B.W. Gane, and W.G. McIntire. 1976. Barataria Basin: geologic processes and framework. Sea Grant Publ. No. LSU-T-76-006. LSU Center for Wetland Resources, Baton Rouge, La.

Allen, K.O., and J.W. Avault, Jr. 1970. Effects of salinity on growth and survival of channel catfish, *Ictalurus punctatus*. Proc. Annu. Conf. Southeastern Assoc. Game Fish Comm. 23:319-331.

Bailey, G.W., R.R. Swank, Jr., and H.P. Nicholson. 1974. Predicting pesticide runoff from agricultural land: a conceptual model. J. Environ. Qual. 3(2):95-102.

Bedient, P.B. 1975. Hydrologic land use interactions in a Florida river basin. Ph.D. dissertation, Department of Environmental Engineering Science, University of Florida. 261 pp.

Bellrose, F.C. 1976. Ducks, geese and swans of North America. Stackpole Books, Harrisburg, Pa. 544 pp.

Blus, L., E. Cromartie, L. McNease, and T. Joanen. 1979. Brown pelican: population status, reproductive success and organochlorine residues in Louisiana, 1971-1976. Bull. Environ. Contam. Toxicol. 22:126-135.

Bragg, T.B., and A.K. Tatschi. 1977. Changes in flood plain vegetation and land use along the Mississippi River from 1826 to 1976. Environ. Manage. 1:1-343.

Brokaw, H.P., ed. 1978. Wildlife and America: contributions to an understanding of American wildlife and its conservation. Council on Environmental Quality, Washington, D.C. 532 pp.

Butler, P.A. 1973. Organochloride residues in estuarine mollusks, 1967-72--National Pesticide Monitoring Program. Pt. I. General summary and conclusions. Pt. II. Residue data--individual states. Pestic. Monit. J. 6(4):238-315.

Chabreck, R.H. 1964. The relation of cattle and cattle grazing to marsh wildlife and plants in Louisiana. Proc. 18th Annu. Conf. Southeastern Assoc. Game Fish Comm.

Cheah, J.L., J.W. Avault, Jr., and J.B. Graves. 1980. Acute toxicity of selected rice pesticides to crayfish Procambarus clarkii. Prog. Fish Cult. 42(3):169-171.

Conner, W.H., and J.W. Day, Jr. 1976. Productivity and composition of a bald cypress-water tupelo site and a bottomland hardwood site in a Louisiana swamp. Am. J. Bot. 63(10):1354-1364.

Conner, W.H., J.G. Gosselink, and R.T. Parrondo. 1981. Comparison of the vegetation of three Louisiana swamp sites with different flooding regimes. Am. J. Bot. 68(3):320-331.

Craig, N.J., and J.W. Day, Jr. 1977. Cumulative impact studies in the Louisiana coastal zone: eutrophication, land loss. Final report to Louisiana State Planning Office. Center for Wetland Resources, Louisiana State University. 58 pp.

Craig, N.J., R.E. Turner, and J.W. Day, Jr. 1979. Land loss in Louisiana. Pages 227-254 in J.W. Day, Jr., D.D. Culley, Jr., R.E. Turner, A.J. Mumphrey, Jr., eds. Proceedings of the third coastal marsh and estuary management symposium. Louisiana State University, Division of Continuing Education, Baton Rouge.

Davis, J.T., and J.S. Hughes. 1977. Channel catfish farming in Louisiana. Louisiana Wildlife and Fisheries Commission. 47 pp.

Deems, E.F., Jr., and D. Pursley. 1978. North American furbearers, their management, research, and harvest status in 1976. International Association of Fish and Wildlife Agencies, College Park, Md. 171 pp.

Dillon, A.W., Jr. 1957. Food habits of wild ducks in the rice-marsh transition area of Louisiana. Proc. Annu. Conf. Southeastern Assoc. Game Fish Comm. 11:114-119.

Finucane, J.H. 1969. Antimycin as a toxicant in a marine habitat. Trans. Am. Fish. Soc. 98(2):228-292.

Florida Fish and Game Commission. 1972. Upper St. Johns River Basin reports to Florida Fish and Game Commission, 1971, 1972.

Gael, B.T., and C.S. Hopkinson. 1979. Drainage density, land use and eutrophication in Barataria Basin, Louisiana. Pages 147-163 in J.W. Day, Jr., D.D. Culley, Jr., R.E. Turner, and A.J. Mumphrey, Jr., eds., Proceedings of the third coastal marsh and estuary management symposium. Louisiana State University, Division of Continuing Education, Baton Rouge.

Gagliano, S.M. 1973. Canals, dredging, and land reclamation in Louisiana. Publ. No. LSU-SG-74-01. Louisiana State University Center for Wetland Resources. 59 pp.

Gary, D.L. 1974. The commercial crawfish industry in south Louisiana. Publ. No. LSU-SG-74-03. Louisiana State University Center for Wetland Resources. 59 pp.

Gill, D. 1973. Modification of northern alluvial habitats by river development. Can. Geogr. 17:138-153.

Gosselink, J.G., E.P. Odum, and R.M. Pope. 1974. The value of the tidal marsh. Sea Grant Publ. No. LSU-SG-74-03. Louisiana State University Center for Wetland Resources, Baton Rouge.

Gosselink, J.G., C.L. Cordes, and J.W. Parsons. 1979. An ecological characterization study of the Chenier Plain coastal ecosystem of Louisiana and Texas. U.S. Fish and Wildlife Service, Office of Biological Services. (Available from National Coastal Ecosystems Team, Slidell, La.)

Gosselink, J.G., W.H. Conner, J.W. Day, Jr., and R.E. Turner. 1981a. Classification of wetland resources: land, timber and ecology. Proc. 30th Annu. For. Symp., LSU. (In press.)

Gosselink, J.G., S.E. Bayley, W.H. Conner, and R.E. Turner. 1981b. Ecological factors in the determination of riparian wetland boundaries. Elsevier, New York. (In press.)

Gray, M.H., and D.H. Arner. 1977. A study of the effects of channelization on furbearers and furbearer habitat. Presented at 31st Annual Conference of Southeastern Association of Game and Fish Commissions, San Antonio, Tex. Oct. 9-12, 1977.

Herke, W.H. 1976. Biologist sees mariculture of motile species as possible threat to natural fisheries. Fisheries 1(6):11-14.

Hern, S.C., V.W. Lamboer, and H. Jai. 1979. Pesticides and polychlorinated biphenyls in the Atchafalaya Basin, Louisiana. EPA-600/4-79-061. U.S. Environmental Protection Agency, Las Vegas, Nev.

Hinshaw, R.N. 1973. Pollution as a result of fish cultural activities. EPA-R3-73-009. U.S. Environmental Protection Agency, Office of Research and Monitoring, Washington, D.C. 209 pp.

Hobbie, J.E., and B.J. Copeland. 1977. Effects and control of nutrients in estuarine ecosystems. Pages 257-274 _in_ Estuarine pollution control and assessment: proceedings of a conference. Vol. I. U.S. Environmental Protection Agency, Office of Water Planning and Standards, Washington, D.C.

Hofstetter, R.P. 1977. Trends in population levels of the American Oyster (_Crassostea virgineca_) on public reefs in Galveston Bay, Tex. Tex. Parks Wildl. Dep. Tech. Ser. No. 24. 90 pp.

Hopkinson, C.S., and J.W. Day, Jr. 1980. Modeling the relationship between development and storm water and nutrient runoff. Environ. Manage. 4(4):315-324.

Hyde, K.M., J.B. Graves, P.E. Schilling, and F.L. Bonner. 1972. The influence of Mirex bait on production and survival of Louisiana red crawfish, _Procambarus clarkii_ (Girard). Proc. 26th Annu. Conf. Southeastern Assoc. Game Fish Comm. 26:473-483.

Jolly, A.L., J.W. Avault, Jr., J.B. Graves, and K.L. Koonce. 1976. Effects of Matadan on mostly hatched and juvenile Louisiana red swamp crawfish, _Procambarus clarkii_. _In_ Proc. 3rd Int. Crayfish Symp. 3:389-395.

Kemp, G.P. 1978. Agricultural runoff and nutrient dynamics of a swamp forest in Louisiana. M.S. thesis, Louisiana State University, Baton Rouge. 57 pp.

Li, M. 1977a. Pollution in nation's estuaries originating from the agricultural uses of pesticides. _In_ Estuarine pollution control and assessment: proceedings of a conference, Vol. I. U.S. Environmental Protection Agency, Office of Water Planning and Standards, Washington, D.C.

Li, M. 1977b. Pollution in nation's estuaries originating from the agricultural uses of pesticides. Pages 451-466 in Estuarine pollution control and assessment: proceedings of a conference. Vol. II. U.S. Environmental Protection Agency, Office of Water Planning and Standards, Washington, D.C.

Likens, G.E. 1972. Nutrients and eutrophication: the limiting-nutrient controversy. American Society of Limnology and Oceanography, Special Symposium. Vol. I. Allen Press. 328 pp.

Linduska, J.P. 1964. Beyond national boundaries. In Waterfowl tomorrow. U.S. Department of the Interior, Bureau of Sport Fisheries and Wildlife, Washington, D.C.

Littlejohn, C. 1977. An analysis of the role of natural wetlands in regional water management. Pages 451-476 in C.A.S. Hall and J.W. Day, Jr., eds., Ecosystem modeling in theory and practice: an introduction with case histories. John Wiley, New York.

Livingston, R.J. 1978. Short and long-term effects of forestry operations on water quality and the biota of the Appalachicola estuary (North Florida, USA). Sea Grant Tech. Pamph. No. 5. University of Florida, Gainesville.

Lynch, J.J., and J.R. Shingleton. 1967. Values of the South Atlantic and Gulf Coast marshes and estuaries to waterfowl. Pages 51-63 in J.J. Newsom, ed., Proceedings of the marsh and estuary management symposium. Louisiana State University, Division of Continuing Education, Baton Rouge.

Mac, M.J., L.W. Nicholson, and C.A. McCauley. 1979. PCBs and DDE in commercial fish feeds. Prog. Fish Cult. 4(4):210-211.

MacDonald, P.O., W.E. Frayer, and J.R. Clauser. 1979. Documentation, chronology, and future projections of bottomland hardwood habitat loss in the lower Mississippi alluvial plain. Vol. I, Basic report. HRB Singer, Inc., State College, Pa. 133 pp.

McGinn, L.R. 1963. Ecological factors that influence the loss of seeds that serve as major waterfowl foods on rice fields of southwest Louisiana. M.S. thesis, Louisiana State University, Baton Rouge. 112 pp.

McHugh, J.L. 1976. Estuarine fisheries: are they doomed? Pages 15-27 in Estuarine processes. Vol. I, Uses, stresses, and adaptation to the estuary. Academic Press, New York.

Mitsch, W.J., C.L. Dorge, and J.R. Wienhoff. 1979. Ecosystem dynamics and a phosphorus budget of an alluvial cypress swamp in southern Illinois. Ecology 60:1116-1124.

Mulholland, P.J., and E.J. Kuenzler. 1979. Organic carbon export from upland and forested wetland watersheds. Limnol. Oceanogr. 24:960-966.

Neely, W.W. 1967. Planting, disking, mowing, and grazing. Pages 212-221 _in_ J.D. Newsom, ed., Proceedings of the marsh and estuary management symposium. Louisiana State University Division of Continuing Education, Baton Rouge.

Newsom, L.D. 1972. Some implications of two decades of use of synthetic organic insecticides for control of agricultural pests in Louisiana. Pages 439-459 _in_ N. Taghi Farvar and J.P. Milton, eds., The careless technology. Prepared for Conservation Foundation and Center for the Biology of Natural Systems. University of Washington, Natural History Press, Garden City.

Odum, W.E. 1970. Insidious alteration of the estuarine environment. Trans. Am. Fish. Soc. 4:836-847.

Paille, R.F. 1980. Production of three populations of red swamp crawfish, _Procambarus clarkii_, in southeast Louisiana. M.S. thesis, Louisiana State University, Baton Rouge. 41 pp.

Plummer, A., and Assoc. 1979. Evaluation of non-point sources of pollution in Louisiana. Prepared for Louisiana Stream Control Commission, Department of Wildlife and Fisheries.

Schmitt, C.J., and P.V. Winger. 1980. Factors controlling the fate of pesticides in rural watersheds of the lower Mississippi River alluvial valley. Trans. 45th North Am. Wildl. Conf. Pages 354-375.

Schnick, R.A., and F.P. Meyer. 1979. Announcements of compounds registered for fishery uses. Prog. Fish Cult. 41(1):36-37.

Scorgie, H.R.A., and A.S. Cooke. 1979. Effects of the Trizine herbicide Cyanatryn on aquatic animals. Bull. Environ. Contam. Toxicol. 22:135-142.

Seaton, A.M., and J.W. Day, Jr. 1979. The development of a trophic state index for quantification of eutrophication in the Barataria Basin. Pages 113-125 _in_ J.W. Day, Jr., D.D. Culley, Jr., R.E. Turner, and A.J. Mumphrey, Jr., eds., Proceedings of third coastal marsh and estuary management symposium. Louisiana State University, Division of Continuing Education, Baton Rouge.

Sternitzke, H.S. 1976. Impact of changing land use of delta hardwood forests. J. For. 74:25.

Turner, R.E. 1977. Intertidal vegetation and commercial yields of penaeid shrimp. Trans. Am. Fish. Soc. 106:411-416.

Turner, R.E., and J. Bond. 1982. Urbanization, peak river flow, and estuarine hydrology near Baton Rouge, La. Louisiana Academy of Science. (In press.)

Turner, R.E., and N.J. Craig. 1981. Recent areal changes in Louisiana's forested wetland habitat. Louisiana Academy of Science.

Turner, R.E., S.W. Forsythe, and N.J. Craig. 1981. Bottomland hardwood forest resources of the southeastern U.S. Bottomland Hardwoods Workshop Review Papers. Elsevier, New York.

U.N. Food and Agricultural Organization. 1979. FAO yearbook of fishing statistics. U.N. FAO, Rome.

U.S. Department of Agriculture, Forest Service. 1980. An assessment of the forest and range land situation in the United States. U.S. For. Serv. FS-345. 631 pp.

U.S. Department of Commerce. 1972. Fisheries statistics of the United States, 1972. Statistical Digest No. 66. National Marine Fisheries Service, Washington, D.C.

U.S. Department of Commerce. 1975. The coastline of the United States. Pamphlet. National Oceanic and Atmospheric Administration, Washington, D.C.

U.S. Department of the Interior. 1970a. National estuary study. Vol. 1. U.S. Fish and Wildlife Service, Washington, D.C.

U.S. Department of the Interior. 1970b. National estuary study. Vol. 5. U.S. Fish and Wildlife Service, Washington, D.C.

U.S. Department of the Interior. 1972. National survey of fishing and hunting. U.S. Fish Wildl. Serv. Resour. Publ. 95.

U.S. Department of the Interior, U.S. Department of Agriculture, and U.S. Environmental Protection Agency. 1979. Irrigation water use and management, an interagency task force report. Washington, D.C.

U.S. Water Resources Council. 1978. The nation's water resources 1975-2000. Vol. 2, Water quantity, quality, and related land considerations. Washington, D.C.

Van Sickle, V.R., B.B. Barrett, L.J. Gulick, and T.B. Ford. 1976. Barataria Basin: salinity changes and oyster distribution. Sea Grant Publ. LSU-T-76-02; LSFC Tech. Bull. No. 20. Center for Wetland

Resources, Louisiana State University, Baton Rouge, and Louisiana Wildlife and Fisheries Commission. 22 pp.

Vollenweider, R.A. 1968. Scientific fundamentals of the eutrophication of lakes and flowing waters, with particular reference to nitrogen and phosphorus as factor in eutrophication. Tech. Rep. DAS/CSI/68-27 to the Organization for Economic Cooperation and Development, Paris.

Williams, E., F.S. Craig III, and J.W. Avault, Jr. 1977. Some legal aspects of catfish and crawfish farming in Louisiana: a case study. Agric. Exp. Stn. Bull. 689. 16 pp.

Woodwell, G.M., C.F. Wurster, and P.A. Isaacson. 1967. DDT residues in an East Coast estuary: a case of biological concentration of a persistent insecticide. Science. Pages 821-823.

Woolhiser, D.A. 1976. Hydrologic aspects of non-point pollution. Pages 7-29 in B.A. Stewart et al., Control of water pollution from cropland. Vol. II, An overview. EPA-600/2-75-026b. U.S. Environmental Protection Agency, Athens, Ga.

Appendix A
Major Trends in Agricultural Land Use by Geographic Regions

Appendix A summarizes by geographic regions the major trends in agricultural land use identified by the Committee. Any prediction is based on information available at a specific time, and therefore it represents a single perspective on a dynamic process. Actual future events and their timing will reflect a complex interaction of economic, social, and political forms, changes in science and technology, and how information is interpreted and adopted. Prognostication is hazardous, but if forecasts are viewed with appropriate caution, it can be helpful in suggesting at least the direction, if not the magnitude and timing, of change.

APPENDIX A

	West		Northeast
	Pacific	Mountain	
Cropland and forage	1. Some increase in land cropped 2. Minor increases in irrigated land 3. More double cropping and interplanting 4. Reduced water application per hectare; more sprinkler and drip irrigation; better preparation of land for irrigation	1. Modest increase in area dry-farmed as rangeland is converted to cropland 2. Modest increases in area dry-farmed as irrigation becomes too costly in specific areas 3. Less fallow acreage in some regions and planting of high-value, low-water-consuming crops 4. Localized expansion in supplemental irrigation	1. Continued gradual reduction in cropland and forage acreage 2. Increased seasonal vegetable production
Pastures	1. Small irrigated pastures developed in conjunction with rangeland 2. Improved dryland pastures on suitable sites should increase	1. Improved dryland pastures on suitable sites should increase	1. Decline in pasture acreage

	West		Northeast
	Pacific	Mountain	
Rangeland	1. Irrigated plots in range areas to improve output from all feed areas 2. More intensive use by all users, particularly grazing 3. More investment in improving rangelands for grazing by clearing, water development, fencing, and seeding; extent dependent on government policy	1. Some rangeland on higher quality soils will be converted to crop production 2. More intensive use of range, both public and private 3. More investment in improving rangelands for grazing but extent depends on government policy	
Forests	1. More intensive farming of private forest lands with improved species and practices 2. More chemical application as fertilizers and pesticides	1. More intensive management of private forests 2. More chemical application as fertilizers and pesticides	1. Increased utilization of hardwoods for a wide range of purposes 2. Continued lack of adequate management of forests
Wetlands and aquatic uses		1. Some further drainage of prairie potholes	

APPENDIX A (continued)

	North Central		
	Northern Plains	Lake States	Corn Belt
Cropland and forage	1. Increased average cropped 2. Less tillage 3. Localized expansion of supplemental irrigation 4. Some switch to higher value crops on specific sites 5. Some additional fertilizer and expanded application of herbicides	1. Question regional crop diversification, if not on individual farms 2. Extensive increase in supplemental irrigation 3. Reduced tillage and greater use of herbicides 4. Fertilizer continued at higher levels, pesticides declining slightly 5. Increased double cropping and intercropping 6. More on-farm live-stock and more intensive forage management	1. Question regional crop diversification, if not on individual farms 2. Extensive increase in supplemental irrigation 3. Reduced tillage and greater use of herbicides 4. Fertilizer continued at higher levels, pesticides declining slightly 5. Increased double cropping and intercropping 6. More on-farm livestock and more intensive forage management
Pastures	1. Improvement of pastures and possible increased acreage 2. More intensive management	1. Improvement of pastures and possible increased acreage 2. More intensive management	1. Significant increase in pasture as a rotation crop 2. Diversification of agriculture will involve pasture

	North Central		
	Northern Plains	Lake States	Corn Belt
Pastures (continued)			3. More intensive management
Rangeland			
Forests			
Wetlands and aquatic uses		1. Continued drainage of potholes	1. Continued drainage of wet areas

	South		
	Southern Plains	Delta States	Appalachian
Croplands and forage	1. Reduction in irrigated croplands in the higher elevations 2. Shift to lower water-consuming crops 3. More supplemental irrigation 4. Declining application rates for agricultural chemicals except for herbicides 5. More intercropping and double cropping 6. More reduced tillage	1. Increase in cropland at expense of forests and wetlands 2. Increase in ponds for aquaculture 3. More supplemental irrigation 4. Increased levels of fertilizer and chemical use but declining application rates per hectare 5. More intercropping and double cropping 6. More reduced tillage	1. Increased fruit and vegetable production 2. More intercropping and double cropping 3. More supplemental irrigation 4. Reduced tillage and expanded use of herbicides 5. More intensive forage management to support expanded livestock production

APPENDIX A (continued)

	South		
	Southern Plains	Delta States	Appalachian
Pastures	1. Some return to native pastures from irrigated farming; some will receive supplemental water	1. Land in pasture will increase 2. More intensive management 3. Improved pastures	1. Increased planting and more intensive management
Forests		1. Clearing of hardwood forest areas for cropping	1. Increased production of softwood 2. More intensive cultural practices including fertilization and pest and disease control and thinning 3. More intensive utilization of forest products 4. More single species planting 5. Increased grazing of forested areas 6. Loss of forested areas to cropland
Wetlands and aquatic uses	1. Continued drainage of wetland areas	1. Further drainage of wetlands 2. Channelization of natural waterways	

Appendix B
Common and Scientific Names of Birds, Mammals, and Plants Mentioned Frequently in the Text

BIRDS

Bittern, American	*Botaurus lentiginosus*
Bittern, least	*Ixobrychus exilis*
Bunting, lark	*Calamospiza melanocorys*
Coot, American	*Fulica americana*
Crane, sandhill	*Grus canadensis*
Eagle, bald	*Haliaetus leucocephalus*
Gallinule	*Gallinula* spp.
Goose, Canada	*Branta canadensis*
Grouse, ruffed	*Bonasa umbellus*
Grouse, sage	*Centrocercus urophasianus*
Grouse, sharp-tailed	*Pedioecetes phasianellus*
Hawk, marsh or harrier	*Circus cyaneus*
Loon	*Gavia* spp.
Owl, short-eared	*Asio flammeus*
Owl, spotted	*Strix occidentalis*
Partridge, Chukar	*Alectoris graeca*
Pelican, white	*Pelecanus erythrorhynchos*
Pheasant, ring-necked	*Phasianus colchicus*
Prairie chicken, Attwater's	*Tympanuchus cupido attwateri*
Prairie chicken, greater	*Tympanuchus cupido*
Prairie chicken, lesser	*Tympanuchus pallidicinctus*
Quail, bobwhite	*Colinus virginianus*
Quail, scaled	*Callipepla squamata*
Rail, sora	*Porzana carolina*
Rail, Virginia	*Rallus limicola*
Turkey	*Meleagris gallopavo*
Warbler, Swainson's	*Limnothlypis swainsonii*
Woodcock, American	*Philohela minor*

MAMMALS

Bear, black	*Ursus americanus*
Bear, grizzly	*Ursus horribilis*
Chipmunk	*Tamias* spp.
Coyote	*Canis latrans*
Deer, black-tailed or mule	*Odocoileus hemionus*
Deer, roe	*Capreolus capreolus*
Deer, white-tailed	*Odocoileus virginianus*
Elk	*Cervus canadensis*
Gopher, pocket	*Thomomys* spp.
Hare, snowshoe	*Lepus americanus*
Lion, mountain	*Felis concolor*
Mink	*Mustela vison*
Moose	*Alces alces*
Muskrat	*Ondatra zibethicus*
Nutria	*Myocastor coypu*
Otter	*Lutra canadensis*
Porcupine	*Erethizon dorsatum*
Pronghorn (antelope)	*Antilocapra americana*
Rabbit	*Sylvilagus* spp.
Raccoon	*Procyon lotor*
Squirrel, Abert's	*Sciurus aberti*
Squirrel, flying	*Glaucomys* spp.
Squirrel, golden-mantled ground	*Callosspermophilus lateralis*
Squirrel, red	*Tamiasciurus hudsonicus*

PLANTS

Acacia	*Acacia* spp.
Alder	*Alnus* spp.
Alpine fir	*Abies lasiocarpa*
Arrowhead	*Sagittaria* spp.
Aspen	*Populus* spp.
Blueberry	*Vaccinium* spp.
Bulrush	*Scirpus* spp.
Cattail	*Typha* spp.
Cinquefoil	*Potentilla* spp.
Cottonwood	*Populus deltoides*
Creosote bush	*Larrea divaricata*
Crested wheatgrass	*Agropyron desertorum*
Currant	*Ribes* spp.
Cypress	*Taxodium* spp.
Douglas fir	*Pseudotsuga menziesii*
Eastern red cedar	*Juniperus virginiana*
Englemann spruce	*Picea engelmannii*

Harvard shinoak	*Quercus harvardii*
Hawthorn	*Crataegus* spp.
Hickory	*Carya* spp.
Honeysuckle	*Lonicera* spp.
Jack pine	*Pinus banksiana*
Juniper	*Juniperus* spp.
Longleaf pine	*Pinus palustris*
Mesquite	*Prosopis glandulosa*
Northern white cedar	*Thuja occidentalis*
Oak	*Quercus* spp.
Pinyon pine	*Pinus edulis*
Ponderosa pine	*Pinus ponderosa*
Sagebrush	*Artemesia* spp.
Sand sagebrush	*Artemesia filifolia*
Sedge	*Carex* spp.
Serviceberry	*Amelanchier* spp.
Soybean	*Glycine* spp.
Sugar maple	*Acer saccharum*
Tarbush	*Flourensia cernua*
Tree cholla	*Opuntia imbricata*
Water-hyacinth	*Eichhornia crassipes*
Whitebrush	*Aloysia lycioides*
Willow	*Salix* spp.
Yellow birch	*Betula alleghaniensis*
Yucca	*Yucca* spp.